JUST FREEDOM

GOVERNMENT AND POLITICS IN THE SOUTH

UNIVERSITY PRESS OF FLORIDA

Florida A&M University, Tallahassee
Florida Atlantic University, Boca Raton
Florida Gulf Coast University, Ft. Myers
Florida International University, Miami
Florida State University, Tallahassee
New College of Florida, Sarasota
University of Central Florida, Orlando
University of Florida, Gainesville
University of North Florida, Jacksonville
University of South Florida, Tampa
University of West Florida, Pensacola

JUST FREEDOM

Inside Florida's Decades-Long Voting Rights Battle

DANIEL RIVERO

Sharon D. Wright Austin and Angela K. Lewis-Maddox / *Series Editors*

UNIVERSITY PRESS OF FLORIDA/Gainesville/Tallahassee/Tampa/Boca Raton
Pensacola/Orlando/Miami/Jacksonville/Ft. Myers/Sarasota

Cover: Photo of the Florida Rights Restoration Coalition; Brandi Hill Photography.

Copyright 2025 by Daniel Rivero

All rights reserved

Published in the United States of America

30 29 28 27 26 25   6 5 4 3 2 1

LIBRARY OF CONGRESS CATALOGING-IN-PUBLICATION DATA
Names: Rivero, Daniel author
Title: Just freedom : inside Florida's decades-long voting rights battle / Daniel Rivero.
Description: 1. | Gainesville : University Press of Florida, [2025] | Series: Government and politics in the South | Includes bibliographical references and index.
Identifiers: LCCN 2025013255 (print) | LCCN 2025013256 (ebook) |
 ISBN 9780813081168 paperback | ISBN 9780813073965 ebook
Subjects: LCSH: Ex-convicts—Suffrage—Florida | Political rights, Loss of—Florida | Suffrage—Florida | Voting—Florida | Florida—Politics and government |
 BISAC: POLITICAL SCIENCE / Civil Rights | LAW / Legal History
Classification: LCC JK1846 .R55 2025 (print) | LCC JK1846 (ebook) |
 DDC 324.6/209759—dc23/eng/20250708
LC record available at https://lccn.loc.gov/2025013255
LC ebook record available at https://lccn.loc.gov/2025013256

The University Press of Florida is the scholarly publishing agency
for the State University System of Florida, comprising Florida A&M University,
Florida Atlantic University, Florida Gulf Coast University, Florida International
University, Florida State University, New College of Florida, University of
Central Florida, University of Florida, University of North Florida, University
of South Florida, and University of West Florida.

University Press of Florida
2046 NE Waldo Road
Suite 2100
Gainesville, FL 32609
http://upress.ufl.edu

GPSR EU Authorized Representative: Mare Nostrum Group B.V., Mauritskade 21D,
1091 GC Amsterdam, The Netherlands, gpsr@mare-nostrum.co.uk

TO MY GRANDPARENTS RITA, ALEJANDRO, NENA, AND PEPÍN; AND MY PARENTS, ALEJANDRO AND MARIA. My family came to this country to give us the freedom to question and to criticize the government loudly and publicly. They instilled in me the dual instincts of curiosity and skepticism, the ability to reason, and the conviction to speak my part. I owe them my everything.

CONTENTS

Preface / ix

1. The List / 1
2. The Backlash / 8
3. Clinging to the Past / 23
4. The Reformer / 33
5. No Rules / 46
6. Let My People Vote / 58
7. A Very Big Problem / 71
8. Poll Tax? / 84
9. "An Administrative Nightmare" / 103
10. The Trial / 119
11. Mask Off / 130
12. The Long Game / 149

Notes / 161
Index / 191

PREFACE

All it took was one letter to shift the center of gravity for the 2020 election to the state of Florida, if only for a short news cycle. The letter, sent Wednesday, September 23, 2020, was penned by Republican Attorney General Ashley Moody.

In it, she accused one of *Time* magazine's "100 most influential people" and a future MacArthur Foundation "Genius Grant" recipient of being involved in a criminal scheme to benefit Democrats and potentially steal the election.[1]

In 2018, Desmond Meade helped lead the charge for the passage of Amendment 4, a grassroots ballot initiative that overnight ended Florida's policy of placing a lifetime voting ban on people with felony convictions. The passage of the item was estimated to have impacted about 1.4 million Floridians. It was lauded by Georgia-based voting rights activist and Democratic hero Stacey Abrams as "the largest expansion of voting rights in a half-century."[2]

That was the rose-colored-glasses take on what Meade and nearly two decades of Florida activists' work had accomplished. The reality was much more complicated. In the wake of the ballot amendment winning by a landslide at the ballot box, the state legislature constructed a system in which someone with a felony conviction could only vote if they paid all fines, fees, court costs, and restitution associated with their case. As a result, the majority of those who thought the 2018 vote might give them a voice in the political process once again found themselves silenced. Detractors likened the law to a "poll tax." A court case about whether the law was or was not a "poll tax" or an "other tax" of the kind prohibited by the Twenty-Fourth Amendment dragged on for the better part of two years. In the end, the state won. If you had a felony conviction on your record and you wanted to vote, someone—anyone—needed to pay the money owed to the state. The state wanted that money.

That's where the letter from Ashley Moody came in.

In a letter sent to the FBI and to the Florida Department of Law Enforcement, the state attorney general called on an investigation into Meade's organization, the Florida Rights Restoration Coalition, for "potential violations of election laws."[3]

Just a day earlier, billionaire Michael Bloomberg announced that he helped raise more than $16 million to help Floridians with felony convictions pay their fines and fees to regain their right to vote. The money was to be given to Meade's organization to help people who owed money become eligible to vote. For Moody, this amounted to potentially buying votes. She included criminal statutes in a packet sent to federal and state law enforcement that likened Bloomberg's work to bribery, for giving people an illegal incentive to vote in a certain way.[4]

The call for an investigation had a mad kind of logic to it. Throughout the previous two years, the State of Florida had maintained the position that forcing someone with a felony conviction to pay money to become eligible to vote was a matter of making sure the court system itself had proper funding, and making sure the criminal sentences had been completed. But now, as someone stepped in to help Floridians complete their criminal sentences and pump money into the court system, the state cried foul. Included in the shifting stance was an inherent legal threat. Anyone who accepted help paying fines and fees could now come under legal scrutiny.

"It's hard not to see this as a bit of voter intimidation," said Danielle Lang, an attorney with the Campaign Legal Center who represented plaintiffs in a class-action lawsuit against the state. "There is no criminal investigation to be had here."[5]

It was a clarifying moment for the State of Florida. The facade of legalese was stripped away, and the ugly underbelly of the thing was exposed. Meade and his group had worked by the book, according to Florida law and according to the position the state took during the federal lawsuit. Then, just over a month before a major election, when the Republican machinery of the state caught wind that millions of dollars might be pouring into the effort to pay off the fines and fees of returning citizens, it insinuated the payment of that money could be illegal.

Virtually all of the money raised by the Fines and Fees Fund, including any Bloomberg money, would soon be pumped into the struggling state court system, a system that was in the midst of a historic budget crisis due to the COVID-19 pandemic. County clerks of courts offices in Florida's sixty-seven counties were seeing average budget cuts of around 50 percent for the entire state.⁶ Budgets for public defenders' offices, victim services, and alternative court programs were under threat because of the shortfall. If nothing else, the money from the fund was an infusion of cash into the struggling system, the very "interest" that Florida sought to protect in the federal lawsuit. But no longer. No matter how you looked at it, it now appeared the state simply did not want to let this class of people cast votes.

By the time of Moody's announcement, the Florida Rights Restoration Coalition had been raising money for its Fines and Fees Fund for more than a year. It was not a secret. More than forty-four thousand people had already paid into it, pumping more than $5 million into the court system and helping more than four thousand Floridians get their voting rights back.⁷ Yet it was only with Bloomberg's announced donation of $16 million that the fund was coming under investigation.

With help from sloppy journalism, the state cherry-picked a *Washington Post* story to justify its new position.⁸ A story written by reporter Michael Scherer strongly suggested the only people who would benefit from the Bloomberg money were Black and Latino. The piece cited an internal memo from Bloomberg's team that talked about how much more likely Black voters are to support Democrats. For Bloomberg's team, the article said, this meant targeting Black voters, who could help Joe Biden in the race against President Trump.

Yet in the same article, Meade stated in no uncertain terms that if Bloomberg gave the money to his group, the billionaire would have no influence over how the money was spent, and he would not be able to insert politics into the process. "No person really dictates how we are operating," Meade told the paper.

Florida's Republican Congressman Matt Gaetz pounced on the article. He went on *Fox News* and alleged Bloomberg was "cheating" in order to steal the election.⁹ Republican Governor Ron DeSantis followed, appearing on *Fox News* and confirming a state investigation into Bloomberg was under way.

"He's discriminating on the basis of race, he's only paying off if you're a certain race," DeSantis said. "Under Florida law, that very well may run afoul of that. We'll have to see."¹⁰

President Donald Trump piled onto Bloomberg on a *Fox News* radio show. "It's totally illegal what he did," said Trump. "I guess it's a felony. He's actually giving money to people—he's paying people to vote. He's actually saying, here's money, now you go ahead and vote for only Democrats."¹¹

PREFACE xi

Meade posted a fiery video online, shooting back at that entire line of attack for what he called "innuendo" and an attempt to "try to intimidate people from supporting our efforts." After years spent keeping his cool and trying to stay above the political fray, the anger seeped from his pores.

"They say we got to pay, and when American citizens come together and stand up for democracy, they get mad about that," said Meade. "What we're seeing is not an attack against a returning citizen, it's not just an attack against Black people, or Spanish people, this is a deliberate attack against the democracy that we want in this country. Democracy that we expect in this country."[12]

Many months later, when the high drama of the presidential election was over, after insurrectionists stormed the US Capitol on January 6, 2021, and as Democrat Joe Biden was well into his four-year term, the Florida Department of Law Enforcement released the results of the investigation.

State officers sorted through 7,614 pages of subpoenaed documents and reached out to more than one hundred people who had their fines paid by Meade's group to reach their conclusion. And their conclusion was this: No crime had been committed. The group never conditioned payments on voting for a particular party or candidate. It took the officers a total of 706 total work hours to figure this out.[13]

But it gets worse.

All those hundreds of hours of work by investigators also uncovered another factoid: Bloomberg never even sent the money. Not only was there no crime, the alleged action that police investigated never even happened in the first place. There was no predicate.[14]

The entire episode was a political fairy tale, imagined into existence to rile up public anger and cast doubt on the work done by the Florida Rights Restoration Coalition. Florida Attorney General Ashley Moody, Representative Gaetz, Governor DeSantis, and President Trump all played their roles in willing the scandal into existence.

With the chaos of the election season safely behind him, and with the investigation officially closed, Meade later looked back on the episode with clarity. "It really slowed our ability to operate in our fullest to the fullest extent of ourselves because we were busy trying to defend a falsehood," he told me. "All it did was create even more confusion on the ground. It hampered our ability to raise money to help people who are too poor to pay.... That whole ordeal was an example of what happens when politics come into play," he said.[15]

The story of Florida's Amendment 4 is a story of triumphs and pitfalls. It is a story of politics and those who dared to dream of a world in which politics could be postpoliticians. It is a story of relentless activists who would not rest until they saw historic wrongs turned right. It is a story about mistakes made, redemption sought, and about the thing that casts its shadow over the entire criminal justice system and, therefore, over American democracy itself: money.

Over the course of several years I have conducted countless interviews on the subject, talked to the main characters and activists involved, reviewed thousands of pages of court records, internal documents and public reports, and grilled politicians at the center of it all.

Taken in its entirety, the full scope of the tale requires a wholesale re-evaluation of how governments at the state and local levels run, where they get their money, whom they penalize, and on what basis. Over the broad course of the narrative, the story that unfolds doubles as an explanation of the current nature of Florida politics and, on some level, our national politics.

When I first heard about the grassroots effort to pass something like Amendment 4 in 2016, it seemed to me like a bit of a pipe dream, a grand idea that could never get enough traction to effect the necessary change. The political class was so entrenched in its ways, in its power, that to dream of such a thing coming to pass required a suspension of disbelief, an unbelievable triumph over authority. I was wrong. And yet, I was also correct.

Ultimately, the story that follows is about the ugliness and cynicism of our political polarization, and how, despite it all, the people are still the moral center of this country. I hope we can learn something from the struggle.

JUST FREEDOM

1
THE LIST

In a world filled with fake stories and disinformation about widespread stolen and rigged elections, our story starts with the rare case of certified voter fraud. The episode was painfully on-brand for South Florida, and it set the scene for the decades to come.[1]

We begin in November 1997 with shady men plotting to rob the Miami mayoral election. One of the candidates was Joe Carollo, the incumbent. By then he had already acquired the nickname "Loco Joe," owing to his fiery temper and a face that betrayed all of his emotions. Running against him was his nemesis, Xavier Suarez, a former mayor who wanted another moment in the spotlight.

On Election Day, Suarez won. But then the drama started to unfold. Months into Suarez's term as mayor, a judge voided the election results, citing "a pattern of fraudulent, intentional and criminal conduct" in the way hundreds of absentee ballots were cast. Dead people cast votes. Elderly voters were found to have had their ballots manipulated. "This scheme to defraud, literally and figuratively, stole the ballot from the hands of every honest voter in the city of Miami," the judge wrote in his opinion. Neither of the candidates was directly implicated, but a wave of indictments came, and the two Cuban American candidates made simultaneous claims to the mayor's office until a new election could be held.

Not to be outdone by his "Loco Joe" predecessor, Suarez would soon come to be known as "Mayor Loco" after pulling stunts like showing up unannounced to a sixty-eight-year-old constituent's Little Havana home at 10:30 p.m. to talk about a critical letter she sent him. She answered the door with a pistol and refused to let him in.[2]

"He looked mad," she later explained, "really really mad."[3] The letter she wrote to him was in reference to the unfurling fraudulent ballots scandal that had captured attention nearly five hundred miles away in Tallahassee, the state capital.

The *Miami Herald* published a lengthy report scrutinizing yet another class of illegal ballots that were being cast: A total of 105 people with felony convictions had also voted in the overturned mayoral race.[4] This was illegal under state law.

Local officials asked for help preventing the people with felony convictions from voting again. If it happened here, where else was it happening?

The *Herald* had identified 2,800 people with felony convictions who were registered to vote in the county. But when Dade County Clerk of Courts Harvey Ruvin ran the numbers himself, he found 7,000 ineligible voters whose names his office had mistakenly never shared with election officials. Five of them had voted in the invalidated mayoral race. "There's a pressing need for a full systemic review of the process," Ruvin told the paper.[5]

The lists that were being sent to elections officials were incomplete and inaccurate. Only felonies committed within the county were being reported. Someone who committed a crime in neighboring Fort Lauderdale, or another part of Florida, was not being captured in the lists. Neither was someone with a felony case that came through the federal court system, or felonies that were committed in other states, for that matter. Collectively, Ruvin said, those cases fell through a "huge black hole."

A handful of the people who cast the illegal votes talked about it openly. One forty-one-year-old man blamed his mother, who pushed him to vote. "Take my rights from me," he told the *Miami Herald*. "But don't mess with my mother."[6]

Some illegal voters were unaware that they had broken any law. Some blamed the system itself for allowing them to vote. Others were flatly defiant. "Isn't voting the right and responsible thing to do?" asked a thirty-one-year-old who cast a ballot in the mayoral race. "I thought the whole point was to get us back into society."[7]

In Tallahassee, state elections officials made a swift decision. They were urged on by local officials like Ruvin, and the US Attorney's Office for the Southern District of Florida, which announced it was looking into "loopholes" that might have allowed for the illegal ballots to be cast.

The State of Florida would create a new database to make sure no one with a felony conviction could ever again slip through the cracks and violate the state's Civil War–era voting ban. They would roll it out quickly, before the 2000 presidential election.

Largely composed of the Florida Keys, the island communities that make up the county at the bottom of the peninsula have the feel of subtropical frontier towns, an end of the road for an entire nation. Tourists flood the islands of Monroe County by the millions, looking for boats, beers, and mischief. But the people who live there full-time keep the small-town connections that can at times feel as much like rural Missouri as they do like Caribbean fishing villages.

By 1999, Harry Sawyer had been the supervisor of elections in the Florida Keys for more than ten years. He lived and worked in Key West, a tiny city by most standards but that still qualified as the largest city in the island chain, with about twenty-five thousand residents. Before running for office to become the local elections chief, he spent years there as a local police officer. He knew the drinking town and its famously colorful characters well.

And so it was strange when Sawyer received a list of local residents from the State of Florida Division of Elections whom he was supposed to remove from the voting rolls. The list purported to show 150 people who had committed felonies and who were, therefore, not eligible to vote.[8]

He looked at the list and saw familiar names. One was an election employee that he had hired. One was another employee's husband. And then he saw another name that he recognized on the list: his own father.[9]

"There were people they had on there as convicted felons that were not, people who were dead were alive," he later remembered. "It was just useless, so we actually just put it in an envelope and mailed it back to the Division and told them we were not going to use it."[10]

On the top end of the peninsula, Linda Howell got a different kind of surprise. She was the elected supervisor of elections in Madison County, just a stone's throw from Valdosta, Georgia. One day Howell opened up the mail to find a letter from the Florida Department of Law Enforcement, the state police. The letter said that she had a felony conviction and that the department would soon "notify your supervisor of elections that we have data indicating that you meet the criteria of a convicted felon."

Howell *was* the supervisor of elections that the department said it would soon notify. She had no such felony conviction. If she had, she would have never been eligible to run for office in the first place. "Needless to say, I was very upset," Howell later said. "It seemed they were taking their job too lax. You could ruin a person with something like that."[11] "The thing that really upset me was that . . . they were not taking their job seriously," Howell said of the state.[12]

In the wake of Miami mayoral election scandal, Florida election officials contracted out the job to an Atlanta-based company called DBT Online to fix the problem. The state paid the company $4 million in 1998 and started feeding it voter data along with statewide law enforcement information. The idea was to cross-check multiple databases and to spit out a list of people who should be banned from voting. After identifying them, the process of removing people from the voting rolls would begin.

Except, the system was flawed. Local elections supervisors, like Sawyer and Howell, had known something like this was coming. In fact, several had voiced concerns about the program directly to state officials.

In early 1999, local election officials met with state officials to discuss the state contract with DBT Online. Anyone who had a 90 percent match with someone who had a felony conviction would be declared ineligible.

George Bruder, the vice president of DBT Online, would later say this rubbed the officials on the other side of the table the wrong way. The local elections supervisors wanted "to be as exacting as possible on the matches," he said. "If I condense it down to a major concern, that was what they were looking for."[13]

The state and the contractor stood their ground. Perfect matches were not the standard they wanted. Word started to spread across the supervisor of elections grapevine that there were doubts about the list that the state was getting ready to send out.

In June 1999, there was another meeting with state officials, this time in Key West, and all sixty-seven supervisors of elections from across the state were invited. By then the DBT list had already been circulating around the state. Sawyer had already received the list with his own father's name on it, and Howell had already received a letter stating that she was ineligible to vote.

"There was much discussion of the inaccuracies of the list," said Jane Carroll, the supervisor of elections of Broward County.[14] At first Carroll tried to give the list a shot in her county. She tried to do some groundwork to verify the information with Florida's Executive Board of Clemency, to see if any of the listed people had in fact had their rights restored or did not in reality have felony convictions. But she found the board was "very understaffed" and unable to do what she needed. "So we opted not to remove anybody that was on that list," she said. "We chose not to use it."[15]

Near the Georgia border, Howell was frustrated, and she described herself as being put in an impossible spot. "We have a law that says that a felon cannot be on your rolls, and if I remove that person, you know, from information that I've received and I've done it improperly, then I'm violating a person's right to vote," she said. "Where is the middle ground here?"[16]

Many counties decided to press ahead with removing people from the voter rolls. David Leahy, the supervisor of elections of Miami-Dade County, described the whole thing as "kind of a reverse process," since someone would have to prove that they were innocent instead of being assumed innocent until proven guilty. Despite his misgivings, Leahy moved forward and removed people from the rolls if they didn't respond to a letter he sent to their last known address. If the would-be voter did respond, they would be granted a hearing where they could defend themselves. But many notices simply went unanswered.

"We're removing a lot of people from the rolls when I know for a fact based on the appeal forms that I get back that this is not a truly accurate list," said Leahy. "It's drawn off the Florida Department of Law's database and that database was never intended for this purpose, but it's being used for this purpose."[17]

"I am concerned that we may be removing people through the administrative hearing process that are truly not convicted felons, and that will cause them a problem when they show up to vote in the next election," he said.[18]

In Hillsborough County, the home of Tampa, the supervisor of elections also pressed ahead with removals. "Some of those people may not even know to this day that they have been taken off the rolls," said Pam Iorio, the county's elections supervisor.[19] That may have been true for some people. But come the day of the contentious presidential election between Al Gore and George W. Bush, many found out.

The mistakes came all at once, as they tend to come on an Election Day.

Matt Frost was a thirty-three-year-old Al Gore supporter in Tampa. The Hillsborough County elections office had already sent him a letter saying he would not be able to vote unless he proved that the list was wrong. He wrote back with an appeal and soon after received a notice in the mail that his polling location had been changed. He assumed this meant everything had been cleared up. He was wrong.[20]

When Frost showed up to the new polling location that Tuesday to vote for Gore, he was told that he was a convicted felon and would not be allowed to vote. "Right in front of a bunch of people," Frost later told the *Palm Beach Post*. "The more I'm going to protest, the more it looks like I've got something to hide."[21]

The ordeal embarrassed him profoundly. Before walking away from the polling location without being able to cast a ballot, he grabbed an "I Voted" sticker to put on his shirt and show off to the world with phony pride. "God, it was humiliating," he said.[22] Frost's problem was one of the cases of mistaken identity. His name had been used as an alias of another man in the Tampa area who had been convicted of fraudulent use of a credit card.

Faulty information also kept Floredia Walker from voting. Walker, another Gore supporter, walked into Pleasant Grove Church in St. Petersburg to cast her ballot as she had done for years. She was told that her name had been taken off the voting rolls because she was a convicted felon. "I was devastated," she said. "I've voted in every election. I've even worked the polls. There was never a problem in the past."[23]

Walker worked for the Florida Department of Corrections, a job that required periodic background checks. She had no record to speak of. A month before the election, she had even been mailed a new voter registration card.

A clerical mix-up was to blame. Years earlier, in 1986, a thief stole Walker's purse and used her driver's license when she was arrested on theft charges. When she heard about it, Walker told the Florida Department of Law Enforcement and her employer about the mix-up and assumed it was over. She had voted without incident ever since. "I thought it was all taken care of," she said.[24]

Sandylynn Williams had also passed a background check for her work as a military contractor. Yet the Black Tampa resident was also wrongfully labeled as having a felony conviction and prevented from voting when she showed up at her polling location. "I don't feel like it was an honest mistake," she told the *Los Angeles Times*. "I felt like they knew most of the minorities was going to vote against Bush."[25]

In Miami-Dade County, with the largest population in the state, 66 percent of people on the erroneous felon list were Black. In Hillsborough County, which includes Tampa, 54 percent of people on the list were Black. Across the state, similar versions of this same scenario played out.[26]

By the time night had fallen in Florida, though, this hardly registered in the local, state, or national consciousness. The state immediately became the center of the political universe for the dizzying number of things that went wrong in that election.

A whole lexicon of new words, phrases, and concepts immediately entered into the American vocabulary: butterfly ballots, hanging chads, manual recount, "too close to call." The nation split at its political seams, hanging onto every development. Protesters and Republican political operatives took to Florida city streets to support a victory for Bush, while the Gore campaign pressed for a full recount in several South Florida counties. "It's like a world gone mad. Regular people hand-counting ballots to make sure the right vote was cast. A process rife with fraud and Democratic voodoo mind reading," deadpanned Will Ferrell, playing George W. Bush on an episode of *Saturday Night Live*.[27] "I'm sure just like me most of you have been very edgy and wetting the bed."

A mob of Washington insiders masquerading as local protesters mobbed the polling headquarters in Democratic-leaning downtown Miami, yelling, "Stop the fraud!" and "Let us in!" in a successful last-ditch attempt to stop the recount in its tracks. Miami-Dade Supervisor of Elections David Leahy acceded to the demands shortly after. The full recount was never finished. The question of whether to complete the recount went up to the US Supreme Court, and the court declined it. The final record reads that George Bush achieved victory over Al Gore by an official margin of 537 Florida votes.

When the dust settled on the chaotic election, answers were expected. What had just happened? As it stood, the world knew that elections in the state of Florida were fundamentally broken, an unacceptable state of affairs for what had emerged as the most important swing state of them all.

By the time George W. Bush took his oath of office on January 20, 2001, a panel of federal investigators had begun to dissect all the failures of Florida's voting system. Elsewhere, a civil rights activist started to lay groundwork for an issue that would one day turn into a movement.

2

THE BACKLASH

When we talk about civil rights, exactly what we're talking about changes with every generation. In the 1920s, it was the right to vote for women and Native Americans.[1] In the 1960s, it was poll taxes and racial equality. In the 2000s, we're increasingly talking about lesbian, gay, bisexual, transgender, and queer rights. There's a crescendo to these movements, and if you close your eyes, you can almost see the arc of the moral universe that Martin Luther King Jr. once spoke about.

For Howard Simon, the trajectory of a lifetime of advocacy started with words from King himself. Simon is a white bespectacled Bronx native who still talks in a thick New York accent despite living outside the city for most of his adult life. He was mostly raised by an aunt whose husband was an American history teacher, and the history lessons he imparted stuck with Simon ever since.

At City College of New York in Harlem, he was serving as the vice president of the student government, when one day a telegram from King came through, addressed to student leaders.

"He said: 'I'm hoping that allies of the civil rights movement will come to Selma, Alabama, to help us crusade for the passage of the Voting Rights Act of 1965,'" Simon told me. Simon had to convince his parents to let him leave college to go along for the trip; just the previous summer, three college students were killed in Mississippi as they helped Black residents register to vote, during what came to be known as the Freedom Summer. One of the students, Andrew Goodman, went to his college.[2] Ultimately, Simon prevailed over his parents' fears: "We got on a bus, we went down there and we stayed for quite some time."[3]

The time Simon spent in Selma overlapped with the moment when King and his allies were in the midst of one of the landmark events of the civil rights movement, one that would define the practice of nonviolence to achieve political goals: a series of marches from Selma to Montgomery, the

Alabama state capital, to protest widespread disenfranchisement of Black citizens.

A newcomer, Simon was given the mundane but important task of running a mimeograph machine in the stuffy basement of Brown Chapel AME Church, the unofficial headquarters of the civil rights movement. The mimeograph was a crude precursor to the Xerox machine, and it allowed the activists to print thousands of fliers to distribute across the South and spread word of the pending action.

Simon stayed back while King, John Lewis, and others crossed the Edmund Pettus Bridge, a bridge that was named after a former Confederate soldier and Alabama leader of the Ku Klux Klan. Once the crossing was complete, Simon and others were bussed to the far end of the bridge to catch up with the others for the rest of the journey to the state capital. The full march took place over several days and long nights spent in sleeping bags. "I remember the tension once we entered the city limits of Montgomery, because there were people who were on the side of the street watching the marchers and sometimes saying bad things. But mostly, silent. Silent and hostile," he said. At the Alabama Capitol, Simon watched in awe as King spoke under a Confederate flag that had been slung up above even the American flag.[4]

The experience in Alabama intoxicated Simon. He graduated from City College of New York, then spent a few years teaching philosophy and ethics at a college in Indiana before turning back to social justice work. Simon first moved to Detroit with the idea of studying law. Instead, he took what he thought would be a temporary job at the American Civil Liberties Union (ACLU) of Michigan. He ended up staying there for twenty-three years.[5]

During his years as the executive director of the ACLU in Michigan he fought the death penalty and secured equal pensions for men and women. One of the most explosive cases he oversaw at the advocacy group brought him back to Alabama, in fact, back to the very civil rights march a young Simon attended in 1965 as a student activist.

After the crowds watched Martin Luther King Jr. speak under the Confederate flag at the Alabama Capitol, Viola Liuzzo, a white Michigan resident, was helping shuttle a fellow civil rights activist back to Selma when another car rammed her off the road and she was shot and killed. In a separate case, from 1961, two busloads of Freedom Riders were assaulted by the Ku Klux Klan on the way to Birmingham. Klan members beat the bus riders with baseball bats and chains, and set one of the buses on fire.

More than a decade into his stint in Michigan, Simon unearthed documents that showed an FBI informant assisted the Ku Klux Klan in tracking the movement of the activists, an explosive discovery. For the 1961 attack, the federal government provided an FBI informant embedded inside the Klan with information about the location of the incoming buses. That informant shared the details with the rest of the Klan members prior to the attack. Worse still was a deal reached between the Klan, the local police department, and the FBI, in which the Klan was granted fifteen minutes to beat the activists before authorities would arrive. Three years later, that same FBI informant was inside the car from which the gunshots that killed Liuzzo came.[6] All of this came to light in 1978, when Simon helped Liuzzo's family shake loose the damning records that tied a man on the federal government's payroll to the murder.

"The passage of the Voting Rights Act was greatly speeded up as a memorial to Viola Liuzzo," noted Simon.[7] As history and chance would have it, he was there in Alabama the day her murder happened, and he has since made a career picking up where the transformative Voting Rights Act left off.

After more than two decades in Michigan, in late 1997, Simon moved down to Miami to become the executive director of the ACLU of Florida. During the aftermath of the debacle of the 2000 election, Simon quickly became one of the loudest voices calling attention to issues with how Florida officials managed the state voter lists. The issue would dominate a bulk of his tenure in Florida.

Simon came into the world of activism fighting for voting rights. Even if it was the last thing he did before retiring, he had his sights on addressing voting rights in his newly adopted state of Florida.[8]

Now that the state was enforcing its lifelong ban on voting for people with felony convictions, the reality of the situation came into clear focus. The sheer scale of voter disenfranchisement was outsized in the southernmost state.

"It's more serious in Florida than any other state in the country," Simon told the *Miami Herald* days before Bush was sworn into office.[9] At the time, Simon estimated 600,000 potential voters had been left out of the democratic process because of their criminal records. About 200,000 of them were Black men and women.[10]

"This is the mass deprivation of voting rights. A felony record already leaves a permanent stain on people's chances to find work but it shouldn't mean losing the vote," he said. "I don't think there is any moral or legal justification for depriving anyone from voting once they serve their time and pay their debt to society."[11]

Simon began to brainstorm what he could do to push the state to fix its voting rights system, and he decided to partner with local activist groups. By late January, the ACLU and local groups hosted the first meeting on voting rights restoration at the African Cultural Arts Center in Miami's Liberty City neighborhood, a predominantly Black area.

About 150 people showed up to learn how they could start the process. Glenn Stepherson was one of them. The former police officer's life had years earlier spun out into a frenzy due to a cocaine addiction and a stolen car. He did three years in prison but had since stitched his life back together. He got married, had five kids, and had another one on the way.[12]

"The way the last election went down, it gets personal," Stepherson said at the meeting. "I work every day, pay taxes like anybody else."[13] "But I can't vote," he said.

The only way to get his rights back was to put in a request to the governor's office in Tallahassee. Volunteers at the event helped Stepherson fill out the necessary forms, but even then, it was no sure thing. It was a daunting process and could take an unknown number of years to get an answer, positive or negative.

"I'm gonna give it a shot," Stepherson told a *Miami Herald* reporter. "I know I'll get shuffled around, but I'll stick. And I'll get it done."[14]

"There's a reason the process is complicated," offered Simon. "Because a lot of people don't want you to get your vote back."[15]

That idea stuck as an early rallying cry: The people in power don't want you to vote. They were scared of the democratic power of the disenfranchised masses. "Everyone knows if we restore rights to felons, they're going to vote Democrat," suggested Democratic State Representative Frederica Wilson, who years later became a US congresswoman in Miami.[16]

Another state representative who was at that first meeting offered a sobering statistic. Over the years, Democratic State Senator Kendrick Meek said his office sent in paperwork to help 175 people with felony convictions get their rights back. Only nine had their rights restored.[17]

Florida didn't have to be like this. It didn't have to reflect the worst clichés of the South, of the thinly cloaked racism, playing games with the right to political representation, the weaponization of the state bureaucracy.

It could have been, should have been, an outlier in the region. More than any other state in the nation, Florida's population has always grown through people moving there from somewhere else.[18] From the Northeast, from the Caribbean, from Canada. And so the stubborn Southernness of its politics is less tradition than choice. As an example of this, a 1976 poll showed that a whopping 75 percent of Republicans in the state were born outside the South.[19] No corollary poll was done for Democrats. But born in the South or not, Florida was still then a land of Dixiecrats, even if some only embraced Southern postures after moving there from elsewhere.

In the 1970s, the state's thirty-seventh governor went to great pains to try to turn the state into something more than just South Alabama. Oklahoma native Reubin Askew was the kind of progressive governor Florida Democrats in the 2020s can only dream about. He took office in 1971 with a cushy mandate and set his sights on broad reforms that define the state to this day. At the top of his list was creating a new corporate tax to help pump more revenue into the state government. He took the battle to the state's largest corporate interests and won it by a 70–30 margin when the issue was put before voters.[20]

Also passed during his tenure: major environmental protection reforms; a constitutional amendment requiring full financial disclosure from public officials and candidates; and increased funding for Florida's public school and university systems.

Over the years Askew developed such a close connection with the state and exhibited such integrity in the office that he came to be known as simply "Reubin the Good." His popularity was such that for his successful reelection campaign he was able to pull an early Bernie Sanders and limit campaign contributions to one hundred dollars per person.[21] "He has exhibited a kind of morality in office that causes people to have faith" in the government, lamented one longtime political foe.[22]

On race, Askew was decidedly forward-looking.

When he took the stage for his inaugural address in 1971, it was only a few short years after the Voting Rights Act of 1965 passed, and he set the tone for his terms in office there and then. "Equal rights for all our people, rural as well as urban, black as well as white," he said. He supported busing in order to integrate Florida's schools at a time when it was a hot-button wedge issue, and when some other Southern Democrats were clinging to segregation. Askew wasn't crazy about the idea of busing itself, but he saw no other way to mend the ills of the Jim Crow era. "The law demands, and rightly so, that we put an end to segregation in our society," he said.[23]

One of the first things Askew did when he came into office was order his aides to conduct a survey of state employees. The results found that most Black employees were in subordinate positions and that 89 percent of them received salaries that were below the poverty level. Outraged, Askew issued an executive order instructing state agencies to use affirmative action to correct the wrongs, and to start filing annual reports. By the time the first report came back, the number of Black employees had doubled, salaries had increased, and some Black employees had started to move up the management chain.[24]

Askew appointed Joseph Woodrow Hatchett to the Florida Supreme Court, making him the first Black justice ever to serve in the body. "I want to, in some specific ways, give some hope to young Black people that the establishment is not inherently hypocritical," Askew said at the time.[25]

Astonishingly, one of the boldest policies Askew signed into law during his tenure as governor seems to have received no contemporaneous media coverage. For days I poured over newspaper clippings and microfiche files and could find no mention of it whatsoever: no op-eds, no partisan mudslinging, no letters to the editor. Nothing. But the thing is a fact. It happened.

In 1974, Askew signed a bill ending Florida's lifetime voter disenfranchisement for people with felony convictions. The policy had been in the state constitution since 1868, just after the end of the Civil War and just as Black Floridians would cast their first votes.[26] Whether the policy was created with overtly racist motives is contested, but the outcomes were racist. Florida elected its first Black congressman, the formerly enslaved Republican Josiah Walls, in 1870, but as Jim Crow–era "Black Code" laws that disproportionately impacted African Americans went into cumulative effect, Black political power was diminished. The state would not send another African American to Congress until 1992.[27]

The revolutionary bill reached Askew's desk by way of a massive criminal justice reform effort that was sponsored by State Senator Richard Pettigrew, a progressive Miami Democrat. Tucked into the mass of paper was a provision stating that all civil rights, including the right to vote, would be "automatically reinstated" after someone completed parole, probation, or their prison sentence, whichever was the final step.

Decades later, just weeks shy of his ninetieth birthday, Pettigrew laughed when I brought up the subject with him. Even he couldn't remember that the provision was ever in the law, though he was still sharp as an iguana claw. "I don't precisely remember the discussion about this particular provision, but it seemed not to be that controversial," he said.[28]

The bill was mostly drafted by staffer Janet Reno, a Miami Democrat who later became the first female US attorney general, under President Clinton.[29] The main point of the bill was revamping the state's penal code and getting inmates access to educational and training programs that would help them when they were released. In retrospect, Pettigrew figured that giving voting rights back to inmates after they finished their sentences was a natural outgrowth of his main goal: a total revamp of the criminal justice system. "That's a part of completing rehabilitation, and it aids in developing a sense of self-worth," he said. "I fundamentally realized and recognized that most people who are sent to prison come back out."

"I made up my mind that we had to have major chapters of Florida law addressed comprehensively and in a coordinated fashion so they're not inconsistent provisions. My suggestion was: Go for it. Don't just piddle around with it. Go for it," said Pettigrew.

So, he went for it, and the legislature followed with a massive omnibus bill. Askew signed the legislation. He supported the bill. But he had reservations about the provision that would automatically restore voting rights for people with felony convictions.

The right to grant clemency and restore civil rights had always been left up to the executive branch under the Florida Constitution. A simple statute can't override the state constitution, so Reubin the Good felt he was in a bind. He wrote a letter to the Florida Supreme Court. In it, he asked for an opinion on whether the new law was in conflict with the state constitution, even though he had already "approved this legislation by signing it into law."[30]

In Florida, the governor can ask the top court for an "advisory opinion" like this one. No lawsuit has to be filed and wend its way up through the courts; the justices simply hear about a topic and issue a ruling, almost performing the role of a legal consultant.[31]

The ruling that the Florida Supreme Court sent back to Governor Askew on January 6, 1975, was bad news for people with felonies on their record. In a 6–1 decision, the justices ruled that the power to restore rights back to criminals was "exclusive" to the executive branch and that "the legislature cannot exercise such power."[32] The automatic restoration of rights under the law was essentially nullified.

Casting the lone dissenting vote, Justice Richard Ervine had a different view, one that seemed to point to the future and what could happen if this issue wasn't resolved right then and there. "After a citizen who was convicted of crime has paid his debt to society, I think it lies within the inherent reserved power of the Legislature as a constitutional responsibility to formally restore his civil rights. It should be done speedily, automatically and routinely," wrote Ervine. "To deny one citizen restoration when others of the same class are not denied would be invidious discrimination. One should not be tainted of crime further after serving his sentence fully. It is necessary to equality of citizenship that there be prompt restoration of civil rights after conviction sentences are completed."[33]

He continued, stressing that the legislature was doing the right thing by helping people avoid the "delay and expense and red tape" that would come with having to ask the governor's office for a pardon. Better to just make it automatic, he wrote.

The Associated Press reported at the time that in the previous ten years, 72,000 people had come out of the state prison system, and only 6,000 had their rights restored.[34]

Askew was not happy with the outcome of the advisory opinion, even though he instigated it. He liked the idea of automatic restoration of civil rights, but by nature he wanted to color within the lines of the law. And so, automatic restoration is what he did. Using the power of the governor's office, Askew created a brand new branch of the executive government, called the Florida Board of Executive Clemency.[35]

Executive power works differently in Florida. Unlike every other state in the nation, the executive branch of the government is shared between a group of people known as the Florida Cabinet. Members of the cabinet are all elected statewide at the same time as the governor, and they all run their own fully independent executive offices of government.

Together, this group of politicians is the Florida Cabinet. Not the governor's Cabinet. The Florida Cabinet. For certain executive decisions, they vote alongside the governor. The system was created in the years following the Civil War as a way to provide an internal check on possible abuses of executive powers that might come with investing all the power in one person.[36]

The Florida Board of Executive Clemency that Askew created was made up of the members of the cabinet. As a clever workaround, the group devised a set of rules for the board that did what the invalidated part of Pettigrew's law could not do: The board made restoration of voting rights automatic.

Between 1975 and 1991, Florida had automatic civil rights restoration, with the exception of the right to carry firearms. All someone had to do was fill out a form and send it to the board when they got out of prison showing they were now eligible for restoration.[37]

Education Commissioner Ralph Turlington hailed the rule change as a victory over bureaucratic red tape, but the rule change was not unanimous at the cabinet. The secretary of state and comptroller voted against it, losing 4-2. "This will destroy whatever effectiveness the restoration of civil rights has in the minds of the public," said Bruce Smathers, the Democratic secretary of state.[38]

A year after the rule change, at the December 8, 1976, meeting, Smathers noted disapprovingly, "Since the automatic restoration of civil rights went into effect in November of 1975 we have had almost—a little over 4,900 cases where civil rights have been automatically granted by this Clemency Board."[39] At that meeting, the rules were slightly tweaked to allow a cabinet member to object to restoring any one individual's civil rights.[40]

But automatic, it was. One of Florida's biggest and most divisive political battles of the twenty-first century was fought over mere access to the ballot box for people with felony convictions—hardly a revolutionary concept, even in Florida. Including Askew, three Democratic governors of the state kept the automatic rights restoration policy intact, along with one Republican governor, Robert Martinez. Then some Democrats blew the whole thing up.

Attorney General Bob Butterworth never said where the grudge came from when he lit the fuse at a Florida Cabinet meeting in 1991. It could have been anyone in a long list of corrupt Florida politicians, but if he had any names in mind, he kept them to himself.[41]

"We have public officials who end up serving time, who misused their office, who automatically get their civil rights back when they get out again. That's not right," said Butterworth.[42] The Democrat urged the Florida Cabinet

16 JUST FREEDOM

to adopt a new set of rules for people with felony convictions: If someone wanted to get their rights back, they would have to go to a hearing in front of Democratic Governor Lawton Chiles and the rest of the cabinet. Only then could a convicted corrupt politician run for office once again.

"If they breach the public trust, they should have to go through a little more review," said Butterworth. "I'm not saying they won't have their rights restored, it's just not automatic anymore."[43]

Unfortunately for posterity, the full record of what exactly took place in the subsequent meeting after Butterworth dropped the bombshell—the words said, the cases addressed—is not accessible. At the Florida State Library and Archives in Tallahassee, you can physically hold a copy of the cabinet meeting recording in your hands, but there is no machine that can run the tape so you can actually hear it. The recording was made on a Dictaphone machine, an obscure relative of the standard cassette. The State Archives has no Dictaphone machine through which it can be played.

Nonetheless, Governor Chiles and the rest of the cabinet adopted the rules, and immediately the whole game changed. For the meeting that took place on September 19, 1991—just before the change was adopted and automatic restoration was still in effect—a box in the archives contains a list of people whose rights were automatically restored. The list consists of twenty-nine full pages of names, with twenty-four names each, making for 696 people getting their rights automatically restored at that meeting. For the meeting immediately following the rule change, on December 19, 1991, the word "automatic" no longer appears on the paperwork. The list of people who had their rights restored has shrunk down to a single sheet of paper, with a measly six names.

With automatic rights restoration out the window, the cabinet would now need to rule on each case individually. A backlog of pending cases quickly began to stack up, and the rules for the Board of Executive Clemency became a game of political football.

Between 1991 and the 2000 election, the rules were changed three more times, but automatic restoration was never in the cards.[44] By the time the 2000 election came around, hundreds of thousands of people were waiting to get their voting rights back.

This reality was unacceptable to Howard Simon. He held the meeting in Miami and did a few more across the state. Even after all of that, only a few dozen documents had been sent up to Tallahassee, and only God knew what Governor Jeb Bush and the cabinet would do with them. He needed to mount a multipronged attack.

In March 2001, the ACLU of Florida under Simon took part in a class-action lawsuit against the director of the Florida Department of Corrections, demanding the state help inmates fill out complicated rights restoration forms as they were let out of prison. The suit was filed in the name of the Florida Equal Voting Rights Project, a group created by the ACLU after the 2000 election.[45]

"Until there is support for automatic restoration of rights, the Department of Corrections has a legal obligation to help people have a fighting chance to get their rights restored," said Simon.[46]

The duty of state officials to help former inmates get their rights back was already required by Florida law. Simon simply wanted them to do their jobs. It was clear that they weren't. In a deposition for the lawsuit, a state probation administrator called Larry Hamilton copped to it, admitting to a colossal, all-of-government failure dating back nearly two decades. Officials used a computer program dating back to 1982 that automatically submitted names of released inmates to clemency investigators. The problem was that they never made a necessary update to the program. The mistake meant that more than fourteen thousand people with felony convictions were erroneously not assisted by state employees in filling out clemency forms over the previous three years alone. "We were not notified," Hamilton said in a sworn statement. "Over the years, the [computer] program was not changed."[47]

The lawsuit against the state was ultimately successful, and state officials agreed to play a more active role in helping newly released inmates ask for their rights back.[48] "I do think it's appropriate to reform the system so that felons can get their rights back so they can vote," Governor Bush said when a settlement was announced. "[But] I don't think it should be carte blanche."[49]

Black lawmakers, civil rights organizations, and even public opinion had begun to coalesce around the issue. By February 2001, a poll conducted by the *St. Petersburg Times* found that nine out of ten Black voters agreed that "The law should be changed so that convicted felons in Florida automatically regain their right to vote at some specific time after they've repaid their debt to society."[50]

Passions flared on the topic even before the public came to learn the true scale of failures of the 2000 election, much of which tied back to this very question.

A series of hearings were conducted in Tallahassee and Miami by the US Commission on Civil Rights that January and February, as the botched election was fresh in the mind. The independent commission was created by the Civil Rights Act of 1957, and since inception it has focused attention on voting rights in the South. With all eyes on the state of Florida after the election, the commission wanted to understand what went wrong and how to prevent it from happening again. Commissioners listened to thirty hours of testimony from more than one hundred witnesses and reviewed more than 118,000 pages of subpoenaed documents.[51]

Some news reports gave a sense of what was brewing, but when the commission released its report, it was laid out on the table: Florida's attempt to enforce its lifelong ban on voting for people with felony convictions played a major role in the overall election debacle.

In the commission hearings, contractors at the company hired to maintain the state's felon list came clean about the overly broad search criteria they were asked to use. George Bruder, the vice president of DBT Online, told the commission that the list of potential felons his company created was knowingly sent out by the state with "false positives," or people who in reality did not have a felony conviction. He testified that the state "wanted to go broader and we did it in the fashion that they requested," according to the report. The hope was that local election officials would whittle the names down after the fact. In the original contract with DBT Online, it was understood that the company would only check for felonies that were committed and prosecuted within the state of Florida, he said. But in June of the election year, the assistant general counsel for the Florida Division of Elections emailed the company directing them to cross-check the names with felon lists from other states, even if those other states automatically restored voting rights.[52]

As a result, Floridians who had felony convictions in Texas, Connecticut, South Carolina, Illinois, and Wisconsin were told that they were ineligible to vote, even though they still had the right to vote. The US Constitution itself specifies that each state should give "full faith and credit" to the judicial proceedings of other states, the commission wrote in its report. Those people factually had a right to vote.

THE BACKLASH 19

The list of problems with the list went on and on. Letters to people who appeared on the potential felon list were sent out by each different county, and the tenor of the communication depended on where in the state you lived. In Miami-Dade County, the letter said that state records indicate that "you have a felony conviction" and that "your name will be removed" from the voting rolls if you didn't prove otherwise. In Leon County, the entire framing was different. The letter sent out there underscored the potential inaccuracy of the list.[53] "We do not know if this list is accurate," read the Leon County letters. "If you have never been convicted of a felony, we want to help you clear this up."

The racial impact of the plain errors became an item of debate, with each side clearly drawing the battle lines. In its report, the liberal-led commission wrote that the 2000 election had seen "patently unjust removal of disproportionate numbers of African American voters" from the voter rolls. As evidence it pointed to the most populous county in the state, Miami-Dade, where African Americans made up only 20.4 percent of the population but accounted for more than 65 percent of the names that showed up on the purge list. Of the African Americans who contested their presence on the list, over half were brought back onto the voter rolls. Many never attempted to resolve the problem. "In the November 2000 election, voters lost their rights because of these provisions and how they were implemented," noted the report.[54]

There were other problems too, with numerous testimonies of Black voters showing up to the polls and simply not being listed. Police checkpoints set up in predominantly Black neighborhoods could have been seen as intimidation. Across the state, about 180,000 ballots were later "spoiled," meaning that they were deemed invalid. African Americans only made up about 11 percent of the state's voters, and yet 54 percent of those "spoiled" ballots were from Black residents. An estimated 14.4 percent of Black voters' ballots were simply not counted in the election, according to a county-level statistical analysis.[55] Considering the rate at which Black residents vote for Democrats, the unstated upshot was that Al Gore should have won the election.

"The Commission's findings make one thing clear: widespread voter disenfranchisement not the dead-heat contest was the extraordinary feature in the Florida election," the commission wrote in its executive summary.[56]

But in a lengthy dissenting statement written by two conservatives, the disproportionate number of African Americans on the list was chalked up to "the sad fact that African Americans are greatly over-represented in the population of persons committing felonies—in Florida and in the United States as a whole." The dissenting opinion pointed out that while about half the African Americans who contested being on the Miami-Dade County list were let back in, a higher proportion of white voters who did the same were allowed to vote. Of the 4,678 African Americans who were on the list in Miami-Dade County who objected, 239 were allowed to vote. At the same time, 125 of the 1,264 white voters on the list objected and were later cleared to vote. "Thus, the error rate for whites was almost double that for blacks."[57]

The dissenting report went on. Florida has a decentralized election system, with independent elections supervisors for every one of its sixty-seven counties, and the Florida secretary of state at the head of it all. Rigging the election to make sure Black voters couldn't vote "would have required the cooperation of these local officials," reads the dissent. To dig deeper into the unstated innuendo that there was a Republican-led partisan element of the effort, the group analyzed the political affiliations of the local elections supervisors. Surely, if there was a partisan motive at play, then Republican-run counties would be the worst offenders when it came to the overall disproportionate racial impact of the main report's findings.

"Of the 25 Florida counties with the highest rates of vote spoilage, in how many was the election supervised by a Republican? The answer is zero," reads the dissenting report. "All but one of the 25 had Democratic chief election officers, and the one exception was in the hands of an official with no party affiliation."[58]

To a certain degree, both sides approached the problem with their own motives. The Democrats had just lost a major election. The Republicans had just won a narrow victory and needed to stand up for the integrity of a discredited state election system. No one said it, but this dynamic turned the inquiry into a political Rorschach test. The conclusions were incompatible abstractions founded in the same set of facts, but with wildly different interpretations. Nobody on either side of the commission actually knew how many eligible voters did not—or could not—vote because of issues with the state's felony list. It was impossible to have granular, comprehensive data about something as inherently private and protected as casting a ballot, or not casting a ballot. The known anecdotes could only say so much.

Estimates range from a few hundred to several thousand eligible voters who were impacted. And along the way, reporting from the *Palm Beach Post* and the *Miami Herald* found that many people with felony convictions still slipped through the cracks and cast ballots, despite all the state's efforts.

Yet the commission report set the tone for the coming years, and centered the conversation around accusations of racism. The state already had the largest population of people who had lifetime bans on voting because of their criminal records, and now addressing this stubborn fact carried political and racial baggage.

Either Florida was stubbornly clinging to its racist history, or the state election system was utterly incompetent. Or maybe it was a bit of both.

3
CLINGING TO THE PAST

Katherine Harris was the secretary of state of Florida during the 2000 election, charged with running elections in the state. She was also the cochairman for the George W. Bush campaign in Florida. In her 2002 book, Harris wrote that accusations of her purposely keeping African Americans from voting was the "most painful" aspect of the postelection storm.[1]

She cast the blame for the mix-ups entirely on local elections supervisors. "They were the *only* officials who had *any authority* to remove the names of citizens from the registration rolls," she wrote about local officials. She did this while defending her erroneous list: "To develop the comprehensive list the legislature mandated, it was necessary to establish broader matching parameters than an exact match of names. Persons use aliases and different variations of names in public records, which a procedure that looked for only for exact matches of names could not detect."[2]

Defiant, Harris wrote that thousands of felons slipped through the cracks and voted, in fact influencing the election "in favor of former Vice President Gore." This, because the "number of illegal voters far outnumbered the persons who allegedly could not vote" after mistakenly being removed from the rolls, she wrote, citing a study from the *Palm Beach Post*.[3]

It's an odd argument. Errors connected to the list her office oversaw unquestionably led to eligible voters being blocked from casting votes. Harris herself did not deny this. But, she argues, if the election system she oversaw had done the job correctly, without issues, Bush would have won by a much larger margin. She slammed the majority report by the US Commission on Civil Rights that opened questions on racism. "It is regrettable that its majority sullied the commission's august reputation by crafting a battle plan for politicians interested in wielding the sword of racial division," she wrote.[4]

The release of the US Commission on Civil Rights report, contested as it was, produced immediate results. Two weeks after the report dropped,

Governor Jeb Bush and the Florida Cabinet instituted major changes for how someone with a felony on their record could get their civil rights restored.

The rules passed unanimously. People who have served prison time, had nonviolent offenses, and who were not classified as habitual offenders would be able to get their civil rights restored without having to go before a full hearing in front of the cabinet. Those rights included the right to vote, the right to serve on a jury, the right to hold elected office, and the right to practice law, or to hold other similarly regulated state licenses. The cabinet would still have to sign off on someone getting their civil rights back—it would not be automatic—but the process was simplified: Instead of having to fill out a twelve-page form, applicants had to fill out a four-page form.[5]

Notably, the changes also applied to people with more than one thousand dollars of outstanding fines and court costs connected to their felony cases. They too, could get their civil rights restored without a full hearing. If someone still owed money on restitution, the rule did not apply.[6]

"We've seen people who haven't paid $48 in court costs not be able to get a nursing license," said Attorney General Bob Butterworth, the clemency board's only Democrat. Butterworth supported the changes, ten years after pushing to stop the automatic restoration of rights. He explained, "I think this is going to do a lot to make sure people who can rehabilitate themselves can do so more quickly."[7]

In explaining why he supported the rule change, Governor Bush said it was a question of redemption. "A lot of the people who come here [to the clemency board] are drug addicts. They commit a whole multitude of offenses, yet, they get their life together," Bush said in the meeting.[8]

Questions remained about if the new process would be race-neutral or not. A December 2001 *Palm Beach Post* investigation found that in the year 2000, the state only granted clemency to 1,067 people, the lowest number in twenty-five years. Only 272 of the people who got their civil rights back were Black, a difficult thing to explain in a state where nearly half the prison population was Black. Similar imbalances persisted when it came to who was receiving full pardons. Black Floridians were statistically overrepresented in the criminal justice system, and statistically underrepresented when it came to rights restoration and pardons.[9]

"This is the first I've heard of it," said Jimmie Henry, the chairman of the three-member Florida Parole Commission, the agency that oversaw the clemency process.[10] In 2001, the state was only starting to gather computer records and data on these sorts of things, and it had never run the analysis itself. Henry was Black. The remaining two parole commissioners were white.

"I can guarantee you that no recommendation is made from this office on the basis of race. We at the commission don't look at race," Henry told the *Post*.[11] Speculating, he suggested that the imbalance might be due to financial differences between Black and white former inmates. Under the old rules—the ones changed by Governor Bush and the cabinet—the emphasis on having to pay all fines and court costs before applying for restoration of rights probably had a cumulative effect, he said. "I would imagine—and this is just me speaking—that based on the old rules the white population had the means to pay court costs and restitution and not be disqualified under the financial restrictions," said Henry.[12]

The overall complexity of applying to have rights restored under the old system also led to people being forced to hire attorneys to get through the process. Attorneys estimated those costs alone could stack up to from five thousand to fifteen thousand dollars in legal fees.[13] Critics stressed that the combination of factors stacked the deck against Black Floridians. Even if the rules were race-neutral, Black residents had less wealth and less income on average. Once you added money as a factor, the racial gap was to be expected in the outcome.

Under Bush, the cabinet changed these rules, and the expectation was that things would over time become more equal. But the lessons learned from the *Palm Beach Post* investigation were important. Nearly two decades later, many of these same issues would crop up once again.

Along with the US Commission on Civil Rights, other bodies were busy trying to crack the code of Florida's broken election system. The investigations often started in Florida, but the implications often went well beyond it; Florida was now a poster child of electoral dysfunction, a one-word geographical punch line.

You name it, they investigated it, or at least talked about doing so. The US Government Accountability Office,[14] congressional hearings, task forces of every name and stripe. The federal government started the US Election Assistance Commission as the smoke cleared from the 2000 election.[15] No state wanted to be the next Florida. States updated voting equipment, paid more attention to ballot design, and started reevaluating the management of voter databases.[16] Congress passed the Help America Vote Act of 2002, which created new mandatory national standards for election administration and pumped federal money into states to meet those standards.

In Florida, Governor Bush convened a task force that looked at the 2000 election. It was a bipartisan group of twenty-one that met six times in four different cities over the course of two months. The members heard from experts about how to make elections better in Florida, and also from the residents themselves.

The group had ten Republicans, ten Democrats, and one member without a partisan affiliation. It consisted of five African Americans, fourteen white non-Latinos, and two Latinos.[17] One of the two Latinos was future US Senator and Secretary of State Marco Rubio, when he was a twenty-eight-year-old, first-term state representative. "This task force is just a start," Governor Bush said at the time. "Real electoral reform means not only updating our technology and clarifying our standards. It also means reaffirming our commitment to make sure every citizen has faith and confidence in our electoral procedures, even when the margin of victory in a race is very close."[18]

The recommendation for new ballot machines was a given. The rest of the agenda was largely up in the air. Democrats worried aloud whether some of the reforms they wanted to see would be addressed, such as the use of outdated machinery in majority-minority districts; voters being turned away from the polls if they didn't have the proper identification; and the voting list that erroneously listed some residents as felons. They wanted an open discussion.

"I just hope the script isn't already written," said Chris Smith, a Democratic state representative from a majority-Black Fort Lauderdale district who served on the commission.[19]

One political observer at the time told the *Miami Herald* that Republicans were "between a rock and a hard place" with the work that the commission was doing. "They have to do something," said political scientist Lance deHaven-Smith of Florida State University, who was not involved in the work of the commission. "To the extent that they fix the problems, they're going to be adding Democrats to vote totals in the future, because that's where the problems are—they're in the Black precincts."[20]

One frustrated expert who spoke to the task force was Pat Hollarn, the Republican elections supervisor in Okaloosa County, in the northwestern corner of the state bordering Alabama. At a meeting in a downtown Orlando hotel, she slammed the process for the restoration of voting rights, and said the state managed its voter rolls database in an overly complicated way.

"The whole process of the central voter file is fraught with error," Hollarn testified. "Our records change by the minute. What we're doing is taking 3-month-old information and sending it to Tallahassee. The pain we have caused people . . . has been grievous."[21]

In the end, the task force adopted recommendations for things like prohibiting punch cards across the state and allowing people to vote by mail for any reason whatsoever. The group punted on the issue of voting rights restoration. The task force only recommended a "separate and independent analysis" of the contract with DBT Online more generally regarding the voting rights for people with felony convictions.[22]

"The Florida Legislature should review issues related to the restoration of voting rights to ex-felons with completed sentences, whether convicted in Florida or elsewhere, especially when voting rights have been restored in other states, and recommend possible changes that might be required to the Florida Constitution or to statutes and rules and regulations of the Clemency Board," read the final report. That's it.[23]

Many of the proposals put forward by the task force were made into law. But some never quite made it there.

The legislature even came close to finally addressing the problem of restoration of rights at one point. A 2001 proposal to put the automatic restoration of civil rights on the ballot, to be decided by a popular vote, seemed to hold promise. A busload of people with felony convictions on their records came in from South Florida to plead their case, and—surprisingly—they persuaded a House committee to pass the item unanimously. Both political parties seemed to support it.[24]

The item was sponsored by Chris Smith, the Democrat who feared the fix was already in on the postelection task force. The proposed ballot amendment specified that a person could vote one year after the completion of all parts of a felony sentence, and went on to define what that meant. Completing a sentence meant that the person "has achieved or completed all nonmonetary terms and conditions of community supervision imposed by a court." A prison sentence counted. Probation counted. Money owed to the state did not count. That was an entirely separate concern.[25]

In pushing to keep the apparent bipartisan support for the proposal intact,

Kendrick Meek, a Black Democratic state senator from Miami, urged them to make history. "If you want to be the party that erased a major blemish in Florida history that was essentially designed to keep people of color from voting... you have a trophy," said Meek. Two of his very own cousins could not vote because they had felony convictions, he added. "This hits my family."[26]

Smith pleaded with his colleagues. "The question before us is at the heart of our democracy," he said during a committee hearing. "This is an issue in Florida, which along with a lot of other issues, has been a black eye on Florida."[27]

Despite passing the first committee with unanimous bipartisan support, the effort sputtered out and died. In any case, the very public debate and the prospect that voters could actually have a say in the matter pushed the civil rights battle into new terrain.

Ever since 1993, Broward County Democratic State Senator Mandy Dawson had quietly been pushing for change. For more than a decade, she filed a bill every session seeking to ease the process of restoring voting rights, to no avail.

Finally, Dawson decided to go it alone: She would start to gather signatures to do what elected officials would not do in the Republican-controlled state. "There are laws on the book based on the convenience of the oppressor," she said. "It is ridiculous someone has to pay for something over and over. The conservatives are quick to call themselves the Christian Right and talk about faith-based initiatives. Jesus forgives, and so should the state."[28]

Dawson registered her effort with the state in September 2003. As originally conceived, the question was supposed to come before voters in the 2006 midterm elections. "If we get the signatures, I think there's a good chance an amendment would pass," she said.[29] The proposal would allow for someone to vote or hold office "upon the completion of sentence," sidestepping the standard rights restoration process through the cabinet.

Dawson's effort coordinated closely with Howard Simon's ACLU of Florida. Along with dozens of local, state, and national organizations, the ACLU formed the blanket group the Florida Rights Restoration Coalition (FRRC), under its umbrella. The coalition hosted a series of workshops in 2003 to help people submit their paperwork to the state to get their rights back. Organizational funding from the ACLU played the role of glue, keeping the separate groups focused on the common goal.[30]

The effort to gather signatures managed to raise only $3,500 total, all of which came in October 2003, much of which came from a historically Black port workers' labor union in Miami.[31] Volunteers gathered petitions, but it soon became apparent that it was a hopeless moonshot, to the point that organizers failed to file a single valid petition signature with the state. To get on the ballot, they would have had to gather 611,009 valid signatures.[32] "It was more passion and devotion to the issue than it was a realistic financial analysis," conceded Simon.[33]

Regardless, Simon made a bold stride that would reap benefits many years later. During the aborted effort, for the first time he created a paid position whose sole focus was to run the Florida Rights Restoration Coalition. The coalition was in its infancy, but it began to emerge as a collective, powerful voice for change.

"We knew strategically that getting a ballot initiative for constitutional change was not viable at that time," remembered Muslima Lewis, the second paid staffer of the FRRC. "So our efforts were devoted to changing the rules of clemency."[34]

While the group couldn't realistically get a question on the ballot, it continued to organize meetings across the state in an effort to give voice to the very people who were directly disenfranchised. When enough of them gathered, when enough of them raised their voices together, elected officials would eventually have to respond to the strength of their numbers.

"One goal of the FRRC was in fact to transition leadership over to people who were directly impacted, and to get people directly impacted very much involved in the work of the coalition in deciding its focus, how we work, really getting directly impacted people in leadership," said Lewis.

Simon explained about the earliest work of the FRRC: "One of our goals was to make this a major issue confronting anybody who would be running for statewide office, or any political office. To bring this from out under the table, and try to demonstrate that this was the principal civil rights issue confronting the state of Florida."[35]

By the time the next presidential election came around, Governor Bush wanted the world to know he was a believer. He announced in June 2004 that under his Clemency Board rule changes, about twenty thousand Floridians had their civil rights restored without a hearing in a single year and that they would be newly eligible to vote for the November election. It was by far the most rights restored in a single year since automatic restoration of rights was ended in 1991. The high number also accounts for Howard Simon's ACLU forcing the state prison system to help newly released inmates with applications to get their rights back. The settlement agreement from that lawsuit was hard at work; Simon's multipronged approach to tackling the issue was starting to pay dividends.

The governor's fellow Republicans worried that the newly eligible voters could swing the state more Democratic for his brother's presidential re-election campaign, a sentiment he downplayed. "We have a duty first and foremost, and I intend to carry out that duty, and I don't worry about the ramifications of that," Bush said, referring to his role in helping people get their rights back. "I'm comfortable with this process . . . I think it's a fair process."[36]

At the same time, critics said the announcement was only intended to deflect attention from a mounting scandal: The state was once again using flawed felon voter lists.

Just a month earlier, the state election officials sent county supervisors of elections a list of forty-eight thousand registered voters who should be removed from the voting rolls because they had felony records. Registered Democrats outnumbered Republicans three to one. Nearly half the list was made up of Black voters. Worst of all, dogged reporters revealed that for some reason "Hispanics" were not included as a category in the list, in a state at a time when Hispanic voters favored Republicans. As a result, only sixty-one Hispanics out of more than forty-eight thousand names were included in the list. Then, the *Miami Herald* reported that at least two thousand Floridians were erroneously placed on the list altogether.[37]

History—recent history—was repeating.

When enough bad press about the flawed list spread about, the Bush administration dropped plans to use it entirely. The Bush administration said it was a perfect storm of honest mistakes; politicos called foul.

"This is a typical South [tactic], denying the right to vote based on race and class," Reverend Jesse Jackson told a Miami radio station about the scandal.[38] While the Bush administration emphatically maintained it all was a mistake, the *Sarasota Herald-Tribune* found what looked like a smoking gun in an email: A state law enforcement official wrote to a colleague that Governor

Bush was explicitly warned that he should "pull the plug" on the flawed list. Election officials were not confident in the work of a state contractor that put the list together, wrote the official. The governor overrode the recommendation and only "pulled the plug" on the flawed list when it became a scandal.[39]

"This isn't functionaries making decisions below the governor. This is the governor directly overruling the recommendations of state employees," snapped Ralph Neas, an attorney who headed a group that did legal work for the NAACP. "This shows a direct, personal involvement of the governor in the decisions of state employees directly related to the conduct of elections. It is nothing short of astonishing."

In 2005, Governor Bush convened yet another commission. This time, it was called the Governor's Ex-Offender Task Force. The goal was to make recommendations about how to help the estimated thirty thousand people who leave prison and reenter Florida society each year. "Florida is committed to the ideal of America being the land of second chance," Governor Bush wrote in the executive order that created the task force. "Without successful re-entry into one's community, recidivism is likely to occur."[40]

The final report, released two years later, made it as a finding of fact that having a felony record makes it harder to get a job, a finding that should have surprised nobody. Apart from the stigma associated with having a record, a whole slew of careers were off the table because state licensing laws effectively made entire career paths "off-limits" for someone with a felony record. The only way to get around this was by having the Clemency Board give someone their full civil rights back.[41]

The group recommended that the legislature should change the laws to remove this employment barrier. Instead, there should be a single background check law, with a simple list of "offenses relevant to the occupation, license, or place of employment." That way it would be less of a blanket ban, and more targeted. A convicted bank robber, perhaps, should not be allowed to work as a bank teller. But why stop them from studying to become a registered nurse or a lawyer later in life?

The state should create a "transition authority," the group suggested. This new government service would coordinate across all levels of state government to better help someone transition into civil society. The very mission statement of the Florida Department of Corrections should be changed to "explicitly address successful reentry," the group suggested. And before someone is released, they should be given a "discharge handbook" that would include an "individualized reentry plan and the programs and services available in his home community." Few of these recommendations were followed. Many remain outstanding to-do items in Florida's criminal justice system.

At the end of its report, the task force made a long list of items that it wasn't able to get to. So, it made one of its recommendations that the task force should be reconvened for yet another session, and it made a long list of things that should receive "further study." Studying the racial disparity in state prisons was one suggestion. Then, the group recommended more study of the "constitutional, statutory and regulatory barriers to the restoration of civil rights" in Florida—rights including the right to bear arms, the right to hold certain jobs, the right to serve on a jury, and the right to vote.

For the second time, a commission convened by Governor Bush had the opportunity to investigate Florida's lifelong ban on voting. Instead of actually studying the issue when it had the chance, though, the group kicked the can down the road, recommending further study.

The Governor's Ex-Offender Task Force never reconvened. The final report was issued in late November, after a gubernatorial election was held in 2006. Bush had already served eight years as governor, and he was termed out. On the horizon came a new brand of Republican governor that would soon change everything.

4
THE REFORMER

The Republican running to succeed Jeb Bush in the governor's office was not known to Floridians as a soft-on-crime guy. For a few years in the 1990s, Attorney General Charlie Crist was on a short list of the toughest-on-crime politicians in the entire nation. Nowadays, when you bring up this chapter of his story, Crist backs into that stubborn fact with a bit of a wind-up.

"I was in the state Senate at the time this occurred. And we were number one in violent crime in America," Crist told me. "Every three minutes and forty-five seconds another violent crime was happening in Florida.[1] Murder, rape, robbery. Violent, violent crime. I took it upon myself as a public servant to try to find a way to stem the tide of violent crime that was happening to women and men and senior citizens all over the state."[2]

In 1995, Crist sponsored a state Senate bill that would have brought chain gangs back to Florida for the first time since the 1940s.[3] An omnibus corrections bill that year passed with Crist's bill tacked onto it as an amendment. The section explicitly required that some inmates "perform labor wearing leg irons in chain gang work groups."

He wasn't really a fan of chain gangs, he explained years later. "I'm not a fan of the death penalty either. But I understand there are times when certain punishments will deter people from killing our fellow citizens, or raping them or robbing their home. And so I was fine with it. I saw it as right versus wrong."[4]

The most far-reaching accomplishment Crist had as a state senator was sponsoring a law that required state prisoners to serve a mandatory 85 percent of their sentences, capping gained time for good behavior at 15 percent. Florida's prisons were overcrowded at the time, and to make room for new inmates the Department of Corrections had started to release inmates early. Sometimes they served less than a third of their sentence.[5]

Even in the tough-on-crime 1990s, Crist's uncharitable passion for punishment and justice was enough to make him stand out. The way he approached the problem earned him a nickname that still shadowed him when he won the Republican nomination to become the governor of Florida in 2006: Chain Gang Charlie.

The very act of filing his documents to run for governor seemed to be an extension of this public persona. The paperwork was hand-delivered to elections officials by John Walsh, the host of *America's Most Wanted*. Walsh's son was kidnapped and murdered in Florida in 1981, and since then his name had become synonymous with being tough on crime. "He is a multi-issue man," Walsh said as he turned in Crist's paperwork. "I think Floridians will know he is a staunch law-and-order candidate, which is a good thing."[6]

As sharp-edged as he was on the issues, Crist was never quite a fire-spewing demagogue. In conversation he's a soft-spoken, upright descendant of Cypriot-Greek ancestry. His complexion wears the subtropical Florida sun like his ancestors wore the beaming Mediterranean, and for most of his public life he's sported a trademark head of white hair atop his boyish face.

He was looking good in the polls mere weeks before the 2006 gubernatorial election, when he surprised the political establishment by letting on that he supported an unthinkable policy. As he told the editorial board of the *Tampa Tribune* in an interview: If elected, he would support giving people with nonviolent felony convictions their right to vote back. Automatically, without the need for any hearing.[7]

"I was a Republican at the time, mind you," he remembered, foreshadowing the backlash that followed.[8] As Crist tells it, he received calls from his Republican colleagues immediately after the interview was published. "'Why would you commit to that policy?'" he paraphrased. "And I said, 'I don't know, why not?' They were concerned that that might be mostly Democratic voters, and I said, 'Look, if you really want to know my answer why I'd do that it's quite simple. I just believe in forgiveness. And I think we should all believe in forgiveness. I mean, who among us doesn't need a second chance or a third chance, or even more?'"[9]

Crist himself had been part of the Florida Cabinet for years, overseeing clemency decisions while serving as the elected attorney general of the state. He had never expressed this side of himself. Across the ideological spectrum, the shift was a head-scratcher.

"From Chain Gang Charlie to 'people deserve to have their rights restored' is a significant evolution," said Howard Simon. In that professed switch, Simon saw an opening for the ACLU to make a real impact.[10]

Crist credited his grandfather who taught him about forgiveness, and he also cited a certain strain of campaign fatigue. After political events held across the state, he would find himself chatting up members of the audience, making his final pitch for their vote one-on-one. But over and over again, he said, the cold truth would come out.

"Pretty soon the pattern was so clear. As soon as I would ask—'I would appreciate your vote,' they would sort of look down and say, 'I can't vote,'" he said. "And so I knew what the answer was if I were to ask why. I almost stopped asking it because it was so prolific that 'It's because I made a mistake' is how they would usually phrase it."[11]

The most surprising thing about Crist's newfound openness to the idea of restoring voting rights is that he actually did something about it once he won.

Three months into his term as governor he decided to bring a proposal on automatically restoring civil rights to people with felony convictions before the Florida Executive Board of Clemency.[12] The cabinet after the 2006 election was politically split. Crist, the governor, was a Republican. So was Attorney General Bill McCollum and Agriculture Commissioner Charles Bronson, while Chief Financial Officer Alex Sink was a Democrat. The politics of Florida's cabinet make these aspects of executive power something like a negotiation. Even if the governor wanted to give every last person their voting rights back, he still needed two other members of the cabinet to agree with him. With a bipartisan cabinet, a vote can always go one way or the other, for political or other reasons.

Sink made it clear that she would support Crist on the measure. Attorney General McCollum wrote a scathing editorial against automatically granting people their civil rights back. He wrote that since an estimated 45 percent of offenders would commit another crime within five years, granting rights only to revoke them again would create a "revolving door" that "would diminish the integrity of our democratic government and the rule of law."[13]

Not only would they be able to vote, McCollum argued, but a whole range of new employment opportunities might open up for them. "Felons will be able to acquire a state-licensed job, whether as a household pest-control exterminator, residential-building contractor or alarm-system installer, allowing felons to regularly access people's homes," he wrote disapprovingly. "They will be eligible to sit on a jury to carry out our system of justice. Felons will have the same vote at the ballot box as law-abiding citizens."[14] McCollum's concerns flew in the face of the Ex-Offender Task Force report, which was released just a few months earlier.

The only civil right that Crist's proposal would not grant was the right to own a gun. For that, someone would have to come before the board and ask. But first, the politics of the situation had to be addressed. Sink was a *yes* and McCollum was a *no*. That left Republican Agriculture Commissioner Bronson.

Bronson is a Central Florida–born cattle rancher, tracing his lineage in that part of the state to some of the earliest white settlers from the decades after Florida first became a state.[15] The Native Americans and free Black settlers had been pushed into the southern swamps by the reign of terror that was the Seminole Wars, and in their place came the cattle ranches.

Crist couldn't put his finger on where Bronson might swing on the issue. During the normal course of business as the agriculture commissioner, Bronson was concerned with controlling wildfires and the health of the state's citrus industry. He didn't comment much on hot-button issues. Bronson was a former reserve police officer. Would he reflexively side with a hard-line law-and-order approach like McCollum? Howard Simon didn't want to leave it to the flip of a coin. He hired a lobbyist specifically to whisper in Bronson's ear before the vote.[16]

The day of the cabinet meeting, Governor Crist opened the gathering with a prepared speech. Most of the public in attendance was Black, waiting to see if an issue they had worked on for so many years would at long last see resolution.[17]

"If a person is working he or she is less likely to commit a crime. Only a few states do not restore civil rights," Crist said. "Like Florida, many Southern states struggled through the Jim Crow era, resisted calls to change laws, continued to deny the restoration of civil rights. Since then, most states have realized the historical underpinning for not repealing these unjust, unfair laws. It is time for Florida to make the same realization and leave the ranks of this offensive minority. Justice delayed is justice denied. And people are waiting."[18]

At the time he made the speech, the backlog of people waiting to get a hearing before the Board of Executive Clemency had reached absurd numbers. About one hundred thousand Floridians were on the waitlist, waiting to plead their cases one by one before the group that had just convened.[19]

The list grew faster than the Board of Executive Clemency could make its way through the cases. It had become so infamously long and hopeless that many never bothered to apply to have their rights restored at all. If nothing was done, the numbers were on track to continue to grow.

"Some have argued that restoration of civil rights is somehow weak on crime. For more than a decade I have worked to ensure that criminals are held accountable for their actions with very strict sentencing. With chain gangs, even," Crist continued. "The ultimate goal of these laws is justice. This is not about punishment, but this is about fundamental fairness."[20]

During the meeting, Bronson slipped Crist a handwritten note, suggesting a provision be added to the governor's proposal for automatic restoration of rights. If someone regains their rights but then commits another crime, they should not be able to regain their rights again for a ten-year period. "I don't mind giving people a second chance," Bronson argued. "But if they blow that second chance, I don't know why we ought to give them a third chance."[21] Sink countered with a modification that would allow people who committed less severe crimes to keep their rights but that would keep the spirit of Bronson's idea intact. Crist, Sink, and Bronson were on the same page. The proposal was passed.[22]

The rules adopted by the board had three tiers: one for nonviolent crimes, one for violent crimes, and a final, more arduous tier for people with murder or sexual offenses. People in the second tier could apply to have their case reviewed as soon as they got out of prison. Those in the first tier could get their rights automatically restored, so long as they paid all their restitution, fines, and court fees.

Attorney General McCollum, the only *no* vote, attacked the automatic restoration of civil rights, calling it the worst possible insult he could conjure up at the moment. He said, "I think it's a very liberal thing we did today."[23]

For Howard Simon and his small but growing team dedicated to the cause at the ACLU, the vote represented a major victory. "This plan is a good first step, but there is much more work to be done," Simon said at the time.[24]

Democrats were ecstatic about the move. They painted McCollum as part of a fading remnant of the reactionary Republican Party, and they felt optimistic about such a major bipartisan victory a few short months into Crist's governorship. "I think we have a progressive governor, someone who can move us along into the 21st century," remarked State Senator Al Lawson, a Black Democrat from Tallahassee.[25]

In an interview with National Public Radio (NPR) after the vote was taken, Agriculture Commissioner Bronson explained why he went along with the vote, despite the objections of the attorney general and other Republican hard-liners. He didn't agree with giving people who committed violent crimes their rights back automatically, he said, but he didn't want to give too much weight to the various numbers of repeat offenders that got tossed around in the process.

"Roughly 50 percent of felons who get out will reoffend and go back in. You know, I said if I was Solomon and I could tell you who those 50 percent were, it'd make it easy for me to make a better determination," Bronson said. "But I didn't feel that lumping all 100 percent of the people—those 50 percent that do want to go back in society and do the right things—I didn't think they needed to be punished along with those who were going to re-offend."[26]

It was April 2007, weeks before Barack Obama formally announced his candidacy for president. But chatter about the next election cycle was already swirling in the increasingly dark last days of the George W. Bush administration. The prospect of adding potentially tens of thousands of eligible voters to the rolls in time for the next presidential election in the most notorious swing state in the nation was a captivating concept. In the NPR interview, Bronson was clear about this. Would the unknown number of people affected by the board's vote be able to cast ballots in 2008? "Oh yes, I think the majority of these numbers are going to," said the Republican. "At least those who are qualified now will be eligible to vote in the next election."[27]

Crist got a small amount of after-the-fact help from Democrats. Shortly after the clemency rules were changed, then State Senator Frederica Wilson slipped fifty thousand dollars of one-time funding into a bill to help implement the new policy. The money went to the Florida Parole Commission, the independent state agency that took care of investigations for rights restoration. The new money was used to notify as many people as possible of the new hearing-free restoration process, open a toll-free hotline where people could call for information about restoring their rights, hold staff trainings, and put together outreach events across the state, from Gainesville and Fort Lauderdale to Eatonville and Palatka.[28]

The Parole Commission is the smallest agency in the entire state government, and in 2007 it had the measly budget of only $10.2 million—making it cheaper to operate than a single state prison.[29] With the newly approved rules, the Parole Commission had its workload for clemency cases explode overnight.[30] By the end of 2007, the state was restoring civil rights to an average of 5,100 people per month, up from the previous year's average of only 1,000 people a month. Yet staffing at the Parole Commission had *decreased* by 20 percent from where it was in 2001. To keep up with the investigations and get people their voting rights back quickly, the commission estimated that it would have to hire forty-two new people to work their way through the slog, to the tune of $1.8 million.[31] The agency sent a request to the state legislature to provide the new resources. Howard Simon sent a letter to state elected officials urging them to approve the much-needed new hires.[32]

But while State Senator Wilson earmarked some funding to help the commission work its way through the deluge, the governor's colleagues in the Republican Party took steps in the opposite direction. During the next legislative session, a bill was proposed that would transfer all the work of the Florida Parole Commission to the Florida Department of Corrections, the notoriously underfunded state prison system.[33] A House staff analysis found that this change would save taxpayers $1.9 million a year as a result of the "consolidation" of state agencies.[34]

Monica David, the head of the Parole Commission, warned a House committee that the move would directly impact the thousands of Floridians whose rights were slated to be restored. "This proposal would delete all of those positions of those people who are currently doing the job, who have the expertise to do so," she said, referring to the investigations needed to complete the procedure. "It would slow down the process."[35]

The Florida House of Representatives, led by House Speaker Marco Rubio, passed the bill. It was a largely party-line vote, with most Republicans supporting the measure. In a statement and open letter sent to Crist, Rubio, and others, Howard Simon warned that if passed by the Senate and signed into law, "perceived cost savings" could undermine the governor's "commitment to address Florida disenfranchisement crisis."[36]

The bill did not pass the Senate. Rather, it became an object of political ping-ponging in that year's budget negotiations. By the end of that process, the Parole Commission was an ailing agency. The damages were tallied in the commission's annual report for that year.[37] "While the Commission remained intact as an independent state agency, the Commission lost $2 million in funding and 17 full time employees were laid off," reads the report. The agency had more work than ever, and fewer people to do it.

Since being elected to the Florida House in 2000, Marco Rubio had risen quickly through the ranks, a trajectory that culminated in him being elected the first Cuban American Speaker of the House in Florida history. He cultivated a close relationship with Governor Bush and seemed to have a bright future ahead of him.

Rubio and Crist were two of the top Republicans in the state. They maintained a working relationship, but deep down each felt the other was a political rival. Both had competing visions of what good Republican governance looked like: Crist was the unabashed middle-ground-seeking populist, whereas Rubio charted a more hard-line, libertarian approach. Bush had worn off on him.

In 2005, as he was sworn into his position of House Speaker, Rubio declared that he wanted to help chart a path for the future direction of the state. He gave each lawmaker who was there a copy of a blank book and asked them to fill it with ideas of how to make the state better.[38] As he took the podium, Rubio announced that he would start holding "Idea Raiser" events across the state, opportunities for everyday people to suggest changes to the state government. Those ideas would be collected and printed into a book at the end of the process. Rubio hoped the project would fill in the vacuum of conservatism that he felt Bush would leave when his last term as governor was finished.[39]

Rubio crisscrossed the state, holding more than one hundred "Idea Raiser" events over the next year.[40] The book was published one week before Crist was elected governor.

"Politics needs to become more proactive. Tomorrow's crises are only emerging problems today, and it is easier and less expensive to solve them now," wrote Rubio. "But when problems go unresolved for too long, they become a crisis. Then the options narrow, and the price goes up."[41]

The book features ideas that have never been implemented, like privatizing the Division of Drivers' Licenses; eliminating property taxes for primary residences;[42] converting all of the state's vehicles into a "high fuel efficiency fleet"; curbing "endless" appeals by people convicted of felonies; and giving whistleblower protections to prostitutes so they could help bring down their pimps. But many of the ideas, like mandating a supermajority two-thirds vote in the legislature to raise taxes, collecting DNA from everyone convicted of a felony, and allowing drivers to register vehicles for multiple years have actually been made into law.[43]

Many ideas collected by the effort didn't make it into the book. On August 9, 2006, resident Robert Reinhagen submitted "automatic restoration of voting rights to ex-felons who have completed their sentences" to Rubio's project through its dedicated website.[44] On June 6 of that year, resident Samuel Acosta in Orlando submitted the idea that "a person should not lose their right to vote upon committing their first felony."[45]

When giving his pitch for the guidelines, Rubio liked to say three things would determine whether an idea would make it into the book: It had to be relevant to day-to-day life; it had to have a conceivable impact on the state's future; and it could not expand the role of the government. Anything that met these criteria would be considered.

"The ideas in this book were not written by special interests or by out-of-touch politicians," reads the sleeve of the book. But when you crack it open and look inside, a small note appears just below the copyright information: "This book was paid for and sponsored, in part, by the Republican Party of Florida."

The project presented itself as an open-sourced, rare opportunity for the public to directly take a role in the future direction of the state. In practice, it became a rubber stamp for the kinds of ideas and biases that Rubio and the entrenched Republican Party already shared. Anything remotely coded as Democratic or "liberal" was left out, regardless of whether it met all of the stated requirements.

Despite the task forces, the studies, the federal lawsuits, the protests, the findings of the US Commission on Civil Rights, despite it all, the Republican establishment was in no mood to expand voting rights.

The problem was, Charlie Crist, the Republican governor, was not following the playbook.

President Obama hangs over the tale of Charlie Crist's career in politics like an all-encompassing shadow, swallowing up all the contours of shade and reducing everything to a black-and-white proposition. This is the tragedy of Crist's years as Florida governor. He was the last of his kind: the populist who at times angered his own party and at times electrified the so-called opposition, rallying them behind him in a way that has entirely disappeared from our politics at all levels.

Crist ran on becoming "the People's Governor," and public polls suggest he fulfilled that campaign promise. By his second year in office, Crist was polling with a 66 percent approval rating across the board, including a full 66 percent approval from Democrats.[46] No Florida governor has polled so high on either measure since.[47]

By mid-2008 Crist announced that 115,232 Floridians with felony convictions had regained the right to vote since the cabinet started automatic restoration, a huge increase from business as usual.[48] "That could make an enormous difference in November," the governor told a crowd of law enforcement officials and prison rights activists gathered in Tallahassee.[49]

The governor was pleased with the large number—a milestone—but the budget cuts at the Florida Parole Commission were still holding the progress back. So on August 27, the day before Obama accepted the Democratic nomination for president, Crist issued an executive order to crank up the volume. The order directed the Parole Commission and the Florida Office of Executive Clemency to "use all of its available resources to notify those whose civil rights have been restored." He ordered that the offices should mail a voter registration form to all the people who were newly eligible to vote, and that the state set up an online database where you could check if your rights were restored.[50]

Two days earlier, the *Orlando Sentinel* reported that out of the many thousands who just had their voting rights restored, only about nine thousand people—less than 8 percent of newly eligible voters—had actually registered to vote. The paper found that the state never informed them that they had just gotten their rights back. Crist intended to do something about that.[51]

The presidential election came at last, and the stage was set for Crist's fall from grace within the Republican Party. The problems were twofold. First, Black Floridians were turning out in record numbers across the state to vote for Obama, which spelled bad news for Republicans. In South Florida, news crews showed long lines outside of polling places during the early voting period. The images spread like wildfire, making their way to national news coverage. The second problem was how Crist responded to these images.

Crist issued an executive order expanding the hours of early voting in the lead-up to the presidential election. This was the last thing Republicans wanted. Minorities—especially Black Floridians—tend to vote early. Republicans preferred fewer hours for early voting, and long lines if it had to happen at all. In his book, Crist describes speaking with Republican political commentator Ana Navarro about his decision. Navarro was, at the time, a campaign adviser for Republican nominee John McCain.[52] "I can't believe you just signed that executive order," Navarro told Crist, according to the book. "You just handed the election to Obama." (Navarro later admitted to voicing that sentiment.)[53]

Obama won Florida with an astounding 96 percent support from the Black community, along with 57 percent support from Latinos.

By the time Obama was sworn in, the effects of the Great Recession were already beating the Florida economy down. The state was ground zero for the foreclosure crisis, the aftereffect of a flimsy building boom that propped up the local economy across the peninsula. When the foreclosures came, they came in shocking numbers and with numbing frequency. In Lee County in the southwestern part of the state, one out of ten homeowners was unable to keep up with payments for their homes. In a single zip code there, 42 percent of properties went into foreclosure, a real estate data firm estimated.[54]

Lee County was the backdrop for the nail in the coffin for Crist's working relationship with the Republican Party. President Obama traveled to Fort Myers to give a speech urging a federal stimulus package to soften the blow and to ease the number of foreclosures. President Bush signed a large stimulus package a year earlier, and there was a growing consensus that a second package was needed. Governor Crist joined Obama for the event, and he put his two cents in for why Florida could benefit from some of that stimulus money. "It's important that we pass this stimulus package," said Crist. "This is not about partisan politics, this is about rising above that, helping America and reigniting our economy."[55]

The next thing Crist did would change the entire trajectory of his political career. In Florida political circles, it's simply known as "The Hug." YouTube has videos showing the moment in slow motion, on repeat. After he introduced President Obama, the two briefly embraced onstage. They shook hands and patted one another on the shoulder while saying something inaudible between them.

"Governor Crist shares my conviction that creating jobs and turning this economy around is a mission that transcends party," said Obama in his speech. "When the town is burning, you don't check party labels. Everyone needs to grab a hose, and that's what Charlie Crist is doing here tonight."[56]

The embrace lasted all of two seconds, but the reaction to the image was swift and vengeful. Crist had crossed a line. The election of the nation's first Black president set in motion a wave of political anger and thinly cloaked racism that had been unseen for a generation. Republicans were angry and scared about what could happen to the country under Obama, and, in their anger, they sought out the most extreme positions from the most extreme candidates. Any whiff of compromise or playing nice was met with hostility.

A month after "The Hug," Crist announced that he would not run for a second term as governor. Instead, he would run for a US Senate seat that was being left open. At first, the chairman of the National Republican Senatorial Committee, Senator John Cornyn of Texas, endorsed Crist's run for Senate. But the wing of the party that came to be known as the Tea Party soon started to creep out of the shadows. Riding on their backs was Marco Rubio, who had just left Tallahassee after reaching his term limits as a member of the House. He entered the race as a Republican challenger to Crist.

"One wing of the party—I don't believe it is the majority wing of the party—believes that if you can't beat them, join them," Rubio said on *Fox News*. The implication was that Crist had become a Democrat.[57]

"The Hug" featured prominently in Rubio's attack ads. In interviews, Rubio painted him as a sellout to conservative values and too darn cozy with liberals. "He supported the stimulus package," said Rubio in an early MSNBC interview. "He restored the rights of felons to vote automatically here in Florida, he tried to impose a cap and trade system. None of these were part of his platform when he ran for governor in 2006."[58]

Rubio repeatedly used the one-liner that Crist had automatically restored people's voting rights as an implicit attack, while never clearly laying out his own vision for justice.[59] After it emerged that thirteen people—one of whom was a child rapist—mistakenly had their civil rights restored through the process Crist spearheaded, Rubio called for an end to automatic restoration.

"Governor Crist was wrong to support this program's expansion and he has failed to oversee its proper implementation," Rubio said in a statement.[60] "In light of the flaws that have come to light, Governor Crist should suspend this program indefinitely to ensure more of these mistakes are not made on his watch."

The previous year, Rubio voted to slash the budget and reduce the staff of the Parole Commission—the very people charged with preventing those mistakes from taking place. Rubio voted to exacerbate the very problem he now railed against.

Crist, a lifelong Republican, was put in a position where he had to defend his conservative credentials against the mounting backlash. "I happen to be pro-life, I'm pro-gun, I'm pro-family. I'm for the death penalty. You know, you name just about any issue that people care about—especially in a Republican primary—and I'm there," Crist said at the time.[61]

But the push from the right proved too much to handle. In April 2010, Charlie Crist declared that he would leave the Republican Party and continue his run for Senate as a political independent. In the speech he gave making the announcement, Crist acknowledged that he was entering "uncharted territory" by turning the race into a three-way battle.

"My decision to run for the U.S. Senate as a candidate without party affiliation says more about our nation and our state than it says about me," Crist said in his announcement speech. "I haven't supported an idea because it's a Republican idea or it's a Democratic idea, I support ideas that I think are good ideas."[62]

In the end, the governor running as an independent split the vote with the Democratic nominee Kendrick Meek, an early proponent of the restoration of voting rights. Crist won only 29.7 percent of the vote, with Meek taking 20.2 percent, leaving Rubio with the win with the remaining 48.9 percent. The Republican Party at the peak of the Tea Party craze fell perfectly in line with its preferred candidate, Marco Rubio, and the Cuban American was now heading to Washington.[63]

In the race for governor over who would replace Crist, things followed a similar tack. A politically unknown businessman named Rick Scott ran in the Republican primary against Florida's Republican Attorney General Bill McCollum, the one who complained that Crist spearheaded a "liberal thing" in giving people their civil rights back. The businessman walloped the attorney. In turn Scott faced Democratic Florida CFO Alex Sink—also a member of the cabinet, but one who voted to give the rights back. You might say all the liberal things died that November 2 when Scott won the election.

5
NO RULES

If Charlie Crist sacrificed his ideological purity to become the "People's Governor," incoming Republican Rick Scott made the opposite calculation. Scott sacrificed the easy crowd-pleasers of good government to become a divisive anthropomorphized script of Tea Party talking points.

Any Floridian living in the state at the time will recall how—within weeks of his inauguration in 2011—Scott turned down $2.4 billion from the federal government to build a high-speed train line connecting Tampa and Orlando. It was to be the first in the state's high-speed train network. The money was already approved and ready to go. It was a done deal. All the State of Florida had to do was pony up the remaining $200 million for the project and it would be left with a profitable turnkey operation connecting two of the fastest-growing cities in the United States, one of which was the tourism capital of the nation. The state's own Department of Transportation conceded that the plan would be a net moneymaker.

But for Scott, this was a bad idea. At some point, possibly decades into the future, it could cost Florida taxpayers additional money, and this was an ideological line that could not be crossed, no matter the free money and no matter the practicality. Scott denied the dollars. Instead, the federal government sent it to fund a project in Connecticut.[1] The bullet train connecting Hartford to New Haven started operating in 2018.[2]

With the election of 2010, the nation turned a corner. Pragmatism was out the window. Political dogmatism and making President Obama look bad were the new vogue. Florida's system of shared executive government was remade overnight by the political wave that just swept the nation. No longer was the Florida Cabinet a bipartisan body, where compromise was possible. Alongside Scott, in came a full slate of Tea Party politicians who made it known that "compromise" was a four-letter word. Every office and branch of the state government was now led by Republicans who wanted to satisfy the base.

Voting rights was one of the first big-ticket items on the agenda. A month after the new cabinet and governor were sworn in, newly elected Attorney General Pam Bondi surprised the state at the first Board of Executive Clemency meeting. After a parade of people who came before the board were denied clemency or pardons one by one by the board, Bondi announced at the very end of the meeting that the system built by Governor Crist and the former cabinet was unacceptable. The Clemency Board was scheduled to meet again a few weeks later, and Bondi wanted to use that time to shake things up.

"After carefully considering the existing rules I believe there need to be changes. I disagree with automatic restoration of rights," said Bondi, a future United States attorney general. "I believe that there should be a waiting period and that you should have to ask to have your rights restored if you are a felon."[3]

"It's hard to think that there isn't a little bit of politics in this because it's so extreme and the basis for it is so out of line with so much development that we've had here in Florida," Howard Simon told the *Palm Beach Post*.[4]

In a statement, Bondi called the restoration of civil rights an "entitlement," rhetorically linking it to the big-government Tea Party boogeymen programs Social Security and Medicare. Red meat for the base.[5]

The final piece of maneuvering was to stress that public officials convicted of corruption should not be allowed to automatically get their rights back, and thus be able to run for office again. These nameless, faceless corrupt public officials were the same pretext used to turn back Florida's automatic rights restoration in the early 1990s, after it was made automatic in 1975. As if on cue, Florida's new agriculture commissioner, Adam Putnam, put out a statement saying he could get behind the measure "to stop public officials who abuse the electoral trust from automatically being allowed to vote or run for office again."[6]

This was the new cabinet in action. In it, Bondi sat alongside Governor Scott as a power player. Bondi was wise to the cameras, the spotlight, and playing up the drama of the moment. Before running for attorney general she was a prosecutor and media-friendly spokesperson of the state attorney's office in Tampa, a post that regularly brought her onto *Fox News* as a legal commentator.

If Bondi brought spark to the table, Scott was the polar opposite. If there is a true antonym to the word "charisma," Rick Scott would be that word. The governor was a businessman who struggled with public speaking and had a cold, seemingly disconnected, flat affect. What he lacked in personal skills he made up for with money. Scott poured $60 million of his personal riches into his gubernatorial campaign, money earned from his healthcare empire.[7] Years before running for office, he oversaw the nation's largest Medicare fraud scheme in history up until that point. Scott was the CEO of Columbia/HCA as it overbilled the federal government for services, employed illegal kickback schemes, and more. The for-profit hospital company was forced to pay a total of $1.7 billion in criminal fines, civil damages, and other penalties to get right with federal prosecutors.[8] Scott was forced to resign from the company as CEO. As an entity, the company he ran pleaded guilty to fourteen felony charges in total.[9] And now, playing the role of politician, Scott sat in judgment of human beings with felony convictions.

The next meeting of the Board of Executive Clemency arrived, and Bondi's proposed rule change was the only thing on the agenda. Scott opened the meeting with an explanation of the rules that were going to be passed. He spoke of them in the future tense, not the conditional tense. The new rules were going to pass.[10]

Under the new rules, anyone with a felony conviction would have to wait up to seven years before they could *ask* for their rights back. There would be no more automatic restoration of rights, for anyone. If you had a low-level felony, you could apply to have your rights restored without a hearing, but only after five years of having no new crimes and no arrests. Even then, the application could be denied. If your case was denied and you still wanted your rights back, you could get in line with the people convicted of more serious crimes, to appear before the board and ask the group of politicians to give you your rights back.[11]

There was already a backlog of tens of thousands of cases waiting for a hearing at this time, people who were not eligible for automatic restoration of rights. Under the system set up by Crist and the cabinet, they still had to come before the board and plead their case. The newly elected cabinet's proposal would make the backlog problem much worse.

No actual physical proposal was released to the public before the meeting, which ran contrary to Florida's robust open meetings and public records laws. As a result, the public was broadly unaware of the new rules even as people stepped to the podium to offer public comment.

"Keeping those plans and conversations out of the sunshine has essentially locked out the Floridians most impacted, as well as criminal justice experts who could provide needed input on crafting the best possible policy," said Danielle Prendergast, an attorney with the ACLU of Florida whom Howard Simon had hired. "We just ask that you slow down this process. If you have faith in this, you can consider this tomorrow as well as today."[12]

Ion Sancho, the supervisor of elections in Leon County, where Tallahassee is, gave a moving statement about how the issue impacted him on his job. He was a history teacher before he became an administrator, and he used history to make his point. "I must call out the stain on Florida for perpetuating a policy that was developed in the 1868 Constitution, whose sole purpose was to ensure that the former slaves of this state could never reintegrate into society," he said. The ongoing policy created a "permanent underclass" in Floridian society and should be rejected, not reinforced. "I can tell you the most searing thing I ever encounter is to, while I'm doing a voter registration drive, encounter individuals who have been permanently disenfranchised and removed from our society," he said. "My soul is seared when I see the shame on their faces as they avert their eyes."[13]

A group of law enforcement officers from across the state supported the rule change. Chief Peter Paulding, the president of the Florida Police Chiefs Association, said that the leadership of his group "unanimously" supported the rule change. "We are the ones out on the streets who arrest them and charge these felons. With so much recidivism, it's only fair that they prove they are committed to a life free of crime before their civil rights are restored," said Paulding, who was the police chief of Gulf Breeze, a tiny city on the Gulf of Mexico in North Florida.[14] A group of sheriffs came to echo his support.

Three different prosecutors from across the state came to Tallahassee to support the new rules. Jerry Hill, the state attorney for the Tenth Judicial Circuit, in Central Florida, took issue with some speakers saying that the ex-felons had already "paid their debt" to society. "I've heard the term 'paid their debt' until I almost rolled out of my chair," he said. "Part of the debt is the loss of these rights. They knew it going in. It was part of the program. They had to earn—some of them had work hard to get that designation of convicted felon."[15]

In reality, people did not know what they were getting into, argued attorney Dale Landry with the Florida State Conference of the NAACP. These changes were being made after many people already did their time and probation. Now this was something extra. "What you're saying is: 'it's my position that I want to impose further sentencing.' That's what we're talking about doing here, to make that requirement hard for them to get their rights back to vote," said Landry.[16]

After all of the people giving public comment finished, it came back to the members of the cabinet. The push to get the new rules approved was done in such whirlwind form that Adam Putnam, the secretary of agriculture, hadn't even wrapped his head around what it was all about. "I would like us to just kind of walk through exactly what the changes are. I think that would be helpful, because I have, during the course of trying to get up to speed on this, gotten a little confused," said Putnam.[17]

After getting a breakdown about what was happening, Putnam opened his mouth as if to ask a critical question. "Is there a—what's the thinking behind the numbers in terms of how long you'll wait before being able to seek restoration?" he asked. "Is there some basis of some FBI crime statistic that after three years, there's X percent of recidivism, and after five it's Y percent recidivism?"[18]

"Mine is what seemed reasonable," said Scott, echoing a notion that would come to define the following years.[19] The governor took a slight, almost imperceptible pause. He asked: "Any other comments? Does anyone want to make any more comments?" Putnam didn't pipe back up or probe with any more questions. Scott brought the rule changes to a vote. The rule change passed unanimously.[20]

Over the Rick Scott years, the Board of Clemency meetings showed how nonchalant and seemingly random the impulses of these politicians could be. As time went on, the national media started to pick up anecdotal stories of one coldhearted denial after another. The exchanges between the politicians and the citizens pleading for their civil rights back drew all kinds of negative attention for their crassness and apparent lack of empathy. A worst-hits kind of aura started to loom over the meetings, with activists and the media hanging on every subsequent meeting, ready to log yet another mark against Scott and his acolytes. Comedian John Oliver featured the meetings in an excruciating segment of his hit show *Last Week Tonight*.[21]

The cabinet denied rights to a man for drinking alcohol, and in different meetings restored rights to people who admitted to smoking weed after getting out of prison.[22] Scott said one applicant had "the worst" driving record he had ever seen, but his rights were restored on the condition that he went two years without another ticket.[23] By contrast, Scott found a veteran's driving record unforgivable, despite evidence that he had a good job and was no longer involved in crime. "If you look at it from our standpoint, you look at it and you say, gosh this is an individual that doesn't worry about complying with the law," Scott said of the man's driving record.[24]

Scott often justified his decision-making by simply saying he didn't feel "comfortable," without explaining further. In one 2011 meeting, Leon Gillis III came before the board. He was released from prison in 1985 but had voted illegally a few times since getting out. Scott denied his case, and Gillis pressed the governor on when he might be able to reapply.

"What else am I supposed to do if I'm doing everything I'm supposed to do . . . how long am I supposed to wait?" he asked. The governor responded, "I could tell you that answer, but today I'm not. I don't feel comfortable doing it."[25]

In some cases, Scott told people they would have to wait two more years before reapplying to get their rights restored; in others, it was ten more years. In one case, Scott told a fifty-four-year-old man that he would have to wait an additional fifty years before he could ask for his rights back.[26]

Toward the end of his tenure in 2016, Scott said what everyone by then knew to be true, but up to that point had not been made explicit. "There is no law we're following. The law has already been followed by the judges. So we get to make our decisions based on our own beliefs. So there's no 'because you did X or did Y, because it's a certain amount of time,' all these things," he said.[27] "This is simply an opportunity for clemency."

That clemency, more often than not, was denied. No one could figure out the rules because there were no rules. Where there are no rules, resentment grows. And resentment is a precursor to every revolution.

Desmond Meade is a Black man who is built like a cinder block with the eyes of a puppy dog and a heart full of passion. His voice bellows from his gut, and it moves to the rhythm of a preacher fully enthralled with the spirit. There's a whiff of the future in his prose, a future all the more important to preserve because it is not promised.

Meade was born in the US Virgin Islands in 1967 but grew up in Miami.

While working as a helicopter mechanic for the US Army in Hawaii, Meade picked up a drug habit that led to his theft of property from the military base. He got a dishonorable discharge and a stint in a Kansas military prison for the theft and went back to Florida after getting out of prison in 1993. Working as a celebrity bodyguard in Miami, he fell into a cycle of drugs and other crimes that led to other charges, and more prison time. In 2004 he was released from prison when his latest conviction was suddenly reversed on a technicality.[28]

Back on the streets, Meade found himself at rock bottom. The way he tells the story, he stood on the train tracks in a seedy part of Miami contemplating suicide. But the train never came. He took it as a sign and walked a few blocks away to check himself into a rehab program.

Off drugs, Meade's perceptions sharpened. He paid more attention to politics as he thought about his own journey and where he wanted to go. A positive vision of the future slowly revealed itself to him.

In 2006, Meade walked into a monthly meeting with the Florida Rights Restoration Coalition, the group convened by Howard Simon and the ACLU of Florida that was working to make the restoration of voting rights a statewide issue.[29] "When I got there, it was an eye opener," Meade said of his first meeting with the coalition.[30]

Meade stayed connected to the group for the coming years, and he shared a sense of accomplishment for the progress under Governor Crist, even if he himself didn't have his rights back yet. Progress was progress.

But with progress came struggles. The financial crisis of 2007 and 2008 hit the ACLU hard. The Florida retirees who were the base of the local ACLU were forced to tighten their belts across the board. Donations dwindled. "There were a lot of terminations because of that, and we had to cut back expenses every place we could," said Simon. That meant the budget for the Florida Rights Restoration Coalition was on the chopping block.[31]

"It was entirely for financial reasons. We were cut to the bone," said Simon. "Staff said, 'This is one of the areas where—not that we're gonna turn our back on it—but if we could find somebody who could take this on and take this off our backs, that it would help us.'"[32]

Desmond Meade turned out to be that person. He assumed control of the FRRC and took it off the hands of the ACLU. Now at the helm of the untethered coalition, Meade watched in horror as Governor Scott and the cabinet undid the hard-fought civil rights victories of the Governor Crist era.

"Seeing that rollback was very disheartening," said Meade. "To think that politicians could actually have that much power to decide which American citizens get to vote and which American citizens don't get to vote. Just with a stroke of a pen."[33]

If the destiny of people like Meade depended on the whims of politicians, what they did to better their own lives didn't count for much. The governor could deny Meade his rights just because he felt like it. And it would stay that way unless Meade and the FRRC had something to say about it.

Meade registered the FRRC as an independent nonprofit group in Florida in December 2011, making it capable of taking tax-deductible donations.[34] The little bird now had its wings.

Meade gave Simon a call. He wanted to get together a group of people to engage in a grand mission. In essence, Meade called for a second round of the failed ballot initiative from 2003. "I think he convened the right people, the legal team," said Simon. Simon himself wasn't a lawyer, but by then he had spent decades supervising them and more or less knew how to think like one. Along with a few attorneys, Simon himself was on the legal team of the new endeavor.[35]

Over the next year and a half, the group met by phone, trying to hammer out what they wanted to get done. It meant writing different drafts of the constitutional language and then running it all by a group of three constitutional scholars. "You put words on paper, you gotta see whether it does the trick," said Simon.[36] The legal scholars included Jon Mills, who served as a Democratic Speaker of the Florida House of Representatives in the late 1980s, and Myrna Pérez, a voting rights attorney at the Brennan Center for Justice who would later become a federal appeals court judge.[37]

Beyond writing the language, the fledgling campaign spent the next few years doing early polling on how Floridians felt about the issue. After the first rounds of polling, it was clear that sacrifices would have to be made. People would not vote for an item that restored civil rights to people who had been convicted of murder or felony sex offenses. Simon recalled that this realization alone was a hard sell for the different groups that were supporting the effort, who were opposed to any kind of carve-out. As he saw things, there was no way around it. Separating people with murder and felony sex convictions from the rest was clearly the only way any version of the ballot amendment would pass, the group found.[38]

Another thing that was clear by 2014: Voters would be more likely to pass the initiative if it restored rights to people only after completing their "full sentence" rather than just "post time served." Opponents to the initiative could argue that the recent inmate "didn't pay back" their full debt to society if it only related to time served, the group wrote in a memo. The rhetorical difference between the two might mean fewer people would get voting rights restored, according to internal memos.[39]

The fledgling campaign to put a new voting rights restoration provision in the Florida Constitution soon adopted the motto, "When a debt is paid, it's paid."

If Florida politics was a sitcom and Desmond Meade a character, those seven words would be his tag line.

Ever since the Clemency Board was created in 1976, no governor restored the rights of fewer people than Rick Scott. Jeb Bush restored more than 9,000 a year on average, while Crist restored nearly 39,000 annually, adding up to more than 150,000 during his four-year term. By comparison, Scott granted clemency to an average of 412 per year. Objectively, it was a paltry sum.[40]

Beyond the hopeless raw numbers, an investigation published by the *Palm Beach Post* as Scott ended his second term in 2018 laid out the full extent of damage that was done through Scott's administration. Under his tenure, the Clemency Board restored rights to twice as many white applicants as those who were Black, and three times as many white men as Black men. Of the people who had their rights restored, Scott "restored rights to a higher percentage of Republicans and a lower percentage of Democrats than any of his predecessors since 1971," the reporters found. "I have never and will never ask an applicant their political views," Scott said at a Clemency Board hearing that September. "That sort of information has absolutely no bearing on my decisions in these clemency cases."[41]

Even unconsciously, all kinds of information can be used as a proxy for political affiliation. Whether someone goes to church, whether they drink, whether they live in a big city or a rural area. If they are Black. And the fact is the numbers showed that thousands of individual decisions that Scott made over the years had the net effect of almost certainly tipping the featherweight scale on Florida's swing-state politics in favor of Republicans.[42]

In total, the *Palm Beach Post* reporters estimated, Scott personally denied the voting rights of 16,000 Floridians.[43]

Toward the end of his tenure as governor, Scott faced a federal class-action lawsuit on behalf of Floridians with felony records that hoped to burn the whole thing down. The central sticking point of the whole thing was that the cabinet admittedly created its own rules as it wished, and they could grant or deny applications based on how they felt when they woke up that morning.

"This setup violates our Constitution," argued Jon Sherman, senior counsel for the Fair Elections Legal Network, a group that brought the lawsuit. "The right to vote should be automatically restored to ex-felons at a specific point in time—the completion of a sentence—not whenever a politician decides you've earned it."[44]

By the time the suit was filed in March 2017, the statewide backlog of people who had applied to plead their case before the cabinet had grown to 10,513. Since the board was only meeting four times a year and handling only 52 cases per meeting, it could take more than fifty years to clear out the backlog.[45]

Not everyone was mired in the slog. James Batmasian was a developer and a Republican donor who served eight months in federal prison in 2009 for payroll tax evasion. In 2014, Batmasian was planning to host a fundraiser for Governor Scott at his mansion in Boca Raton. After news of Batmasian's felony conviction came out, Scott canceled the fundraiser.[46]

A few years later, in 2017, Batmasian got a surprise gift. Scott and the cabinet restored the developer's voting rights without a hearing, a truly rare event during Scott's tenure. The *Palm Beach Post* reported that Batmasian had a framed photo of himself, his wife, and the governor hanging in the lobby of his property management firm in South Florida. The governor and the developer denied that they ever discussed the matter before Batmasian's rights were restored.[47]

In short, the federal lawsuit sought to do away with a system in which rich donors to the governor could inexplicably get their rights back whereas others waited blindly for years, with no luck.

The case never made it to full trial. US District Judge Mark Walker issued a summary judgment in the case *Hand v. Scott*. The ruling raked the State of Florida—and Governor Scott in particular—across the coals.[48]

The beginning of that order is worth quoting at length:

Florida strips the right to vote from every man and woman who commits a felony. To vote again, disenfranchised citizens must kowtow before a panel of high-level government officials over which Florida's Governor has absolute veto authority. No standards guide the panel. Its members alone must be satisfied that these citizens deserve restoration. Until that moment (if it ever comes), these citizens cannot legally vote for presidents, governors, senators, representatives, mayors, or school-board members. These citizens are subject to the consequences of bills, actions, programs, and policies that their elected leaders enact and enforce. But these citizens cannot ever legally vote unless Florida's Governor approves restoration of this fundamental right.

The rest of the order consists of a systematic dismantling of the system that Scott had bragged about. It was technically in place under his predecessors, but Scott wielded the power that the process gave him like no one else in Florida history.

The process left open the possibility for "viewpoint discrimination" that knew no bounds, according to Walker. The opening for this kind of discrimination is "deeply antithetical to the Constitution and our Nation's longstanding values," he said. The process depended on nothing in particular, he noted, sometimes with eyebrow-raising results. The judge invoked an incident where a white man, Stephen A. Warner, admitted to the cabinet that he voted illegally—for the governor himself. That right there was admittedly another felony that had been committed.[49]

"I voted for you," Warner told Governor Scott in that incident. The governor reacted with a quick grin, adding, "I probably shouldn't respond to that." The governor then gave Warner his rights back.[50]

The judge noted that at least five other Floridians were denied the restoration of their voting rights explicitly *because* they had illegally voted. "It is not lost on this Court that four of the five rejected applicants are African-American," wrote Judge Walker.[51] Walker declared that "The unfettered discretion that the Clemency Board possesses over a former felon's re-enfranchisement violates the First Amendment." "All the component parts of the vote-restoration process that Defendants wave like shiny objects to distract from potential viewpoint discrimination—the investigations, case analyses, and hearings—mean nothing if the Governor *alone* has final authority to restore Plaintiffs' rights," he wrote.[52]

If the state decided to ban *all* people with felony convictions from ever voting again, it has that explicit right under the US Constitution. But if the state opened up even a sliver of a process for someone to get their rights back, it had to make some kind of sense. The state couldn't just decide to give Florida Seminoles fans their voting rights back and keep Miami Hurricanes fans away from the polls. If the state was going to do this thing, there had to be some kind of baseline logic to it, some form of criteria. Otherwise, Floridians would be spinning their wheels in place for decades on end, not knowing if they would have a good governor or a bad governor when their name was finally called, not knowing if a single-word slip-up was what got their case denied, or praying that a political connection was their golden ticket.

After decades under this kind of regime, Judge Walker ended it at once. By the time he wrote his order in February 2018, an estimated 1.7 million Floridians were unable to vote because they had an *F* next to their name. The broken process was no longer. The Florida Cabinet was charged with creating a newer, fairer process. But if the political class failed, Floridians themselves would have to decide what came next.

6
LET MY PEOPLE VOTE

The thing I remember the most about that day is that it was hot, and I was wholly unprepared to be on camera. I was working for a cable television network and website, primarily as a writer for the web, focused on criminal justice issues. And I really had no idea what I was doing.

It was October 2016, a few weeks before a presidential election that would flip everything upside down. As the company's resident Florida man, I was looking into a few issues that could impact the vote in my state. If not this election, sometime in the future.

The scene was at the Robles Park Village housing projects in Tampa, where I met with the resident council president Reva Iman. As she guided me through the courtyards and the buildings of the complex, all kinds of people greeted her with a familiar warmth. All of them were Black.

"Hi, Ms. Reva!" a squad of kindergarten-aged children screamed in unison. Iman waved to them and waved to their parents. She bantered with them, asked about their families, and asked if they had registered to vote.[1] That last part was increasingly starting to worry her.

A few weeks before my visit, a member of Democrat Hillary Clinton's campaign visited, and Iman agreed to give them a tour. Iman took to the task openheartedly and open-mindedly, connecting dots and introducing friends to the visitor.[2]

The segment of Florida between Orlando and Tampa is known as the I-4 Corridor, for Interstate 4, which connects the two cities and financial centers. This area was long known as something of a swing region within the swing state. Win this area, and you win the election, goes conventional political wisdom. More specifically, win Hillsborough County—the home of Tampa—and you win the whole election. As we spoke, that math had carried true for every presidential race since 1960.[3] Robles Park Village was in the heart of this magical region, which explains why a visitor from Clinton's campaign thought it necessary to put in some face time that day.

As she started connecting the visitor to fellow residents that day, Iman had a devastating realization, one that opened her eyes to the concrete limitations placed on her neighbors because of past mistakes. "We come to find out that the mass majority of them could not vote," she told me.[4] "It was a great deal of a shock," said Iman. "*That* many people in this area."

So here I was, a few weeks later, for the first time dipping my toes into the topic. My company had me meet up with a duo of Russians who followed me and Iman around the complex with cameras while we talked to people, assuming that I knew how to direct them. I did not. It was a laughable situation in retrospect: The Russians kept trying to get me to direct them when I had no idea what I was doing. I was dripping sweat in the last swampy days of the Florida summer, in no mood or shape for the cameras. I started ignoring the Russians. The poorly planned video piece never aired. But I listened closely to every word the people I met told me.

About half the residents shared the same story. They couldn't vote. "I got a felony," said Mike Johnson, a Black twenty-nine-year-old who sat on a park bench with his friends. "A lot of people out here like that."[5]

What played out before me in Robles Park Village was a showcase of the two-pronged issue of mass incarceration, explained Mike Reed, a Tampa-based local organizer with the nonprofit Organize Now. First, people of color get arrested and locked up at a disproportionate rate, compared to white residents. Then, when members of those Black communities return to their economically and racially segregated neighborhoods, they're further marginalized.

"People get elected, they make decisions, and these people—these neighborhoods—don't have a seat at the table," Reed told me. He saw the same dynamic playing out in mostly Black communities of East Tampa and Ybor City. "After a long time, the neighborhoods start to become apathetic."[6]

But now, people were starting to organize. When I left the housing project that day, I met up with another, unrelated Johnson. Rodney Johnson, a Black man, had been standing in front of a clothing shop in a strip mall in Tampa's Egypt Lake–Leto neighborhood for months. He held a clipboard and a stack of papers and would chum up to anyone who walked past him.

For those who were eligible, he helped them register to vote. He estimated that over the course of a few months he registered six hundred people. Johnson also kept a separate stack of papers. This stack would hold the key to his salvation. It was a petition calling for a statewide ballot referendum that would automatically restore the right to vote for people with felony convictions.[7]

All the groundwork laid out by Desmond Meade, Howard Simon, and the rest of the activists and legal teams was now set in motion. With every signature gathered, the vision of sidestepping politicians and putting the question directly before voters came one step closer to reality.

"I'm unable to vote. I'm a convicted felon," Johnson told me. "The more I do this canvassing job, the more I'm learning about politics. I'm learning that *that's* the way you change things: you have to vote."[8]

Across the state, thousands like Johnson were learning the same lessons, reaching the same realizations. By late 2016, the petition had received enough signatures that the Florida Supreme Court was slated to review the proposal to make sure it was legally valid. If all went well, the referendum would be put up to a vote within a few years.[9]

"When we get our rights back, it's giving us a second chance," Johnson said. "That's important because we might be felons, but at the end of the day, the kids still look up to us for answers."[10]

It was a miraculous thing. A religious person might even venture to call it a miracle. But that miracle was born of blood, sweat, tears, and the tens of thousands of miles Desmond Meade put on his car, driving up, down, and around the peninsula.

At first, Meade would show up anywhere he thought he could get an audience, even just a few people at a time. Anything to preach his gospel. He went on podcasts, talked at an NAACP meeting in Miami. To lawmakers in Tallahassee. He crashed conventions to connect with speakers he thought might be influential or lend a hand, or perhaps they might speak at a future event and draw in a bigger audience.[11] Slowly, methodically, Meade worked his way through the state, staking his claim as a thought leader on voting rights, with vision and perseverance that maybe, just maybe, might make an impact.

It was a skill he learned in college a few years prior. While still living in a three-quarters house, still recovering from drug addiction and homelessness, Meade had enrolled himself at Miami Dade College at a time he later reflected was a "special time and place" for activism. Among his many classmates were Gaby Pacheco, Felipe Matos, Juan Rodriguez, and Carlos Roa, the group of undocumented immigrants that boldly walked from Miami to Washington, DC, and pressured President Barack Obama to enact the Deferred Action for Childhood Arrivals program—or DACA—in 2012. The dream of the "Dreamers"—a name derived from the Development, Relief, and Education for Alien Minors (DREAM) Act, a bill that sought legal status for young, undocumented immigrants living in the United States—was born on that campus in downtown Miami, with Meade in the periphery. In fact, Meade once rode on a bus with all of them to Tallahassee to lobby for additional funds on behalf of Miami Dade College. The group of them were all politically active on campus, pushing for civic participation, civic engagement, personal empowerment, and political action, and the college tapped them to lead the lobbying delegation to the state capital.[12]

"Miami Dade College really created an environment that welcomed unconventional students into that space," recalled Meade. "What sticks out to me is that we were just ordinary people that were experiencing a personal pain, and decided to take control of our lives and address that pain through our own personal experiences, and use it to help other people."[13]

Along the way, he picked up knowledge of how politics really works. About pressure campaigns, about driving public opinion. About how to speak to the media. As the president of the fully independent Florida Rights Restoration Coalition, he put it all to use.

The campaign kicked off in a sense in January 2014, at a small protest rally Meade and the FRRC held in front of Republican Attorney General Pam Bondi's office in Tallahassee.[14] A few weeks later, national politicians started talking about it. US Attorney General Eric Holder compared voting restrictions like those faced by Floridians to Jim Crow–era laws. At the time, the Sentencing Project, a national advocacy group and research group, estimated that one in five Black adults in Florida—and also Kentucky and Virginia, which had similar policies—could not vote because of a past criminal conviction.[15]

Surprising many, the libertarian-leaning Republican US Senator Rand Paul announced that he would sponsor federal legislation to address the issue affecting his home state of Kentucky and beyond, calling it "the biggest problem of voting rights facing our country." At an event with the ACLU that Meade attended, Paul supported calls for reform. "The largest impediment to employment and voting rights is the criminal-justice system," argued Paul. "I don't mean to downplay past challenges minorities have had with voting rights, but I do think this is the biggest problem."[16] Paul's Democratic colleague from Maryland, US Senator Ben Cardin, was also working on federal legislation to address the issue.[17]

The following month, in March 2014, Meade and other members of the fledgling FRRC went to Switzerland to talk to the United Nations in the hope that the international body would shame Florida and other states into changing their tune. The Office of the United Nations High Commissioner for Human Rights issued a statement about the topic, agreeing with Meade and the activists who joined him that the status quo was unacceptable. The body determined that Florida policy in particular was out of compliance with the International Covenant on Civil and Political Rights, an international treaty signed by the United States in 1992.[18] In a statement, the United Nations Human Rights Committee wrote that there was a well-founded "need for international attention on this issue."[19]

Meade was pleased. His pressure campaign was starting to see results. The problem was bigger than many thought. It was so big that it was now on the radar of the United Nations.[20]

Late in 2014, Meade was feeling emboldened. The legal team with Howard Simon and others had done their work, held their workshops. They had an idea what enough people would vote for to make a difference.

In November 2014, Meade finally announced that he would soon launch an effort to gather enough petitions to put the question directly to voters in the coming election.[21] "Once a person has served their time, they should not be made to continue paying for their past mistakes," Meade told a *Sun Sentinel* columnist as he prepared the launch.[22]

This time, he was going to do it for real.

For Neil Volz, his new calling came unexpectedly. The former Republican congressional staffer had been tied up in the Jack Abramoff lobbying scandal that rocked the nation's capital in 2005 and 2006, and he moved to Florida shortly after with a felony record to show for it. He was doing work with local churches and heading the Homeless Coalition in Lee County on the Gulf coast after he arrived, putting his past organizing skills to work.[23]

"I moved to Florida in 2008 not ever thinking I was gonna get involved in politics again," Volz told me. "I was just dealing with my own shame and my own guilt and trying to put a bunch of pieces of my life together after making a bunch of stupid, selfish decisions."[24]

Then, one day in the summer of 2015, Volz found himself at Florida Gulf Coast University, where he was meeting with a young man at a church, trying to give him some guidance. He spotted a flier on a university wall about voter disenfranchisement, saying that Desmond Meade would be there. Volz had no idea who Meade was, but he chose to attend.

"I walk in and there's maybe twenty-five to thirty people there, and right away I sit down and I'm like man, this feels a little progressive-y for me. Like, I was out. I'm thirty seconds away from—I'm just going to kind of kindly, respectfully get up and walk out the door. And then Des spoke. I remember him talking about how there's no individual who has a monopoly on the pain of felon disenfranchisement. This really is an everybody issue, and something that impacts every community in Florida," said Volz. "It really touched me. Touched my heart, and ultimately it opened a door for me."[25]

Volz and Meade spoke for hours after the event. He was sold. Over the next few months, Volz would become one of the core organizers of the signature-gathering campaign. As a white conservative in an increasingly conservative Southern state, he sharpened the pitch for why conservatives should care about the issue. He began doing outreach, building strategies, doing communications for the FRRC, all as an unpaid volunteer.

The campaign urgently needed his help. The League of Women Voters of Florida originally planned to put up funds for the signature-gathering campaign, but in October 2015 the group announced it wouldn't have enough money to maintain support. Running a full campaign of that sort could take $7–9 million, and they just didn't have it. Meade conceded that the entire effort was in peril. The campaign needed 68,314 verified signatures to be reviewed by the Florida Supreme Court. Assuming the item was given the thumbs-up by the court, it would need to collect hundreds of thousands of additional signatures to be placed on the ballot.[26] "We're still alive," Meade told the *Palm Beach Post* about the announcement that funding had been pulled. "But it's not the strongest heartbeat."[27]

At the time, a new wave of political energy was starting to ripple across the nation, bringing hordes of grassroots supporters together for a singular cause: electing Republican Donald Trump as president. As the new resident conservative strategist, Volz took it upon himself to start attending Trump rallies throughout Florida, preaching an audience-tailored flavor of the same gospel perfected by Desmond Meade. Conservatives were impacted by this issue too, he stressed. You can only do so much to support Trump if you can't vote for him. His overall task was twofold. First, he needed to counter the pervasive and untrue narrative that the restoration of voting rights was somehow a progressive, left-leaning issue. Second, he needed to collect signatures.

At a rally in Palm Beach County, Volz spoke to a crowd full of Trump supporters, telling them about his own journey, about how he could not vote. In response, Trump supporters dealing with the very same issues approached him afterward.

A gray-bearded man and his wife, both decked out in American flags and Trump gear, stood out in Volz's memory. The man told him his story, about how it took him four to five years to get back on his feet after getting out of prison on a felony charge. The man owed a business now with about eighty employees, the majority of whom had felony convictions.[28]

The next words out of the man's mouth came to resonate with Volz, signifying the person-to-person approach that would define the early phase of the campaign. "He's like, 'I'm just gonna let you know you don't have to come back to this group, this MAGA group,'" said Volz. "He looked at me and said, 'I got us.' And I'm like, man. This campaign is a powerful thing. This campaign is him too, and his wife. And they happen to have wildly different politics than what people might think of returning citizens."[29] Conservatives were impacted too, and they were jumping onto the organizing train. Volz felt that this created a firewall, insulating the effort from becoming a partisan issue.

To protect that firewall, the campaign instituted the policy that it would not allow elected officials to speak at its rallies, even if they supported the cause. If they allowed it, politics and bias might start to creep in.[30]

"We shun the description of being a bipartisan or even a nonpartisan campaign," Meade recalled years later. "We did not want politicians involved in this. We want this to be a purely grassroots effort."[31]

Meade had the philosophy that because so many individual Floridians were impacted, if every one of them got one eligible voter they knew to sign a petition, that would be more than enough. The hardest part was finding them. Meade believed that the social circles of a forgotten constituency would be the key to grassroots success. For some crowds, he himself could work it. Other crowds needed another messenger.

One example is Gwendolyn's Café, a small diner in Fort Myers, on Florida's

Gulf coast. The café for years had been a gathering place of recovering addicts and the formerly homeless in the community, a spot where meetings were held and where people made new connections. Since he had been involved in antihomelessness efforts in the community before taking part in signature gathering, Volz knew the place was a potential gold mine. Many who frequented the café could not vote, and their signatures would not be valid. But their sponsors, their friends, and their families could vote. If he started there, the concentric circle would reverberate outward in the overwhelmingly conservative area.

"It took off. We collected thousands of petitions through just that one diner. It's just the epitome of relational organizing," said Volz. "At the end of the day it came down to family members, someone who went to school or mosque or church who had a relationship with somebody." "It was legit bottom up," he remembered.[32]

The grassroots effort really was grassroots. By August 2016, the political committee Meade set up to help the effort, known as Floridians for a Fair Democracy, had raised only $12,000.[33] Most of that came from Howard's ACLU of Florida, the Brennan Center for Justice, and Faith in Florida, a nonprofit Black, faith-based organization. Other churches across the state also contributed small amounts. But most of all, sweat from the brow is what kept things moving. Almost all contributions to the committee were in-kind contributions, meaning people were offering their services and labor to the organization free of charge. Thousands upon thousands of dollars in free labor were freely given to the signature-gathering effort, often from people who themselves could not vote. From the top of the state to the bottom, forgotten constituencies were being activated.[34]

With all that effort, the 68,314 signatures needed to spark a review of the ballot language by the Florida Supreme Court were in the bag. The milestone was reached in August 2016. Once the court approved the language, it would be a marathon sprint to gather the 766,200 signatures needed to actually put the question on the ballot for the next election, in 2018.[35]

But that was a lifetime away. Before the Florida Supreme Court could get to the question, voters across the country had to choose the next president of the United States.

Even before Donald Trump won the presidency, the amount of money being donated to Floridians for a Fair Democracy started to pick up steam. The mere fact of crossing the threshold for a Florida Supreme Court review raised optimism that something might actually change.[36]

But it was only after Inauguration Day, as the nation learned to adjust to its brash and outspoken new president, that things truly shifted. Just a week into his presidency, on January 27, 2017, the new president issued Executive Order No. 13769, titled "Protecting the Nation from Foreign Terrorist Entry into the United States." The president and his critics alike called it something else: "the Muslim Ban."[37] Immediately, the order blocked entry into the United States of people from Iran, Iraq, Libya, Somalia, Sudan, Syria, and Yemen. Even lawful permanent residents who hail from those countries were at first barred entry.[38] Syrian refugees were denied entry indefinitely; the rest of the national refugee program was temporarily suspended, and the number of refugees allowed into the country was to be slashed.

Chaotic protests sprung up at airports, in support of those caught in the middle. Hundreds of travelers hailing from the listed countries were detained at international ports of entry, if not sent back to their home countries. The Trump administration estimated that sixty thousand visas to enter the United States were "provisionally revoked."[39]

It was a shock to the system for countless Americans who didn't pay much mind to politics. The nation was entering into new territory, where access to the most basic right to travel, to return home, to reunite with family after an arduous vetting process, depended on where you were born. Who knew what could come next? The new president was incredibly bold, and that was cause for alarm. Many of the provisions that led to the chaos and widespread anger against the Trump administration's "Muslim Ban" were later overturned by the courts. That was in large part because the nation seemed to have an overnight realization that it could depend on a steadfast defender of our collective civil rights: the American Civil Liberties Union. "Suddenly people were donating to the ACLU and joining the ACLU like never before in our history," remembered Howard Simon.[40]

Just a few months earlier, Meade and Volz were breaking their backs to gather signatures to get the question before the Florida Supreme Court, with almost no funding. The court signed off on the ballot language three months into the Trump presidency, after a hearing that took place without drawing too much attention for any reason.

The summary language that would appear on the ballot read, in full:

This amendment restores the voting rights of Floridians with felony convictions after they complete all terms of their sentence including parole or probation. The amendment would not apply to those convicted of murder or sexual offenses, who would continue to be permanently barred from voting unless the Governor and Cabinet vote to restore their voting rights on a case by case basis.[41]

The only obstacle left before them to place that language before voters in 2018 was gathering those 766,200 signatures, something that was far from an easy proposition. All hands, from the FRRC and the ACLU alike, were set on getting the question on the ballot in 2018. While the first part of the campaign was distinctly scrappy, a do-it-yourself, grassroots effort, the second phase would require a massive infusion of funding. The immediate explosion of money pumped into the ACLU after the "Muslim Ban" fiasco played a major role.

"Who was flush with money in 2018? We were. And we were because of guess who? Trump. So Trump helped us," remembered Simon.[42] In 2017, the national ACLU organization held a conference in Denver. The meeting took place under the shadow of Trump, while the organization had more money than it knew how to handle. Simon flew out with the idea of pumping much of the new Trump money into the Florida ballot initiative.

"I got commitment," said Simon. "A million dollars."[43] The national ACLU in fact would contribute much more than that to the cause. The total the nonprofit donated to the campaign, through Election Day on November 6, 2018, was just over $5 million, amounting to over one in five dollars raised for the effort, making it by far the largest contributor. The Sixteen Thirty Fund, a dark-money group that funds progressive causes, donated the next-largest amount, just under $4 million. Coming in third was a single family, that of David Bonderman, the billionaire private equity baron, which donated $3.7 million. Thousands of individual donations flowed into the effort too, with contributions coming from families based in Florida but also Louisiana, Wisconsin, Colorado, Utah, and elsewhere. In total, more than $24 million was raised for all parts of the campaign effort.[44]

All of that money went into gathering the 766,200 signatures needed to officially put the question on the ballot, and later toward the actual campaign to convince people to vote for it. To hit the signature number, the campaign contracted with a petition management firm that hired people to fan out to every part of the state and gather signatures.[45] Hundreds if not thousands of unpaid volunteers continued to contribute their sweat to the cause, mobilized by the promise of ending lifetime voter disenfranchisement in Florida. But the campaign workforce was more or less professionalized at this time, with workers being paid to collect signatures. In the meantime, Desmond Meade, Neil Volz, and other members of the Florida Rights Restoration Coalition crisscrossed the state in a red bus emblazoned with the words "Let My People Vote," holding rallies and meetings and assisting in the effort.

Just eight days before the state deadline of January 31, 2018, the campaign finally turned in the necessary signatures.[46] The question was officially going to go before voters in the midterm elections in November of that year, appearing alongside a contentious gubernatorial race, a tight battle for a US Senate seat, and eleven other ballot amendments.

Over the course of the entire campaign, voices arose to speak against what the effort intended to do. One conservative columnist in 2016 railed against it in the *Orlando Sentinel*, for example, writing that it was simply an attempt to push a "progressive agenda" on Floridians. "Just because many other states have a more-liberal viewpoint on the issue doesn't make it right for Florida to follow suit," wrote George W. Koehn. "I don't want Florida to be like all those other liberal-leaning states."[47]

In the 2018 gubernatorial race, the issue came up in a televised debate between Democratic nominee Andrew Gillum and Republican nominee Ron DeSantis. Gillum expressed support for the effort; DeSantis did not. "I think it's wrong to automatically restore rights to felons who've committed very serious crimes," DeSantis said. "I want people to be redeemed. But you've got to prove that you're getting back with the law."[48]

But the opposition, as it existed, never organized. The Florida Republican Party never took an official position on the question. No political committee ever registered to formally and legally oppose the effort.[49] "There was not one negative ad that was aired on TV. We're unaware of any negative mailers that may have been sent out," Meade proudly recounted years later.[50]

"This has been a tried-and-true citizens' initiative," Meade said just as Election Day approached, as the yearslong effort drew to a close. "If the people put it on the ballot, they're going to vote for it."[51]

On Election Day, I visited a slew of voting locations across Miami-Dade County, talking to voters and generally observing the electoral process. At the bustling Coral Reef Library in South Dade, candidate campaign signs were stacked upon campaign signs, and members of a firefighters' union tried to convince voters to fill in boxes next to their preferred candidates. After that, I made my way about two and a half miles south, to the historically Black, poor, and largely forgotten neighborhood of West Perrine.

There, at Robert Russa Moton Elementary School, I spent an hour without seeing a single voter enter or leave. There was not a single sign for any candidate. Not one. The only election signs in sight were a few that read "Vote Yes on 4," the voting rights amendment. Two Black women stood on a hot street corner waiting alongside me. They were employees of the campaign and were not authorized to talk to the press. On the condition that I not use her name, one of the women explained why—in her view—a few miles north things looked so different.

"People in this neighborhood, they can't vote," the woman told me. "You don't see no signs for no candidates, because the candidates know it's not worth it to campaign here, because so many people can't vote. It's not worth it to them."

She pointed down to her black shirt that read "Let My People Vote." This, she indicated, could change everything. "When this passes, them politicians are gonna *have* to start paying attention to West Perrine. Because they look at it now and don't see no votes. But when the people can vote, someone will have to pay attention," she said.

That night, as voting came to a close and the ballots were counted, a beam of hope shined bright for the thousands upon thousands who participated in the campaign and the overall struggle, going back to the aftermath of the 2000 election.

Amendment 4 received more votes than any political candidate in the state. A large majority of voters approved it, even in some of the deepest-red parts of the state. Overall, the effort only failed to achieve a majority of votes in six out of Florida's sixty-seven counties. Even in those few rural counties where it lost (Union, Suwanee, Lafayette, Holmes, Gilchrist, and Baker), the margins were incredibly close to breaking even. In Holmes County, 3,293 voted against the measure, and 3,272 voted in favor, a mere 21-vote difference.[52]

The ballot amendment passed with 64.55 percent of the statewide vote, surpassing the necessary 60 percent. In a flash, the amendment became the law of the land.

At a campaign watch party in Orlando, Desmond Meade shouted in joy as the results showed a landmark victory. Drake's "Started from the Bottom" blasted from the speakers. He gave a speech surrounded by his loved ones, friends, and supporters. Many shed tears of joy.

"This was a campaign about inclusion," Meade told the crowd in a victory speech. "Those numbers represented what happens when we come together along the lines of humanity and reach each other where we're at. That's what happens when we're able to transcend partisan politics and bickering, when we're able to transcend racial anxieties and discourse, when we're able to come together as God's children."[53]

The outcome of the effort stunned observers across the nation. Voters in Florida seemed to have definitively turned a page away from the vestiges of Jim Crow and toward a more inclusive democratic process. In an article titled "Florida Votes for Democracy" in *The Atlantic,* reporter Conor Friedersdorf wrote, "This is a hugely consequential result. The change will extend the vote to more than 1 million Floridians."[54]

The certainty of that statement was emblematic of the general coverage of the historic victory: The ballot amendment passed, therefore more than a million Floridians will become newly eligible voters. The Associated Press, a definitive outlet of record, followed the same unquestioning logic, as if the end result was preordained, as if the fight had just drawn to a close. The very first line of the newswire service's write-up of the stunning victory stated as fact that "Florida added 1.4 million possible voters to the rolls."[55]

I had my doubts it would be that simple.

7
A VERY BIG PROBLEM

To understand what happened next, we must first talk about the environment. Specifically, the Everglades, that largely undeveloped soggy enigma at the bottom of the state. As Florida's legendary journalist and activist Marjory Stoneman Douglas once wrote, "There are no other Everglades in the world. They are, they have always been, one of the unique regions of the earth; remote, never wholly known."[1]

The unique biosphere was described by Stoneman Douglas as a "River of Grass." By the late 1990s, the river was running dangerously dry. In the early 1900s, politicians urged the US Army Corps of Engineers to drain the wetlands out to the ocean to open up more dry land for development and agriculture. As the years trudged forth, the ecosystem began to collapse and wildlife populations started to decline. Along with the decline of the Everglades came an existential threat to the water supply for millions of South Florida residents. In 2000, Congress passed a landmark bill that would help restore the Everglades to the tune of billions of dollars. It still wasn't enough.[2] The bureaucracy and massive infrastructure projects moved too slowly.

There's a general understanding in Florida that the economy and the environment are connected at the hip. If the environment gets out of whack, tourists—the top drivers of the state economy—won't flock to the beaches. The freshwater fishermen won't come down to the state's interior for the winter. The Midwestern birdwatchers will catch a flight to another destination, deeper into the tropics.

With Everglades restoration work still struggling to catch a foothold, in 2014, Florida voters passed a ballot amendment ordering the state to set aside even more funds for Everglades and wildlife restoration. The idea was simple: The state was hereby directed by the voters to spend 33 percent of taxes collected on real estate documentary stamps on buying and managing land to bring the state's environment back into shape and preserve it for future generations. It was a targeted plan, amounting to less than 1 percent of the state's budget.

That's not what happened. The state legislature declined to spend the money as voters demanded. It was only a lawsuit in 2018 that forced the legislature to follow the state constitution. The judge ruling on the case said that lawmakers had "defied" the clear will of the people.[3]

Defying the will of the voters was, by 2018, an honored tradition in Republican-controlled Florida. In 2010, Florida voters passed two "fair districting" constitutional amendments that aimed to eliminate partisan gerrymandering. The legislature did not pay the new addition to the state constitution enough deference, and it drew overtly gerrymandered maps. Only through a lawsuit were the maps overturned in 2016. Several heavily gerrymandered election cycles had already taken place by the time victory came.[4]

Then, in 2016, Florida voters legalized medical marijuana with 71 percent of the vote. Lawmakers responded by banning medical marijuana from being smoked. That ban was overturned by a state court as unconstitutional.[5] Again, it took a lawsuit for the legislature to follow clear directives passed by Florida residents.

All of this hung in the air when I went to meet Howard Simon at the ACLU headquarters the day after Amendment 4 passed. The offices are on a palm-tree-lined street just south of the Miami airport, in a building named after Chesterfield Smith, the Florida civil rights icon who—ironically—was the chairman of Florida's 1968 Constitutional Convention, which kept Florida's lifelong felon voting ban in place. Simon leaned forward as he spoke, tilting the chair he was sitting on. He still beamed in the afterglow of victory.

"This is the largest extension of the right to vote in America since the constitutional amendment that extended the right to vote to people who are eighteen years old," Simon boasted.[6] He had just overseen the completion of what was effectively his life's work, stretching back to the time spent in Alabama during the civil rights era.

Then I had to change the tenor of the conversation. While national and local headlines marveled at the massive civil rights victory, my mind wandered to the Everglades. That ballot initiative was as straightforward as could be: You take money from this pot, and you put it here. And still, the Republican-dominated state government had refused.

"I'm not naive. It's something that could happen. There are a couple of things that I want to say about this," Simon started. "Our legislature has been hostile to the elimination of the Civil War–era, Jim Crow lifetime felon disenfranchisement. I'm not overlooking that, I'm not naive. I hit that brick wall many times. Our newly elected governor said he was not a fan of Amendment 4."[7]

But there was a line of defense against government intrusion that would seek to stall or reverse it. As Simon put it, it was the result of years of work that was put into the language itself. "It says that voting rights 'shall be restored.' I don't know what is unclear about that, what could be unclear about that. 'Voting rights shall be restored upon completion of all the terms of a sentence,'" he said. "People in the legislature, people in the governor's office, people in the secretary of state's office—there's no role for politicians to decide who gets to vote in Florida and who doesn't get to vote in Florida. You have automatically had your right to vote restored upon completion of all the terms of a sentence."[8]

The only thing that needed to happen for the law to go into effect was for the calendar to hit January 8, 2019, a mere two months later. That was the day newly eligible Floridians could register to vote. "I'm going to presume the best of intentions, but if the legislature tries to erect barriers, if the secretary of state tries to erect barriers, this language of Amendment 4 is so clear it will be great ammunition to try to prevent the legislature from erecting barriers," said Simon.[9]

By the time November was over, it became clear that things would not be so rosy. The entire government of Florida was in a period of transition. Governor Scott had just squeezed through a victory propelling him to the US Senate.

The vacuum of information that formed in the lame duck months of Scott's administration led to widespread confusion about how to proceed. Over the course of a week in late November, I called every election official I could find contact information for. One major issue they repeatedly complained about was the second question on the state's voter registration form. It read: "I affirm that I am not a convicted felon, or if I am, my right to vote has been restored." Before Amendment 4 passed, this was a relatively straightforward question. Now, it was confusing.

"I'm going to have to be given some guidelines. You can't just ignore the question," Joyce Griffin, the supervisor of elections of Monroe County, in the Florida Keys, told me.[10]

In Orange County, the home of Orlando, the head of elections said otherwise. "As far as I know, people will be able to walk into our office on January 8th and check the box that their rights have been restored," he said. "But somebody at the state is going to have to scrub the registrations that come in, and I don't know what that process will look like."[11]

Officials in Miami-Dade, the most populous county in the state, said they had no idea how it would be implemented. In Leon County, the home of Tallahassee, the deputy supervisor of elections told me, when I asked him what would happen on a practical level when Amendment 4 went into effect: "Funny you bring this up. I just left a voicemail with someone at the Department of State about an hour ago trying to get some information on this." Susan Bucher, the top election official in Palm Beach County, a Democrat, flat-out said that the effective date of the amendment, January 8, was not feasible. "The legislature has to provide legislative guidance before that goes into effect."[12]

For its part, the Florida Department of State offered no guidance. A spokesperson simply offered that they would "share more information as it becomes available." A kaleidoscope of state agencies—the Department of Corrections, the Florida Department of Law Enforcement, the Florida Commission of Offender Review—told me they awaited guidance either from the governor's office or from the legislature. Outgoing Governor Scott's office spoke as if those agencies were not publicly seeking guidance on how to move forward. The totality of a response I got from his office about the confusion was, "This constitutional amendment takes effect in January, as outlined in Florida's constitution."[13]

State legislators began to pipe up. Blaise Ingoglia, the chair of the Florida Republican Party and a state representative, hinted on a radio show that something in response to Amendment 4 could be in the works in the Republican-led Florida legislature. "There will be numerous what we call 'implementing bills' that are going to be offered by various members of the House and the Senate," Ingoglia said. "That's a conversation we're going to have to have."[14] For his part, State Senator Dennis Baxley, an old-timey Republican from the heart of Central Florida's interior, told me that some things about the language of Amendment 4 were ambiguous and could require some form of action.

"We need to clarify: When are you clear? It's not just when you walk out of incarceration but it's 'completing of the sentence,'" he told me. Baxley was, at the time, the chairman of the Florida Senate's Ethics and Elections Committee. Any bill about a voting rights issue would likely first pass by his desk.[15] Over the years, the longtime ally of Marco Rubio had developed a reputation as a staunch social conservative who didn't mind taking the heat for controversial policies, and whose pet projects tended to become law. Baxley was the one who introduced and fought for the passage of Florida's Stand Your Ground law, the first in the nation that legalized shooting someone perceived as a threat instead of trying to avoid the confrontation.

The problem with Amendment 4, said Baxley, is that it wasn't universal. That one provision about "completion of the sentence" meant something that was yet to be crystallized. And if the Florida Legislature didn't take immediate action to make the definition equal across the state, each of Florida's sixty-seven different counties could end up interpreting it in their own way. With the Scott administration playing dumb, deaf, and blind, his argument held some weight.

The benefit of every county getting on the same page was to minimize the number of people claiming that they were eligible to vote thanks to Amendment 4 when they really were not, Baxley explained. "What I'm concerned about is how we go about validating them so that they're not signing a false statement," he said.[16]

The criminal punishment for declaring that you are eligible to vote on a voter registration form when you are not carries a particularly harsh punishment in Florida: a felony conviction.

In that moment Baxley forecast that a move was coming without revealing what shape it would take. The legislature would come up with a way of doing *something* with Amendment 4. They would absolutely not "slow-walk it," he assured me. Amendment 4 was going to be a reality. What it would look like was unclear.

By mid-December, newly elected Governor Ron DeSantis threw his hat in the ring, telling a podcast that he didn't "see any way around" the legislature getting involved.[17]

One Democratic state senator thought he knew which way the wind would blow. Jason Pizzo had just been elected to represent an incredibly diverse district encompassing some of the poorest and richest areas of South Florida. Before that, he was a prosecutor in Miami, handling cold murder cases, giving him an insider's understanding of the justice system.

A few days before people with felony convictions could start registering to vote, I met with Pizzo in his Miami office, bordering a hipster gym and one of the best pizza shops in town. A clean-cut, olive-skinned New Jersey native with a broad smile, Pizzo looked a poster child of a politician. But as we spoke, the smile faded into a look of concern. He took no delight in telling me what he told me, but he laid it out flatly, like an attorney confined to the facts of his case.

"In the exuberance and excitement to pass Amendment 4, what was lost was the provision that you must complete your sentence," he told me. "And sentence means any restitution you owed to an individual or an entity, or court costs that you had outstanding."[18]

He pulled up a letter that he sent to Miami-Dade Clerk of Court Harvey Ruvin, dated in mid-December 2018, just a month after Amendment 4 passed.[19] The letter spoke about money. Money, it turned out, would be the biggest talking point of the next several years.

In Florida, the clerk of courts is the money man for the state government's bureaucracy. Parking tickets, civil infractions, criminal court fees, and fines—all of it goes through the hands of the clerk of courts. For the Sunshine State, there are sixty-seven different clerks of court, one for each county. The Miami-Dade clerk of courts office is by far the largest, employing more than one thousand staffers. Tens of thousands of felony cases get processed in Miami-Dade every single year. And that meant that someone who committed a felony back in the 1970s might still, technically, owe money in fees, fines, court costs, or restitution connected to that crime.

What Pizzo wanted to know from Ruvin was, Would you really hold that decades-old debt against someone who is trying to register to vote? "Prior to Amendment 4, I can't imagine it was contemplated that cases older than 5, 10 or even 15 years would see any substantial rush for payment on these costs," wrote Pizzo in the letter.[20] If you go far enough back, surely the debt has to be written off at some point, he argued. Any payments collected from those long-ago cases should be considered "found money," he argued, rather than something that is still on the books. "I'm not arguing it's an unfair cost to the ex-cons that want to get their rights restored; I'm just saying to be fair, this was like loaning somebody money twenty years ago and you never thought you were gonna get paid back," Pizzo told me.[21]

If those ancient debts were still considered active, if they were not written off or canceled, the criminal sentences connected to the debts might not be technically completed. Those people would still be ineligible to vote.

In a mere matter of days people with felony convictions would be signing up to vote on the assumption that they could legally do so. If what Pizzo said held weight, many of them would commit a criminal act in the process.

The Miami-Dade Supervisor of Elections office is nowhere near the urban core of the region. The box building sits on a traffic-plagued road a few miles west of Miami International Airport, in an area best known as the suburban corporate home to companies like Carnival Cruise Line and Univision, down the street from the command center of US military operations in Latin America and the Caribbean. The roads are wide and public transit nearly nonexistent. It's the kind of place where you only end up if you have a damn good reason.

Anthony Bushell had one. During the election that just passed, he estimated that he served as an unofficial chauffeur, driving twenty-eight friends to the polls to cast votes. For several election cycles he did the same, engaging with the process the only way he could. The last election he voted in was in 1992, when he voted for Bill Clinton for president. On January 8, he drove to the far-flung office to be among the first to register to vote under Amendment 4.

"Seeing all these elections go by, whether it's the city, the county, the state as well as the federal government, it kind of hurts not to be able to participate," said Bushell. "I wanted to do my part as soon as possible, versus having to wait and seeing how things go. I put my name in the beginning."[22]

A small trickle of his peers followed, the vast majority of them Black. Jerry Armstrong, a forty-five-year-old with a football player's build, showed up to the scene with his girlfriend, who cheered him on. "That was the first thing he wanted to do today. He said 'I'm gonna register to vote today,'" his girlfriend told me. After filling out his form, Armstrong smiled wide. "I never voted a day in my life," he said. "I feel like I'm a United States citizen, so I want my right to vote."[23]

Lorenzo Latson took a few hours off from his job at the Florida Department of Veterans Affairs to register to vote. The fifty-eight-year-old showed up to the office sporting a Panama hat. "It feels great, it feels outstanding," he said. "Any election coming up, I'm gonna be a participant." He hadn't voted since 2011 and could hardly control himself. Cell phone in hand, he called a friend and put them on speaker, yelling the address into the wind for whomever else might hear it. Lawson's coworker, Clarence Office, joined him for the ride. He wore a navy-blue suit with white vertical stripes and a slight, bashful smirk for the occasion. Not since he helped elect President Obama to office in 2008 had he been able to cast a vote. Ten years had flown by with him standing on the sidelines. He told me putting his name and signature down on the paper felt "like a sense of renewal."[24]

Across the state similar scenes played out.

Desmond Meade rose before the sun to bring his family with him while he registered to vote in Orlando. Before television cameras he reached back into the 1960s to capture the moment. "Moms and dads took their kids to vote with them during the civil rights era," he said. "Not only do I get to vote, but this is an opportunity now to stimulate a conversation about how important voting is."[25]

In Jacksonville, elections for mayor and county sheriff were just two months away, making the new voters in Duval County among the first in the state to be able to exercise their restored rights. Corri Moore said the main thing he wanted to use his vote for was to push criminal justice reform. "Now the people making laws and writing laws are going to be listening to me," he said.[26]

Smiles, hugs, and tears filled every newscast in the state and lined every newspaper the following morning. It was a watershed moment, marking a definitive before and after. Finally, organizers could start gauging how much the momentum of the campaign might translate to the ballot box. No one expected the new voters to be looped back into the political fold overnight, but expectations were cautiously high. The aggregate numbers were not. Out of more than a million people who ostensibly regained the right to vote in Florida, three months later only an estimated 2,000 registered to vote.[27]

The day after Meade, Bushell, and others registered to vote, on his second day in office, newly elected Governor Ron DeSantis stood at the Freedom Tower in downtown Miami making a nomination for an empty seat to the

Florida Supreme Court. The nominee was Barbara Lagoa, a Cuban American woman. DeSantis used the occasion to speak about American ideals, the "rule of law," the kinds of arbitrary justice people in dictatorships face, and the shining city on a hill that is democracy.

During the event, I asked the new governor if he had any words for the Floridians who had just gotten their rights back the previous day. "It is what it is," said DeSantis. The five apathetic words hung in the air as he moved on to the next question, on to the next subject.

Senator Jason Pizzo still didn't have an answer to his question about what would ever happen with those decades-old debts from felony cases.

The office of Clerk of Courts Harvey Ruvin in Miami-Dade County was tasked with verifying voter information during the chaotic and fraudulent 1997's mayoral race in Miami that led to the state enforcing its felon voting ban for the first time in the 2000 election. His office was intricately connected with the core of the matter. Somewhere in that sprawling bureaucracy of records lay the answer to whether many people could vote or not.

I got Ruvin on the phone one afternoon, and he started, "It's a complicated issue, and it hasn't been thought out."[28] Technically, the clerk of courts office functions not just as a repository for records but also as a kind of bank for accepting payments that are later distributed to the state and local governments, according to the different agreements each has, what charge or offense someone has committed, or what service is being rendered. Old debts are never written off, Ruvin told me. No debt whatsoever could just be forgiven because it's too old. The government is not a person; debts don't die off. They just don't get paid sometimes, and there's only so much the government can do about it.

Ruvin had been involved in local politics since 1968, when he was elected as mayor of a small city. He spent two decades on the Metro Dade County Commission before being elected six times as the clerk of courts for the largest county in the state. If anyone did, Ruvin had a good vantage point from which to see the situation in a practical light for local governments.

Come to think of it, he seemed to realize midconversation, Amendment 4 could be good for everyone. "Clearly, if this works out and we see lots of people wanting to get their rights back, this could be a real source of revenue," he told me.[29]

There was a kink in this system, however. Ruvin's office had a contract with debt collection companies that charged an additional 40 percent to collect those outstanding payments. Once the contract was signed, the clerk of court's office washed its hands of trying to collect the money. That was now a corporate matter. If the money was ever collected, the government would get its fill, and the company would take its cut off the top. In essence, what that meant was that if you wanted to pay off an old $1,000 fine, that debt could balloon to $1,400 if a debt collection company was involved. A 2004 Florida law allowed for this kind of arrangement. Ruvin's office was directly involved in pushing to make it a reality. "We got a lobbyist and we got a bill passed," he recalled.[30]

Now that voting rights and the debt seemed to be tied together, corporate profits could stand squarely in the way of democracy. Clarence Office found this out firsthand. After filling out his registration form on the first day he believed he was legally eligible, the soft-spoken man and I had stayed in touch. A week later we met up at a grocery store parking lot close to his job. The clerk of courts website listed an unspecified amount of pending fines for one of his felony cases, and it was unclear if that would affect his voting rights. As we stood under the shade of a young oak tree, he called the debt collection company listed on his account for more information.

The representative for the company informed him, matter-of-factly, that he owed more than a thousand dollars. "This is for an old, old charge. That's what it's for. From '08," he said in frustration after hanging up. After years spent getting back on his feet, Office has a steady job with the Florida Department of Veterans Affairs now, with house and car payments due monthly. A thousand dollars meant a huge chunk of his annual salary that he would not be able to just drop down on the counter.[31]

"I mean, come on, man," he said, to no one in particular. "It shouldn't stop me from being able to vote. I'll get my voter's registration card next week."[32]

That wasn't it, either. Other felony charges stemming back from the late 1980s listed on Office's rap sheet listed outstanding payments. The specific pending dollar amount tied to all those cases, if it was known, was tied up somewhere in the bureaucracy or corporate offices. Or perhaps, a little bit of both.

The light at the end of the tunnel to normalcy, to being a full decision-making member of society again, seemed to be up in the air. But Office was one man. If we multiplied cases like his across the state, exactly how much money would we be talking about?

The Florida Clerks of Court and Comptrollers Association is a tiny hub in an arcane bureaucracy that hardly anyone seemed to know existed. In addition to lobbying for themselves, the principal role of the independent association is to serve as a repository for financial statements from every county across the state. Every year, by law, each clerk of courts office for each county has to send a full financial report to the association.

After crunching the numbers for five years of data, the full scope of the problem started to become clear to me. Not only were the debt amounts

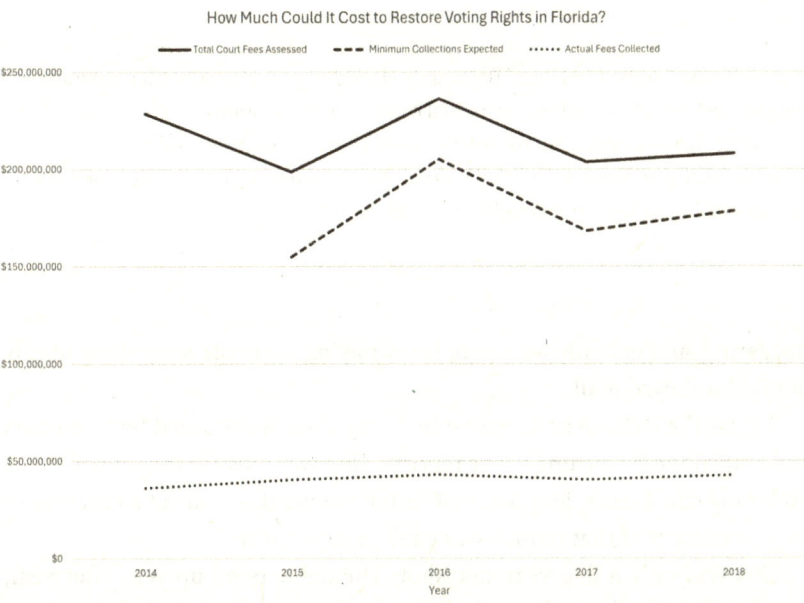

Statewide data show how much money is assessed to defendants in connection to felonies, per year. Starting in 2015 the state began flagging certain debts as having "minimal collection expectations," showing that a vast majority of money is not expected to be repaid. Note: These are year-to-year numbers, but the total amount owed accumulates and carries on to the next fiscal year. Source: Florida Clerks and Comptrollers Annual Assessment and Collections Reports. Credit: Graphic by Anjelica Fabro.

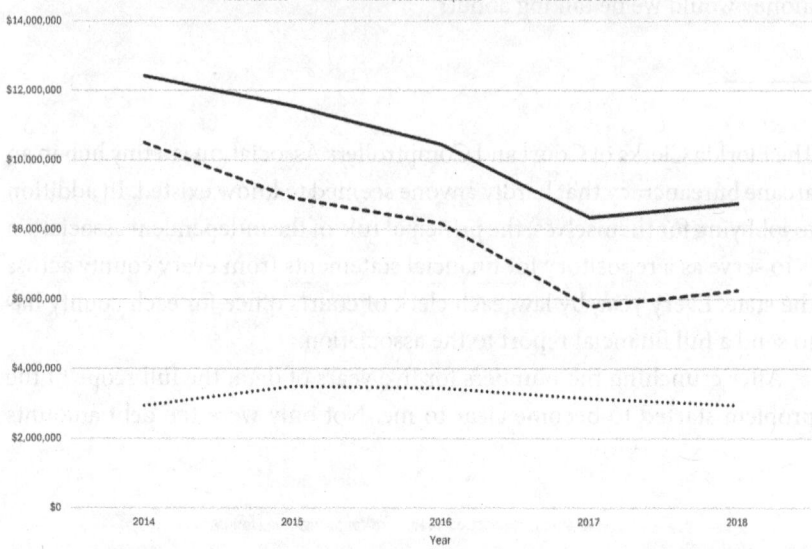

Miami-Dade County–level data. The county clerk of courts started a pilot program, flagging certain debts as having "minimal collection expectations" in 2014. Note: These are year-to-year numbers, but the total amount owed accumulates and carries on to the next fiscal year. Source: Florida Clerks and Comptrollers Annual Assessment and Collections Reports. Credit: Graphic by Anjelica Fabro.

staggering, and not only were people not paying the debts, something utterly illogical followed it all.

Across the state, over $1 billion in felony fines were issued between 2013 and 2018 alone, according to the reports. That was only for the fines alone—excluding court costs, fees, and restitution payments—and yet an average of only 19 percent of that money was paid back per year.[33]

This was only a five-year snapshot. The debts piled up year after year, decade after decade, and snowballed into obscure amounts that were hard to account for, controlling for deaths, changes in the tech used to track the money, and whether interest was added to the balance.

Miami-Dade said a total of $278 million in felony fines alone were still outstanding, but they were only able to make the calculation as far back as 2000. Palm Beach County said a total of $195.8 million was owed in unpaid felony fines stemming from felony convictions for all past years, a number that included interest.[34]

So, that was bad. Even worse was that starting in 2015 the association began marking some of the fines assessed as having "minimal collections expectations," meaning the state knew they should not expect payment on those debts, often because the offender was low income and likely received a public defender. A mind-boggling 83 percent of the debt was described this way, on a yearly average.[35]

Without any stretch of the imagination, this money that the state literally did not expect to collect would balloon to over $1 billion. And the way the rhetoric was headed, this money could serve as the only roadblock that stopped citizens of Florida from exercising the right to vote. The very concept began to evoke fears that Florida would soon institute a system of poll taxes.

This was going to be a very big problem.

8
POLL TAX?

Poll taxes would become a key and divisive phrase over the following months. By the time the amendment to the US Constitution that aimed to ban poll taxes was first proposed in 1962, only five states still had poll taxes on the books: Alabama, Arkansas, Mississippi, Texas, and Virginia.[1] Poll taxes were explicitly defended as a mechanism of white supremacy, since it allowed a way for white elites to block Black voters from exercising their civil rights. One 1939 column in the *Tuscaloosa News* in Alabama proudly declared, "This newspaper believes in white supremacy, and it believes that the poll tax is one of the essentials for the preservation of white supremacy."[2]

When the Twenty-Fourth Amendment was ratified in 1964, it banned poll taxes from preventing anyone from casting a vote in a federal election. President Lyndon B. Johnson called the ratification of the amendment a "triumph of liberty over restriction," adding that "it is a verification of people's rights, which are rooted so deeply in the mainstream of this nation's history."[3]

Poll taxes at the state and local level, on the other hand, would still be permitted. That was a concession for states'-rights advocates who wanted to keep poll taxes on the table in case they ever felt like imposing them.

Federal courts struck down the remaining state-level poll taxes in the years immediately following the passage of the Twenty-Fourth Amendment.[4] But in order to do that, they largely relied on the Fourteenth Amendment—the one that gave formerly enslaved people the full rights of citizenship and gave "equal protection" to everyone within the nation. The most important of these cases was brought to the US Supreme Court by a poor white Virginian named Annie E. Harper. She argued that forcing her to pay a poll tax in order to vote effectively silenced her electoral voice, making her a second-class citizen.

The US Supreme Court agreed. In 1966, in a 6–3 decision, the court wrote that "a state violates the Equal Protection Clause of the Fourteenth Amendment to the U.S. Constitution whenever it makes the affluence of the voter or payment of any fee an electoral standard. Voter qualifications have no relation to wealth."[5]

Along with the unambiguous ban on federal poll taxes enacted by the Twenty-Fourth Amendment, this now equaled a complete and total ban on tying wealth to the voting booth: "Voter qualifications have no relation to wealth" meant what it said.

As Floridians started to grapple with the implications of what was to come, this history was the central frame of reference. Florida was set to take a questionable turn.

A bill was introduced in the Florida House that did what many feared, tying the ability to pay fines, fees, court costs, and restitution connected to a felony conviction to the right to vote. As soon as the hypothetical was put down in writing, the question of poll taxes was unavoidable. It rose and fell in every committee hearing that touched on the subject.

"It's blatantly unconstitutional as a poll tax," said Democratic State Representative Adam Hattersley.[6] If the bill passed, money would explicitly become a barrier to voting for thousands of Floridians. The Florida Rights Restoration Coalition created a website announcing that its key victory was "under attack." The group called the bill "an unconstitutional overreach" that "would restrict the number of people who would otherwise be eligible to vote."[7]

The driving force behind the effort—and its most staunch defender—was James Grant, a libertarian-minded Republican from the Tampa Bay area.[8] A sharp-spoken thirty-six-year-old with a Conan O'Brien–style poof of blond hair, Grant was known to fly into high-minded monologues about the US Constitution, and why he was on the right side of it. He rejected that his proposal amounted to a poll tax, and the accusation angered him.

"To suggest that this is a poll tax inherently diminishes the atrocity of what a poll tax actually was," he said during one hearing.[9] People pushing the phrase had ulterior political motives, he explained to me in a long conversation. "Some people want an inflamed electorate," Grant said. "Some people want to provoke the electorate with talking points to rile them up to accomplish a political goal."[10]

Grant spoke clear-mindedly and with conviction. There was no problem with what he was doing whatsoever. If there was a problem with what he was doing, it was only because there was a problem in the ballot amendment itself, if not with the petition process that put it on the ballot in the first place. State policies should not be created in this way, he argued. "This is not a bill that has gone through the committee process with an idea proposed by a duly elected legislator trying to make good policy. This is the legislature having the responsibility to clean up and define an ambiguous process of making policy in the Constitution," he said.[11] Floridians had had their party with the Florida Constitution, and now he had the responsibility of sweeping the floor and doing the dishes.

At the same time, Grant did not dispute that voters had to make policy decisions inside the constitution only after they tried for nearly two decades to do it through the legislature or through the executive branch with no luck. If he were governor, he would have done things very differently. "I think we're here today because the previous administration refused to use clemency," Grant said in a hearing, referring to Rick Scott.[12]

At his core, the message Grant had for the world was that he was only codifying what was already inside Amendment 4, and was doing no more, no less. Yes, he conceded that attaching the payment of money within the scope of "completion of all terms of a sentence" could "prevent somebody from having their rights automatically restored." But his hands were tied by what voters themselves passed.[13]

"The voters were offered a deal. And the deal—the terms of that deal—said no murder, no felony sex offense, and automatic restoration if the person has completed 'all terms of their sentence,'" he said. "That's what I'm going to maintain fidelity to. Whether or not I think it's the best policy—I'm not going to undo what the voters explicitly voted for."[14]

He lamented that the "poll tax" language was being widely used and that a new nickname had been bestowed upon him: Jim Crow Jamie. "It's important for us to get rid of labels and to judge people by the work product and the intellectual honesty and their actual words," said Grant. "It's never fun to have words like 'Jim Crow' and 'poll tax' thrown around. But if people were not playing politics, if people were truly concerned about this issue, they would have had counsel in front of the [Florida] Supreme Court."[15]

It was now in the middle of the 2019 legislative session, and suddenly a Florida Supreme Court hearing from two years earlier was the most important thing in Florida politics. A deep analysis of the hearing would complicate matters for the opposition that Grant faced.

Once ballot initiatives reach a certain threshold of signatures, they go before the Florida Supreme Court in order to pass a smell test of whether the question meets the criteria for reaching the ballot. Namely, does the question do what it says it is going to do? Every initiative goes through this process, and some seemingly straightforward questions have been killed at this stage, as justices poke holes in the language, at times sharply pointing out logical gaps and at others stretching the bounds of logic into something that more closely resembles activism from the bench in order to kill an initiative. But killing a ballot measure is rare, especially for initiatives that are coherent and represented by real legal professionals.

Back in March 2017, it was the turn of Amendment 4 to go through this process. Attorney Jon Mills was chosen to represent the initiative. Mills was an original member of Desmond Meade and Howard Simon's powwow team chosen to workshop the language of the effort, and he was known across the state as a brilliant legal mind. In the late 1980s Mills served as the Speaker of the Florida House of Representatives as a Democrat. By the time he went before the court, he was officially out of politics and working as a professor of law and dean emeritus at the University of Florida's law school.[16]

In a brief exchange with Justice Ricky Polston, Mills made a concrete statement of how the authors and supporters of Amendment 4 interpreted their own work. Talking about what was included and what was not included in "all terms of a sentence," Polston asked Mills, "So it would also include the full payment of any fines?" To which Mills responded, "Yes, sir. All terms means all terms within the four corners."[17]

The "four corners" is lawyer-speak for what is contained in the actual sentencing document, as in the four corners of a piece of paper. In the exchange, Mills clarified that the sentencing document was the driving factor. Whatever it contained would be included.

Justice Barbara Pariente, the most liberal justice on the bench at the time, elaborated on the implications of what Mills had just laid out. "I'm thinking, this would actually help the state because if fines, costs and restitution are a requirement, then there's—for those that want to vote, there's a big motivation to pay unpaid costs, fines and restitution," she said.[18]

Those two exchanges were seized upon by the Florida Legislature to justify a policy that was getting some serious pushback. The rebuttal to accusations that they were creating a poll tax was right there, in plain language. Video of the exchange was played for lawmakers and broadcast across the state. The argument did not convince everyone. "The colloquy between the lawyer and the Supreme Court Justices is not binding," Mark Schlakman, a professor of law at Florida State University who worked with Florida Governor Lawton Chiles on clemency issues in the 1990s, told me. "This isn't even opinion; the legislature is not bound by that."[19]

Representative Grant admitted he was not bound by the testimony. But the video severely blunted the criticism aimed at Republican lawmakers and gave them ammunition for counterattacks. "What I find offensive is that somebody would suggest that I should have to statutorily be required to take proponents at their word," he said. "I think good politics and good policymaking is being able to take people at their word, and that's exactly what we're doing."[20]

Self-sabotage can happen over the course of decades in politics. A decision made to solve one specific problem at a specific moment in time can later boomerang back and present a new range of problems for a new context. It's the reason that politics is never done, why there's no such thing as a perfect utopian government, why there's no place where all the tough decisions have already been made and where everyone can just smile and live life without political worry. There are problems and then there are solutions. Give it enough time, the solutions become the problems.

He might not have realized it right then, but Jon Mills stepped into this scenario as he spoke to the Florida Supreme Court that March day in 2017. Every twenty years, lawmakers appoint members of the public to form a special group that is unique to Florida politics. The Constitution Revision Commission looks over the state constitution and suggests changes that could make the government work better. The potential changes are voted upon by the group and then placed on the ballot for voters to approve. In the second-ever meeting of this group, in 1998, Mills was appointed by Democratic Governor Lawton Chiles. Some of the decisions Mills made then were directly implicated in the debates about poll taxes swirling around in 2019.[21]

As the 1998 Constitution Revision Commission held listening sessions across the state, in county after county local politicians complained about the cost of funding the state court system. While the state spent less than half of 1 percent of its budget to fund the state court system, many counties spent exorbitant amounts of their local tax dollars to fund courts. The state required counties to pay for operating courtrooms, personnel, and equipment in order to operate all circuit and county courts. Costs for funding the local clerk of courts office, state attorney's office, and public defender's office were left to local governments. The state chipped in hardly anything at all.[22]

The local officials begged the Constitution Revision Commission to come up with a solution to their woes. Many suggested the state pick up the full tab. It was a touchy subject because Florida had for so long prided itself as being a low-tax state with a lean state government and no income tax. Funding the court system from the state budget could require raising taxes across the state; nobody wanted to raise taxes at the state level. In a hearing, Democratic State Representative Shirley Brown suggested a simple solution: Let the counties collect the fines and fees imposed by the local courts, and use *that* money to fund the court system, instead of local taxes. It was this idea that stuck.

Mills headed a special committee in the Constitution Revision Commission that was tasked with figuring it out. For months they labored on how to make the idea work. On February 12, 1998, he presented his solution. "The bottom line is there are only about three areas to draw from: that is, the state taxpayer, the local property taxpayer and the user. That is, the persons who use the court system either through paying their filing fees or through collection of other fines, etcetera," Mills told members of the commission.[23]

"We suggest you construct a system whereby clerks would be funded by fees. This entails raising fees," Mills said.[24] Instead of the general public paying to keep the justice system operating, Mills argued, the very people caught up in the justice system should be the ones paying for it. That could include increasing the fees and filing costs for things like minor traffic infractions and filing fees for civil lawsuits. It could also mean raising fines that were attached to certain crimes. If everything went well, it would give relief to the local governments and local taxpayers, allow the state to avoid raising taxes, and the main person stuck with the bill was the criminal. Who would go to bat for the criminal?

The proposal was placed on the 1998 ballot, and Florida voters overwhelmingly passed it.[25] That move made Florida an early leader in a new phenomenon that began sweeping its way across the nation: something that has become known as "cash register justice."

Most famously, this was the case in Ferguson, Missouri. In the wake of civil unrest following the police shooting of teenager Michael Brown in 2014, an

Obama administration investigation found the city police department was trapping residents in a spiral of debt as a way to raise revenue for the city rather than raising taxes. People had their driver's licenses revoked, served jail time, lost jobs, and generally had their lives ruined by the practice. Overall, it played a huge role in the strained community-police relations that exploded in the city after Brown was shot and killed by officer Darren Wilson.[26]

On a different scale, a similar dynamic played out in Florida, and those who have been around long enough have seen it play out in real time. "When I first started in the system a ticket was like $35. Now it's minimally about $160," said Steven Leifman, an administrative judge in Miami-Dade County Court, talking about a typical traffic ticket. He entered into the system in 1995. "It's a significant jump, and it's not an inflation jump," he told me. "It is philosophy and living in a state with a very low tax rate. People don't understand that you still have to pay for services even if you have low taxes. Whether you're paying it through one-time income tax, or you're paying it through sales tax, or you're paying it through fees, which is what we do generally. It adds up, and for a lot of the individuals there's a huge tax burden on the people that can least afford it."[27]

Lawmakers learned they could add various fines and fees to the criminal justice system to offset regular tax dollars. The amounts involved for some of the crimes are staggering. The fine attached to some classes of drug trafficking offenses was raised to a half million dollars. For lower-level trafficking cases, mandatory fines were set at $25,000.[28] If someone is convicted of stealing a fish or an animal from an agricultural facility, they are fined a mandatory $10,000. As a result, Floridians leaving prison with felony records often leave with crippling debt.

"The debt can be insurmountable," said Phil Telfayan, the executive director of Equal Justice Under Law, a national nonprofit that tracks court fines and fees. "Folks who are living paycheck to paycheck, who are barely making enough to get by, it's not that they're trying to evade court obligations, it's not that they're trying to avoid paying a fine that they may have collected. It's literally they're unable to pay it."[29]

Between 1996 and 2007, the Florida Legislature "created or authorized" more than twenty new categories of surcharges, fees, and other financial penalties connected to criminal offenses, according to a 2010 study by the Brennan Center for Criminal Justice. The report found that the state acted without considering the ability of the average resident to pay and "without considering the effects" it might have on recidivism or "reentry into society for those convicted of crimes."[30]

As Mills stood before the Florida Supreme Court, these two worlds collided. He was a coauthor of Amendment 4. He was also a coauthor and sponsor of the constitutional amendment that could be its undoing.

A companion version of Jamie Grant's bill taken up by the Florida Senate would have solved many of these problems. That version, introduced by Republican Senators Jeff Brandes and Keith Perry, would have considered a criminal sentence complete if the fines, fees, or court costs—but not restitution—were "converted to a civil lien." This was a momentous shift from what Representative Grant proposed. Judges in criminal cases convert unpaid financial obligations to civil liens all of the time. The money is still technically owed, but it lets the defendant close out the criminal case. Thereafter it becomes a matter of civil law. The bill passed its first committee by a 3–2 vote, offering hope that the worst outcome was avoidable.[31]

In social justice circles, Brandes was widely regarded as a champion of criminal justice reform. He spent huge amounts of his political capital over the years in attempts to place limits on police surveillance powers and reforming the state prison system. "It was one area where I saw there was no one else working in it," he told me.[32]

Brandes also questioned the rationale for the state's fines and fee structure that threatened to intrude into the realm of voting rights. For years he had been trying to push through bills that would stop the practice of suspending the driver's licenses of people who could not afford to pay the various fines and fees imposed upon them by clerks of court. As far back as 2016 he was publicly discussing "changing the entire model" of how the court system was funded, because it had long been funded "on the backs of people who can least afford it."[33] He vocally pushed for technocratic, structural changes to the criminal justice system in a way that is rare for any politician, much less for a Republican.

"I think my goal is: What's the philosophy behind our fines and fees structure? What's our goal here? Is our goal to simply penalize? Is our goal to make sure that the state is recouping some of its costs? What are the effective fines and fees strategies from around the country that work? Or are we just throwing numbers at a dartboard and saying, 'Well, this should be a $10,000 fine if you steal a fish?'" he said. "There's no rationale or rhyme or reason."[34]

With his bill's treatment of civil liens as a safety net for poor people who still owed money on their felony convictions, the ACLU, the Florida Rights Restoration Coalition, and their allies sensed an opening. Kirk Bailey, the political director of the ACLU of Florida, took the opportunity to fend off accusations that the backers of Amendment 4 were being deceptive to the public.

"Our position has been that monetary obligations that are within the four corners of a sentence need to be expected to be paid as a part of the completion of terms of sentence," Bailey said at a Senate committee hearing. "However, it's important to note that those fines, fees and restitution—their status changes as a criminal penalty over time. Some are converted into civil liens, some are waived. There are different procedural postures of those fines and fees at different times. And so it is not inconsistent for us to say, yes, they're part of a 'terms of sentence' if they're included in the four corners of the sentence. But it's also true to say that they can be released later."[35]

Tensions between the Senate and House versions persisted. For example, the definition of "murder" in the Senate version of the bill included "attempted murder." On the House side, it didn't. Interpretations ran along different paths, and the very fact of this divergence undermined Grant's central argument that the true meaning of Amendment 4 was largely not up for debate. It was somehow both vague enough to need clarification and specific enough to mean exactly what it said.

Before the final bill came to form, Brandes had sponsored several different versions of the bill, all with different definitions of what it meant to complete a sentence. They passed through committees in the Florida Senate with Republican votes.[36] Although Democrats balked at every version of the legislation, civil rights groups were largely reassured by the direction the bill was taking.

For his part, Grant acknowledged some of the deeper issues with how the criminal court system was funded, but he brushed it off as largely beside the point. "I think those are all very good and meritorious questions that I plan on working on in policy as we move forward," said Grant. "But they're, quite frankly, not relevant to the package that was bundled up and sent to us. They may have ramifications. It may have implications."[37]

The final version of the bill, championed by Grant, would not let people vote if they had financial obligations that were converted to civil liens. The only parts that could be construed as helping an impacted person's voting rights were sections that let a judge convert the money owed into community service hours, and a separate provision that would let a judge go back and modify the original criminal sentence to "no longer require" the payment of some financial obligations.[38] If the judge did that, the person could still vote, even if they never paid that money. As a small fig leaf, the legislation would prevent anyone from being prosecuted for still owing debt if they registered to vote between the time Amendment 4 passed and the moment the new bill went into effect, in July 2019.

The new, more restrictive definition of "all terms of a sentence" contradicted what Brandes was pushing for in his previous versions. Democratic Senator Jason Pizzo asked him a few key questions about it on the Senate floor. The two are close friends of opposite political parties; in Tallahassee they shared an apartment together.[39] In the political context, they worked together when they could and butted heads when they had to. The exchange between the two on the Senate floor just before the legislative session ended spoke volumes.

"Senator Brandes, you believe the term 'sentence' is reflected in this latest permutation of language, correct?" asked Pizzo.

"Yes I do," said Brandes.

"Last week, the version that we had to review, did you think that reflected a sentence?"

"I did, yes."

"And three weeks ago, the version that you presented that we all reviewed, did you think that was a sentence?"

"I did."[40]

And yet the newer, more restrictive version was passed in both houses, along party lines. All Republicans voted for it, and all Democrats voted against it. Brandes voted for it, even after acknowledging it could have been much less restrictive.

The fact is that lawmakers did have a choice in the matter, and they chose the version they chose. Less restrictive options were not only debated, but they also passed multiple committees in the Florida Senate. Nevertheless, the harder line on voting rights won the day. The provisions the bill contained, which many likened to a poll tax, now awaited the signature of Governor DeSantis.

The FRRC and the ACLU fought hard to even maintain those two provisions on community service and letting judges modify a sentence. Desmond Meade and his team worked closely with both Brandes and Grant to keep those pieces intact. Yet after it passed both houses, Meade let it be known he was frustrated that any kind of law was passed in the first place.

"Our elected officials had over 20 plus years to deal with this issue and they did not pick the ball up. They walked off the playing field. What we as citizens and returning citizens did is that we picked up that ball up and we got it across the finish line," he said. "After we got it across the finish line, here come elected officials to try to pick that ball back up. Today they fumbled."[41]

Newly retired, Howard Simon followed the legislative session from his beach home on Sanibel Island on Florida's Gulf coast. As the debates ended and the votes came in, Simon reflected back on when he told me he was "going to presume the best of intentions" from lawmakers in implementing Amendment 4. Watching lawmakers at work will make anyone a cynic, and in this case, it pained Simon to see what they did with his life's work.

"I was wrong," he said. "I think the legislature did whatever they could to limit the effect and limit the number of people who are now newly eligible voters."[42]

"Nobody in their right mind would say, 'Oh I didn't graduate yet because I'm still paying off my student loan,'" said Simon. "I think the courts are gonna have to straighten out a lot of what they did."

From left to right, Lorenzo Latson, Clarence Office, and Jerry Armstrong register to vote at the Miami-Dade Supervisor of Elections office the first day that Amendment 4 went into effect, on January 8, 2019. Credit: Daniel Rivero

A staffer of the Florida Rights Restoration Coalition helps Dolce Bastien register to vote minutes after Eleventh Judicial Circuit Judge Nushin Sayfie restored his right to vote, despite him still owing money connected to a past felony offense. More than a dozen people had their rights restored by the judge on November 8, 2019, thanks to a provision in state law. Credit: Daniel Rivero

Members of the Circle of Brotherhood, a nonprofit based in Miami's Liberty City neighborhood, lead an August 12, 2020, march to the polls for about twenty voters who had their rights restored after the passage of Amendment 4. As they marched, neighbors cheered for them from apartment balconies. Credit: Daniel Rivero

Desmond Meade speaks at a July 18, 2019, event with the Miami-Dade state attorney, the Miami-Dade public defender, and judges in which they announced a new process to help people with felony convictions get their voting rights back, after Amendment 4 was passed. Credit: Daniel Rivero

A handwritten note written by then-Republican Florida Governor Charlie Crist explaining why he wanted to reform Florida's rights restoration process. His reforms passed with a 3–1 vote at the Florida Cabinet meeting that took place on April 5, 2007. Credit: State Archives of Florida

Attorney General Bob Butterworth and Governor Jeb Bush speaking at a news conference on the initial vote recount during the 2000 presidential election. Voter list issues that arose during the contested election sparked activism that aimed to restore voting rights to Floridians with felony convictions. Credit: State Archives of Florida / Mark Foley

Governor Charlie Crist (*second from left*) with members of the Florida Cabinet. Attorney General Bill McCollum (*left*) voted against expanding voting rights for people with felony convictions. Agriculture Commissioner Charles Bronson (*center right*) and Chief Financial Officer Alex Sink (*right*) supported the governor in favor of changing the state policy in 2007. Credit: State Archives of Florida / Bill Cotterell

Clarence Office was surprised to learn that he might not be able to vote in the 2020 presidential election because of unpaid fines associated with a previous felony conviction. "This is for an old, old charge," he said. "This is ridiculous." Credit: Daniel Rivero

Governor Reubin Askew (*center*) signs a bill into law in 1971. On his left is Senate President Jerry Thomas, and on his right, House Speaker Richard Pettigrew. The governor signed a massive criminal justice reform bill into law in 1974, which was championed by Pettigrew. The law provided for automatic voting rights restoration for people with felony convictions, but it was deemed by the Florida Supreme Court to be unconstitutional. Credit: State Archives of Florida

Governor Ron DeSantis during a press conference in 2021. Chief Financial Officer Jimmy Patronis (*right*) and Lieutenant Governor Jeanette Nuñez surround him. The governor signed SB 7066 into law in 2019, preventing anyone who still owed fines, fees, restitution and court costs connected to felony convictions from voting, after the passage of 2018's Amendment 4 ballot referendum expanded voting rights. Credit: Daniel Rivero

Judge Nushin Sayfie, of the Eleventh Judicial Circuit of Florida, restored voting rights to more than a dozen people at a hearing in November 2019. The hope was that the new process allowed by SB 7066 would lead to thousands of people getting their rights restored through similar court programs. In the end, few people were able to do so. Credit: Daniel Rivero

Desmond Meade is the executive director of the Florida Rights Restoration Coalition. He spearheaded the effort to expand voting rights to more than a million Floridians who have criminal convictions that was overwhelmingly passed by voters in 2018. He had been advocating to expand those rights for over a decade. Credit: Daniel Rivero

Neil Volz is the deputy director of the Florida Rights Restoration Coalition. He worked hand in hand with Desmond Meade and others to pass the landmark ballot amendment in 2018. As a Republican who could no longer vote due to his felony conviction, Volz helped sharpen the message to appeal to voters across the political spectrum. Credit: Daniel Rivero

The Florida Rights Restoration Coalition has held rallies in the Capitol since 2014, when it organized a rally outside of Florida Attorney General Pam Bondi's office. The group Desmond Meade is pictured speaking alongside hundreds of advocates from across the state on the steps of the Florida Capitol in Tallahassee. The FRRC's Neil Volz is to his left, and Ángel Sánchez is to his immediate right. Credit: Courtesy of the Florida Rights Restoration Coalition; Brandi Hill Photography

Howard Simon worked on expanding voting rights for people with felony convictions in Florida ever since the issue arose during the botched 2000 presidential election in the state. He served as the executive director of the American Civil Liberties Union of Florida from 1997 to shortly after the 2018 election, in which he finally helped eliminate Florida's lifelong ban on voting, ostensibly expanding rights to more than 1 million people. Simon is pictured here in the ACLU of Florida office in Miami in 2016, as the campaign was underway. Credit: Courtesy of the American Civil Liberties Union of Florida

9

"AN ADMINISTRATIVE NIGHTMARE"

Betty Riddle came a long way from the spot she found herself in after a heated altercation in 1972. Pregnant at the age of seventeen, Riddle said she was attacked by a girl before she responded by stabbing her in the eye. "I went in the house and got a knife and came back out. And that's where I went wrong," said Riddle.[1] The incident ended with her being charged with aggravated assault with a deadly weapon, the first of many felonies she racked up over the following decades. Up and down the peninsula Riddle cycled in and out of the incarceration system for short stints on small crimes and longer sentences for larger crimes. Thefts, drug possession, aggravated assault.

All of that was a lifetime ago, a different person altogether. After serving a ten-year sentence on cocaine-related charges, she stepped out of prison for the last time in August 2008.[2] She was fifty-one years old. Riddle, a lively Black woman with bouncy braids and a wide smile, decided that she had had enough. She wanted her five children to stop worrying about her latest misadventure, and she wanted to be present for her grandchildren. She learned to cook and opened up a restaurant with her daughter.

The wide-openness of her new life raised her self-expectations. Riddle enrolled in college and took paralegal courses. She interned at the public defender's office in Sarasota County, which later turned into a full-time job she holds to this day.

Surrounded by lawyers, when Amendment 4 passed in 2018, Riddle was caught up in the historical sweep of the moment. For her first felony conviction at the age of seventeen, she was tried as an adult. She lost her right to vote before she even had one, and now, reformed and surrounded by twenty-four grandchildren and seven great-grandchildren, the emotional weight lifted off her shoulders.

"I celebrated like 1999," said Riddle. "It was like when I got my degree, when I graduated from college, it was that type of feeling, to be honest. Because I didn't ever think I could go to college."[3]

Riddle never imagined that she could own her own home, and now she did. She never thought she could own her own car, and yet she did. With the passage of Amendment 4, the final part of her impossible dreams came within reach. The first day she could register to vote, on January 8, she did. "Everything was in place in my life," she said.

As the legislature was in session, she started to get nervous about the direction the debates. When the final bill tying the right to vote to paying debts passed, she felt railroaded. Overnight she would soon go from eligible voter to noneligible voter once again.

"I was so angry. I cried because it was like giving you joy and then ripping it from you," said Riddle. "It boils down to money. It was just about money, money, money, money, money, money. And I see how the vicious cycle in the criminal system is all about money, money, money, money, money."[4]

Some in the state had an even worse whiplash: Local elections had already taken place in Tampa and Jacksonville after Amendment 4 went into effect, but before the state law was passed. Keith Ivey, a Black forty-six-year-old car dealer from Jacksonville, registered to vote the first day that he could.[5] He then voted in a March primary and a May runoff election, before learning that he owed $400 in costs. He had no idea until a reporter told him.[6]

Worst of all, Floridians who found themselves in this kind of situation had nowhere they could go to clarify their own situations. The court records for Betty Riddle's first felony case back in 1972 were so old that the case had essentially aged out of the system. Since records were nowhere to be found, they could not be consulted. Riddle estimated that she owed about $2,000 for felonies that accumulated since her last case in 1998, but she had no way of verifying the rest. The fact that she committed crimes in different counties made it that much harder, since each county had its own recordkeeping system.

"It's a complete quagmire of just simply being able to figure out if I can satisfy all that the legislature is now requiring them to satisfy before being able to vote," said Daniel Tilley, the legal director for the ACLU of Florida.[7] Tilley was already preparing a lawsuit to file against the state as soon as Governor Ron DeSantis signed the bill. Riddle, Ivey, and other Floridians were already lined up as plaintiffs. Once DeSantis's pen hit the page, the battle was on.

Governor DeSantis signed the bill into law behind closed doors, and on a June evening he sent out a statement musing about the whole ordeal. The bill, he wrote, "enumerates a uniform list of crimes that fall into the excluded categories and confirms that the amendment does not apply to a felon who has failed to complete all terms of his sentence."[8]

Then the governor went into detail about his own plans and how they differed from the ballot amendment or even the bill he just signed. Florida voters forced the state to change its however-politicians-feel approach to giving people voting rights back. Now there were standards, and they were written down in black and white. But the governor and the cabinet still had the ability to go further if they wanted. DeSantis broached the subject, noting that Amendment 4 "curiously" did not address the restoration of other civil rights, like the right to hold public office or serve on a jury.[9]

"I am considering whether to seek restoration of all civil rights to some of those whose rights were restored by Amendment 4," DeSantis said in his statement. "However, I would only consider restoring rights to those convicted of nonviolent offenses. Amendment 4 restores—without regard to the wishes of the victims—voting rights to violent felons, including felons convicted of attempted murder, armed robbery and kidnapping, so long as those felons complete all terms of their sentences. I think this was a mistake and would not want to compound that mistake by bestowing blanket benefits on violent offenders."[10] DeSantis ordered his administration to implement the ballot amendment and new law.

The lawsuit against the law moved swiftly. In broad strokes, it alleged that the law was racially discriminatory: Because Black Floridians are so overrepresented in both the Florida prison system and among the state's poor, the legislation unfairly prevented Black would-be voters from casting ballots.[11]

The most compelling part of the suit alleged that it was often "difficult—if not impossible"—for the plaintiffs to figure out how much money, if any, they owed to the state in order to regain their right to vote. This was the result of Florida's byzantine system of recordkeeping, spread across sixty-seven counties and different state offices. The suit alleged that this system would "chill voter registration" and democratic participation even among those who *were* able to vote, because eligibility was nearly impossible to verify. The scare factor and risk of prosecution, in effect, would suppress the vote. Then there was the question of whether tying the right to vote to payments was a violation of the federal ban on poll taxes.[12]

Different suits filed by the ACLU and the Southern Poverty Law Center and others were merged into one case, and the plaintiffs asked the court to temporarily block the law before a full trial.[13] During the first round of arguments, in October 2019, the federal judge in charge of the case admonished the state.

"If any of you think that this is a process that is immediately—that is easily applied, you are kidding yourself," said Judge Robert Hinkle, of the US District Court for the North Florida District. "I've tried to look at Florida records for various reasons. The plaintiffs are right. This is very hard sometimes to figure out just what was imposed and how this works." "What we have now is an administrative nightmare," he said.[14]

Born in the tiny Gulf-facing town of Apalachicola in the Florida Panhandle in 1951, Hinkle had been appointed to the court twenty-four years earlier by President Bill Clinton. Even still, he quoted Ronald Reagan in court in his musings on democracy. A Southerner to the core, he spoke more Alabama than most parts of Florida did, with the "whens" sliding into the "winds."[15] In the courtroom, Hinkle developed a reputation for a sharp tongue and for writing with moral clarity.

In the arguments for the voting rights case, Hinkle made it clear that the law raised serious constitutional issues. While he did not say "poll tax," he skeptically used the phrase "other tax" in reference to some of the financial obligations. That "other tax" would still trigger the same section of the constitution that banned explicit poll taxes.

He zeroed in on the fees that became widespread after the 1998 ballot amendment, the money that funded the operation of the court system itself. "The expressed purpose is to raise revenue to fund the government. Why is that not a tax?" he asked.[16]

For its part, the state made a head-spinning argument that "it is not a tax." Attorney Mohammad Jazil argued that instead of framing the money as a tax to pay for a basic government function, the money was required to "bring into good standing a person who has otherwise violated the social contract" and triggered "the operation of the government" in the process. That governmental process simply needed money to operate. Hence, it was not a tax.[17]

The judge did not buy it. "Frankly," he said, "it seems to me that when the judge decides as part of the punishment you ought to pay a fine of $5,000, well, that's not a tax, that's a fine for a criminal act. But some of these fees that are being charged, no judge is exercising any discretion. This is just an amount that the State has exacted automatically to fund the government. This is just that we have chosen to impose it on these people."[18]

"Fines and restitution, I'm okay with," said Hinkle. But the fees appeared to be a carve out. Hinkle poked holes in the argument that people were given the choice to pay off their outstanding debt by doing community service. Lawmakers put a value of ten dollars on each hour of community service worked. "If you had a $25,000 fine in a drug case, nobody's going to work that off through community service hours," he said.[19]

At the end of the hearing the judge made it known that a temporary ruling was coming. The final trial date had already been set for April 2020, a month after the Florida Legislature would finish its 2020 lawmaking session. The law—SB 7066—was a bad one, he said in no uncertain terms, and if they wanted to address his concerns before trial, they had that chance. But if they refused to fix the issues, it would be left to him.

"The Legislature," he said, "can make it a whole lot easier."[20] They never did.

A few months after court proceedings started, a ray of hope emerged from Miami. The law that passed contained a small provision that let judges change an original sentence to "no longer require" things that were originally required. Under that provision, judges could decide to reduce or even entirely waive the money owed for a sentence, clearing a pathway for voting.

In Miami, the local prosecutor's office, along with the public defender's office, the circuit court system, and the clerk of courts office all collaborated to identify people who were too poor to pay their outstanding debts. On a November afternoon, seventeen former defendants gathered in a courtroom to become the first to receive this treatment. Nearly all were Black. Singer and activist John Legend showed up for the occasion, lending a celebrity aura to the event. By the time proceedings got started it was standing-room only. "Today our returning citizens have the right to vote restored," declared Judge Nushin Sayfie at the beginning of the hearing. She said the collaboration between different parts of local government was a "legitimate and efficient process" that would strengthen democracy in the state.[21]

Each person received two printed copies of a court order titled "Order Finding Defendant's Sentence Is Completed for the Exclusive Purpose of

Restoring Right to Vote." As the judge declared, one by one, that the seventeen were now eligible to vote, cheers and applause erupted in the courtroom.[22]

"Today was an unexpected but pleasurable, enjoyable, rememberable, priceless moment in my life," said Carmen Brown, a Black woman who was the first to have her rights restored.[23] Brown filled out a voter registration form on the spot. She planned to cast a ballot in the 2020 election, the first time she would be able to do so since 1995.

"I feel really excited, I feel great, because I've been a convicted felon for so long," said Cynthia Cray, who hadn't been able to vote for ten years. "We got Donald Trump in that presidency. We can't keep having that foolishness. I'll vote because I don't want another Trump."[24]

Dolce Bastien sported a pin on his golden vest to commemorate the Black Voting Rights March, the action that brought about the landmark Voting Rights Act of 1965. "This is the follow-up of what took place years ago, as African Americans struggled to gain the rights to vote," Bastien told me. "I have a second chance to be able to obtain something that they fought long and hard a long time ago for, which is the right to vote and make a difference in this country."[25]

After getting his rights restored, he could hardly contain himself. Bastien also registered to vote on the spot with the help of an FRRC volunteer. "It's a feeling that is hard to even describe, I'm so excited. I feel like my face is about to crack, I'm smiling so much," said Bastien.[26]

Andre Williams hadn't cast a vote since he helped elect Barack Obama to the presidency in 2008. "The next election is gonna be fun. Hooo boy is it gonna be fun," he told me. "Changes are gonna be made. Donald Trump? Hmm. Toodle-oo."[27]

Soon, a total of four counties across Florida announced that they were implementing similar programs: Miami-Dade, Broward, Palm Beach, and Hillsborough. All are Democratic-leaning counties, leading to the question, Would Republicans suffer political consequences at the ballot box for not following suit?[28]

"I think the effect certainly could be dramatic," said Kathryn DePalo-Gould, a political science professor at Florida International University. "Some of these other counties, including some of these very, very red counties who had huge turnouts for Trump in 2016 could be missing out on some of these felons."[29]

For his part, Jamie Grant, the Republican state representative who largely spearheaded the controversial law, expressed frustration that only a select few Democratic-leaning counties were taking advantage of the waiver provision. "I mean, I didn't create the waivers not to be used," Grant told me.[30]

At the same time, Grant said the fact that only Democratic counties were using the provision absolved him of much of the criticism he faced when writing, debating, and later passing the state law. "If I'm trying to suppress the vote, and if I am 'Jim Crow Jamie,' why did I create the waivers that Democrats have been turning around and using? Which one is it?" Grant said. "If the effect of what I passed flips the state blue—so be it, I'm good with that. I did my job."[31]

In making comments about the program in Miami-Dade County, Desmond Meade specifically thanked Representative Grant and Republican State Senator Jeff Brandes for working with them to insert the waivers into the version of the law that passed. "When the legislature first introduced their legislation, we did not cry foul, we did not point fingers, we did not do anything to create a vibe," said Meade, somewhat distorting his group's own words and actions leading up to the final vote. "Rather, what we did is we rolled up our sleeves and we went into the offices of Republican legislators that stood with us as we engaged with the legislature to make sure that the initial legislation that was introduced was fixed and got closer to the will of the people."[32]

Meade took pains to stress that these programs were following the direct language of the law and that they were not some kind of loophole.[33] "At the end of the day, it is the law," said Meade.[34]

Carlos Martinez, the elected public defender of Miami-Dade County, felt emotional that first day when the seventeen people got their rights restored in Miami. Outside the courtroom, he hugged the new voters. "You hear about the politics of being able to vote, but you forget that some of it is the redemptive value of somebody knowing that the government recognizes that they've paid their debt to society, and they've told them: 'You have value again,'" said Martinez. "This was a big deal."[35] In Miami-Dade County alone, Martinez estimated 150,000 people could be eligible to get their voting rights back through the new process.[36]

Judge Hinkle's ruling dropped on the Florida political world like the summer monsoon in Miami. The bottom line was that the state could not condition voting rights on debt that someone is unable to pay.

The state *could* make people pay financial obligations before they vote, he wrote. But their specific financial circumstance needed to be taken into account. On that basis, the judge temporarily granted all seventeen plaintiffs the right to vote, since all asserted they could not pay what was owed. The ruling would hold until a full trial was heard.[37]

By this point Betty Riddle had lost her right to vote decades before, regained it in January 2019 when Amendment 4 went into effect, lost it once SB 7066 went into effect, and then regained it again when the temporary ruling dropped. Beyond her and her sixteen fellow plaintiffs, Riddle saw the ruling as a beacon of hope for the thousands of other Floridians who could either not find out what they owed, or who were unable to afford what they knew they owed. The forthcoming presidential election weighed heavily on her mind. "That opens the door for the other former felons. I really believe that. I believe that this here gives them a chance," she said. "The freedom to vote for the next president."[38]

By this time the DeSantis administration was conducting a slick-talking two-step that amounted to a possible effort to void the voting rights ballot amendment in its entirety.

The ordeal came about as DeSantis and his administration filed an appeal to Hinkle's temporary ruling to the Eleventh US Circuit Court of Appeals. In a statement issued by the governor's office after the temporary ruling came down, his spokesperson said all debt needed to be paid, while at the same time recognizing the need to "provide an avenue" for people unable to pay debts because of "true financial hardship." It seemed to leave open room for a carve out, or an exception.[39]

In the courts, the state took a different tack. "The entirety of Amendment 4 must fall" if exceptions were created for low-income people, state lawyers wrote in a brief.[40]

In a hearing after his temporary ruling came down, Judge Hinkle grew frustrated at the dissonance between public statements and court strategy. He tried to pin down the true position of DeSantis and the state, and he wrestled with attorneys for two hours at a hearing to get them to say as much. "I want to be sure that you don't just bury it in your papers, that you say it here in public," Hinkle told state lawyers.[41]

At last, in bits and pieces and smothered in lawyerly gobbledygook, the truth came out. The argument Hinkle shook out from the legal team was that if Hinkle's decision were to stand, Amendment 4 would no longer be the same thing that Floridians voted to pass in the first place. Since there was no clean way to do away with only one section of Amendment 4, the entire thing would have to be blown up.

"That, we believe, is an absurd outcome," the state lawyer Jazil told Judge Hinkle in a hearing. Instead, the state would prefer to simply ban lower-income people from voting if they could not afford what they owed. That was the nature of the appeal.[42]

The main argument for the appeal was that allowing the seventeen individuals to vote would bring "irreparable harm" to Florida if the decision were reversed at some point, and the plaintiffs later removed from the voter rolls.

At first, a three-judge panel on the appeals court upheld the temporary ruling. The unsigned opinion read as a sharp rebuke to the state efforts. "The long and short of it," the court wrote, "is that once a state provides an avenue to ending the punishment of disenfranchisement—as the voters of Florida plainly did—it must do so consonant with the principles of equal protection." A poor person who finds themselves in the fix of trying to exercise the right to vote would be punished "more harshly" than wealthier people "who commit the same crime," the court wrote.[43]

"The sanction of disenfranchisement cannot be described merely as a one-time revocation of the right to vote; rather, the punishment visits the felon at each and every election," the judges wrote. Those who cannot afford to pay suffer a barrier to full civic participation "repeatedly and indefinitely ... while for those who can pay, the punishment will immediately come to an end."[44]

While the case was winding through the federal courts, DeSantis fired his own shot. He asked the Florida Supreme Court to provide him with an "advisory opinion" on what the drafters of Amendment 4 really meant when they wrote "all terms of sentence." There is no trial for an advisory opinion; there are no findings of fact. Yet in these settings the court can decide to simply "advise" the state government on questions of state law as a matter of guidance. Since the interpretation of the Florida Constitution is not a federal issue, the state court's reading would hold sway. In the Amendment 4 case, Judge Hinkle left that up to the state.[45]

The day before Governor DeSantis took office, three Florida Supreme Court justices retired due to a mandatory retirement age. As it happened, all three of them were appointed in the 1990s by the last Democratic governor of Florida, Lawton Chiles. Despite the fact that Republicans had ruled the state for two decades, the liberal-leaning state supreme court proved a constant thorn in their side, frequently shooting down state actions favored by conservatives.

Within weeks of taking office, DeSantis appointed judges Carlos Muñiz, whom President Trump had previously appointed as general counsel to the Department of Education under Secretary Betsy DeVos; Barbara Lagoa, a state appeals court judge; and Robert Luck, another state appeals court judge. The new makeup of the Florida Supreme Court was decidedly conservative, cementing the rightward shift of the state in the previous decades.[46]

The court heard oral arguments about how Amendment 4 should be interpreted in November 2019, with both sides pleading their positions. Nearly every question at the hearing was asked by the newly appointed justices. Justice Luck offered the most nuanced questions and observations. State law treats court costs and fees differently than fines and restitution, he noted. Grouping them all together presented genuine questions, and just because costs and fees technically appear on a sentencing document did not mean the court should treat them the same. "Is a cost and a fee a sentence?" he asked. "It can't be apples and oranges."[47]

Lagoa seemed to be the most skeptical of the civil rights groups. She mentioned the comments made to the Florida Supreme Court by Amendment 4 attorney Jon Mills that fines, fees, and restitution were included in the "all terms of a sentence" language. "We were told that here, and voters were also told that in different editorials and opinion pieces throughout the state," she said.[48] She cited voter guides distributed across the state that also said as much.[49]

As oral arguments go, the justices were mindful not to show their hand too much. That would have to wait for the opinion itself.

An attorney from the ACLU argued that if the justices found the language in the state constitution ambiguous, then the court should look to the US

Constitution for guidance. Lagoa retorted, "Should we do that or should it be stricken?" As in, perhaps all of Amendment 4 might have to be shot down as unconstitutional.[50]

Depending on how you look at it, what happened next was either an impressive act of cunning or a miraculous coincidence. President Trump nominated both Justice Lagoa and Justice Luck to the United States Court of Appeals for the Eleventh Circuit—the same court where a three-judge panel had just upheld Judge Hinkle's temporary ruling against Governor DeSantis for the federal court case. Within weeks of hearing arguments about the Amendment 4 lawsuit at the Florida Supreme Court, Lagoa and Luck were confirmed by the US Senate.[51]

They were now federal appeals court judges, and their nominations helped President Trump transform that appeals court into a conservative majority body. The court previously had a majority of Democratic appointees.[52]

In the meantime, the Florida Supreme Court issued its advisory opinion, written and signed without Lagoa and Luck. The court unanimously decided that money owed is indeed a part of the sentence under state law.[53] The opinion bolstered Governor DeSantis's assertions that there was nothing wrong with the interpretation of "all terms of a sentence" lawmakers chose, even though they had chosen among a menu of widely varied interpretations.

DeSantis used his Twitter feed to praise the outcome. "I am pleased that @FLCourts confirms that Amendment 4 requires fines, fees & restitution be paid to victims before their voting rights may be restored. Voting is a privilege that should not be taken lightly, and I am obligated to faithfully implement Amendment 4 as it is defined," his account tweeted.[54]

After facing pushback for saying "voting is a privilege," the governor later told reporters it was actually a staffer who used that language. "I don't tweet," he said. "The bottom line is with the felons, the 14th Amendment to the U.S. Constitution, they don't have a right under the 14th Amendment."[55]

"We're going to enforce the law as it is. If folks qualify, they'll be eligible. If they don't qualify," he added, "they wouldn't necessarily have access to it."[56]

Access, it turned out, was the core question. Even for those who were eligible. This reality started to emerge as the attorneys gathered evidence for the full federal trial. Attorneys began taking depositions of senior state government officials, pressing them on details of how the law was implemented. As the depositions became public, it became clear that behind the scenes was utter chaos.

Maria Matthews, the director of the Florida Division of Elections for the Department of State, confirmed that there was no one place where someone with a felony conviction could confirm whether or not they were eligible to vote.[57] "You are talking about agencies that each have systems that are created and need to be able to talk to each other and share data," said Matthews. Efforts to get those systems to talk to each other were "ongoing," she said.[58]

Matthews said her staff was not trained to read sentencing documents, nor to make the kind of judgment calls that the state law now asked them to make. "My staff has not looked at court documents in the way that the law is now going to require us to look at it, so we are trying to get some guidance from the clerk of the courts as to what we see currently in terms of court documents," Matthews said. "Every clerk of court has some different records and format in which the sentence and judgment might appear. So my staff is going to have to look at it at a different—at a more intense level than they have previously."[59]

Some county clerks of court offices did not regularly provide sentencing documents upon request, Matthews said, citing Duval County, the home of Jacksonville, as an example. Other counties, like Brevard, seemed to frequently misplace the necessary documents. In Miami-Dade, a lot of the necessary documents were actually held by the Miami-Dade Police Department, a situation that caused frequent headaches.[60] "What this means is that my staff is then not able to proceed," said Matthews. "We do not have an established relationship with the police department for court records."[61]

The depositions seemed to confirm nearly every red flag that activists and plaintiffs in the court case had raised. Any semblance of an actual system was nonexistent. Anyone who wished to register to vote with a felony on their record was flying blind and ran the risk of winding up on the wrong side of the law.

Toshia Brown, the chief of Voter Registration Services at the Department of State, suggested people should "not register to vote" unless they were certain they were eligible. That was the absurd advice of one of the state's top elections officials: Don't register to vote if you can't get answers to these questions. But don't expect the state to help you find the answers.[62]

Twelve supervisors of election were defendants in the case and many gave depositions. They were equally stumped about how to help would-be voters navigate through the confusion. "If you are absolutely intent on following the word of law, which people who are registering to vote need to be doing, that needs to be their modis of moving forward, they, I guess, should endeavor to try and determine [if they are eligible], but it's going to be a tough thing for them to do," said Leon County Supervisor of Elections Mark Earley.[63] Asked what someone should do if they can't figure it out on their own, Earley offered a few words of advice: "Get a good lawyer."[64]

The posture of Judge Hinkle made some nervous. If he wrote a full opinion that mirrored the logic of his temporary opinion and it was upheld by an appeals court, the entire landscape of the criminal justice system would be changed overnight.

This was especially the case after Hinkle granted class-action status to Betty Riddle and the sixteen other plaintiffs in the federal case. Mere weeks before the federal trial was set to begin, the judge added to the mix every other Floridian who could not afford to pay the money owed into future rulings.[65] Any ruling that allowed the seventeen plaintiffs to vote would impact the voting rights of hundreds of thousands of Floridians.

Other states worried. If Judge Hinkle did what it looked like he was about to do, they might not be able to milk people with felony convictions for money. Instead, they might have to raise taxes. Or find a different kind of way to fund the criminal justice system.

In a court filing, the attorneys general of Alabama, Arizona, Arkansas, Georgia, Kentucky, Louisiana, Nebraska, South Carolina, Texas, and Utah argued that they had a "substantial interest" in the outcome of the case. The reasoning was that, they argued, it could force them into an "all-or-nothing choice." The states wanted to get the debt owed by the would-be voters. They also cared about things like "deterrence, retribution, and restitution." But if some people were allowed to vote before they paid all of the debt, the states would lose out on what little leverage they had; the money could go uncollected. The full sentence for the crime, in their view, would go unfulfilled.

"If States are limited in their ability to pursue reenfranchisement alongside their other interests, some States may well throw in the towel and prohibit any felon from regaining the right to vote," the attorneys wrote.[66]

Florida repeatedly found itself in hot water over the years because it opened the tap for some people to get their voting rights back, but then didn't apply the standards equally. But according to the Fourteenth Amendment, states have no *obligation* to open the tap. If opening the tap meant a flood of unwanted voters, states might just close the spigot.

Many states require fines, fees, and restitution to be paid before someone can vote again. According to the filing, these included Alabama, Georgia, Arizona, Iowa, Arkansas, Kansas, Connecticut, Nebraska, New Mexico, Kentucky, Virginia, Tennessee, West Virginia, Wisconsin, Texas, and Wyoming. And still others like Missouri, North Carolina, Louisiana, California, and Idaho required the completion of probation or parole, often with an attached financial component. Nebraska, for example, considered the full payment of money owed when deciding whether to end probation early. Missouri only lets someone off probation or parole when all the restitution has been paid. And on and on. Reversing the requirement to pay debt before voting would change everything.[67]

In neighboring Alabama, the Florida case was familiar. The state faced a lawsuit about the disenfranchisement of an estimated 286,000 people, nearly 8 percent of the statewide voting population, and more than 15 percent of the Black population.[68] A major part of the suit had to do with the fact that payment of fines, fees, and restitution was required before someone could vote. If Florida's law was shot down in a federal appeals court, Alabama's practice would also effectively be shot down, since Alabama is in the same appeals court circuit as Florida, along with Georgia. Any precedent coming from Florida would directly impact the two neighboring states, without having to go to the US Supreme Court.

Unlike Florida, Alabama banned people from voting if they were convicted not just for felonies but specifically for felonies of "moral turpitude." This vague, Jim Crow–era term was used for generations to deny Black citizens the vote. In 2017, the state declared that white-collar criminal charges for crimes like embezzlement and various kinds of corruption were not crimes of "moral turpitude," whereas crimes associated with low-income communities, like theft and burglary, were.[69]

Georgia also disenfranchises anyone convicted of a "felony involving moral turpitude," but it has never defined precisely what that means.[70] In practice, lawmakers and the courts have interpreted the phrase harshly, with every felony charge leading to a loss of voting rights. That interpretation carries a logical flaw, however: If there are certain felonies "involving moral turpitude," there must be other felonies that do not. But the vagueness is the point, Andrea Young, the executive director of ACLU Georgia, told me.[71]

"It has a chilling effect," said Young, who is the daughter of Andrew Young, one of Howard Simon's mentors from the civil rights era in Alabama. "Like in Florida, if you register when you are not eligible to, then it's fraud," she continued.[72]

Georgia does not ban people from voting for life after being convicted of a felony. It lets them vote upon completing the sentence. The problem is that, despite its modest population, Georgia has long been a leader in the number of people on probation, often for lengthy periods of time, and the sentence is not complete until probation is completed. In 2018, the only state with more people on probation was Texas, the second-largest state by population.[73] Young said some of the questions in the Florida case could prove directly relevant to important voting rights questions in Georgia.

"How do you determine what's a fine and what's a fee?" asked Young. "People get really long probation periods, and you're required to pay fees toward that monitoring. So if you get behind in your fees [and] then they tack on extra penalties, Is that a fee or is that a fine?"[74] If Hinkle's logic carried the day, were those probationers not just paying for the cost of a government service? Was that not a tax by another name?

The frustrating thing was that as Florida, Georgia, Alabama, and other states were concerned about the labyrinthian minutiae of a process that could determine whether someone was able to vote or not, another state quickly revamped the whole thing from start to finish with undeniably simplicity.

Democrat Andy Beshear won the gubernatorial election in Kentucky in November 2019, and he took office that December. Within days of being sworn in, Beshear signed an executive order restoring the voting rights to about 140,000 people convicted of nonviolent felonies. "The fact that someone owes money will not keep them from getting their voting rights back," declared Beshear. "Those that have less money shouldn't have their voices squelched."[75]

Prior to the executive order, about 10 percent of the adult population, and about a quarter of Black Kentuckians, were ineligible to vote because of felony convictions. From there on out, Kentuckians convicted of nonviolent felonies would automatically get their voting rights back after serving their term of supervised release or term of imprisonment. The move effectively made Iowa the only remaining state with a lifelong voting ban for all felons.[76]

For those watching from Florida, there was a particularly enviable point to what Beshear did in Kentucky: Within days, his administration set up a website where all you had to do was enter your name and birthdate, and it told you clear as day whether or not you were eligible to vote.[77]

The simplicity was astonishing. The answer to so many problems was right there in black and white. No questions, no attorneys, no lawsuit, no trial.

10
THE TRIAL

The trial was scheduled for the end of April 2020, when it felt that few things were right in the world. The COVID-19 pandemic had largely shut down the federal court system, save for the most pressing of cases. This was one of them.

The way the trial would work was that the judge, the attorneys, and the witnesses would all communicate over a secure video-conferencing line. The rest of us would be able to call in on a public telephone line. This most logical of twenty-first-century measures was nothing short of a revolution in the federal court system. Under normal circumstances, you can't even bring a cell phone into a federal courtroom in the Northern District of Florida. The only way to listen to any federal district court trial is to be there in person. Recording or broadcasting proceedings is strictly forbidden by court order. But the pandemic had forced the court's hand. In order to keep the ritual public as required by law, the court had to make it public.

Dozens and dozens of people called into the line from across the state and across the country. In the world of voting rights activism and law, the showdown became a blockbuster event. All of the quotes below taken in a court or trial setting come directly from the court transcripts of that trial.[1]

On the one side of the fight were potentially hundreds of thousands of Floridians who were too poor to exercise the right to vote. On the other was a state government apparatus that—as became increasingly clear as the trial unfolded—was incapable of defending its own actions.

Between these two parties sat Judge Robert Hinkle.

The voting rights trial kicked off with a technological hiccup. Hinkle couldn't hear Mohammed Jazil, the attorney representing Governor DeSantis and Secretary of State Laurel Lee.

"I'm not hearing you. I see you on camera trying to get your sound to work," said Hinkle.

The attorney's audio eventually came online, but the state's case never quite dug itself out of that early hole. The state's case throughout the seven days of testimony amounted to a few key talking points that can be summed up like this: The state is working on a system to make it easier for people with felony convictions to figure out if they can vote or not; lawmakers only passed a law that ran exactly parallel to Amendment 4, and so they didn't really do much; and of what they *did* do, their hands were tied by the original amendment. The lawmakers didn't have any discretion!

The first of these talking points collapsed once Maria Matthews, the director of Florida's Division of Elections took the stand. By the time she got there, Hinkle was already wound up. Ten days before the trial, attorneys for the state told him that they had developed a new system to determine whether someone had paid their debts. Instead of requiring payment in full once fees, costs, and collections agency charges are calculated, the state would just try to make sure that someone paid the dollar amount that was owed—even if 100 percent of that money went to these other things and not, say, restitution for a victim.

The way that the state would do this was through some sort of omnipotent formula that would give them immediate access to every court record ever in existence, on top of collections agency records. Once this magical spell was cast, the state would determine if someone paid what they owed, regardless of if it went to a collection agency or a crime victim. Only then would voting rights be restored.

In the case that someone wanted verification of all these things in writing, all they had to do was ask the state for an "advisory opinion," and the government would lay it all out for them in plain English, explained Matthews. You owe X amount of money before you can vote. Or actually, you are already in the clear. "If he seeks an advisory opinion, we will give him that answer," said Matthews, speaking about a plaintiff in the case. Through this new plan, the state promised the steady hand of a functioning government. Clarity, at last.

The proposed plan was fantasy. Once she was on the virtual stand, Matthews was confronted with this reality, and she all but admitted it. As "test cases," the state looked at the felony convictions for the seventeen plaintiffs in the federal lawsuit, she said. She even looked at a few of them herself. An attorney for the plaintiffs asked straightforward questions about how to deal with fines and fees that were paired with a misdemeanor offense: Would that money still have to be paid? Would only half of it need to be paid?

Matthews said she would have to think about it and maybe ask her general counsel for advice. Hinkle stopped her. "You've said the way you would deal with that if it comes up again, is you'd go ask general counsel," snapped Judge Hinkle. "But when it, in fact, came up, nobody even noticed the problem. You didn't check on it. You didn't ask general counsel. . . . You just missed it," he said.

Matthews defended herself. "Well, I can't say we entirely missed it because we haven't—we didn't reach the final part, which is to go ahead and make a final determination," she said. "My staff is not going to know the subtleties of this particular thing. This is something that we would, you know, have to train them with, at least for the reviewer."

The judge was not moved. "I guess my follow-up question is, when are you going to do that? Because this got adopted in November of 2018. The statute has been in effect for now, almost a year. We're a few months out from the August primary," he said. "When are you going to work on this?"

Matthews took this question and dragged her reply on for an excruciating few minutes, discussing protocols and staffing and procedure. Hinkle let it go, and the cross-examination continued until Hinkle's question of "When are you going to work on this?" came up again, and the process started anew.

Finally, Hinkle jumped in and pinned her down in a corner, clearly frustrated at her evasiveness. "It's a time question," he said. "If you don't know, say you don't know."

"I don't know," said Matthews. She did not know when the state would work out its magical formula that would bring clarity to the underlying issue.

The phone line remained silent for a few seconds. Matthews had finally dared to say the forbidden three words she had just danced around for hours. And that was only a part of her worries.

At the time of the trial, roughly 85,000 people with felony convictions had filled out voter registration forms in Florida and were waiting for the state to decide if they were eligible to vote, she testified. After sorting through all the absolute mess of records and paperwork to verify if anyone still had debts, employees at the Florida Division of Elections were only able to process about 57 of those pending forms per day. She said this in open court.

"We were talking about this all being done and in place where people could be able to vote in the 2020 election," said Judge Hinkle. "But this suggests that they wouldn't even be able to vote in the 2024 election."

The question of discretion haunted the trial. Jazil, representing the governor and secretary of state, claimed that the lawmakers had none. The State of Florida was proudly implementing Amendment 4. But in the state law that they passed, he argued, the legislature was boxed in by the language inside that amendment.

"The voters in Florida voted for a generational change—there is no doubt about that—in 2018," said Jazil. "The state intends to defend and implement the will of the 5,148,926 Floridians who voted to approve Amendment 4's clear and unambiguous language that sets the standards for the restoration of voting rights."

This argument was interrogated in-depth on the fourth day of the trial. J. Morgan Kousser, a researcher on racial discrimination in politics at Caltech, took the stand as an expert witness. He discussed, among other things, this nagging question of discretion. For research he spent hours upon hours reading legislative history documents, watching hearings, and analyzing amendments to the bill that was ultimately passed.

He cited the exchange between Democratic State Senator Jason Pizzo and Republican Jeff Brandes on the Senate floor, the one where Brandes admitted that less restrictive versions of the law would also be valid interpretations of Amendment 4's language. "All of this tends to undercut the idea that they were absolutely, by Amendment 4, required to end up with exactly what they ended up in [Senate Bill] 7066," said Kousser, the expert witness.

The judge agreed: There were things in the law that he could not directly and explicitly infer from the language of the ballot. At some point, someone was making decisions on the thing.

After that testimony, a recorded deposition with Desmond Meade was played for the trial. The recording ran more than fifty minutes. Toward the end of the tape the attorney turned to uncomfortable questions: Did Meade think the lawmakers who passed the law acted in bad faith? More specifically, Were they motivated by some kind of racism?

Meade was audibly bothered by the question in the deposition. Up to this point he was clear that the law should have been written in a way to help more people vote. At the same time, he worked directly with some of the sponsors to adopt some form of potential relief. Outside the deposition, he had publicly thanked Senator Jeff Brandes and Representative Jamie Grant for helping insert provisions into the law that allowed judges to alter criminal sentences after the fact.

He took a long wind-up before giving his response. The intention of passing Amendment 4 was that it would be self-executing, he said. So that this sort of conversation would never have to happen.

"We knew the minute politicians touched it, that all of a sudden we're gonna have these lines that divide our state—lines that divide our country—all of a sudden materialize. We were able to blur those lines in passing Amendment 4," said Meade. "Any conversation to the government was just based on that premise. That: Let's keep politics and politicians out of something beautiful that the people have done."

There, in the room where he gave his deposition, it became clear that the ideal had been blemished. Politics was no longer a question only for politicians. It was the bull in the proverbial china shop, and he was fully engulfed in the racket.

"The same Floridians that came together, we're now dividing them simply around partisan lines," said Meade. And with that, he gave his response. "Was it the most ideal piece of legislation? No it wasn't," said Meade. "But it was legislation that we felt we could live with. Fully embrace it? No. There were some improvements that could be made, but we were, we could live with it."

He was asked specifically about Brandes and Grant. Were they motivated by some kind of racism? "I believe the exact opposite to be true," said Meade. "I believe there was some genuine intent between those two legislators to actually try to get this right."

To the casual observer, Meade's testimony would seem to be a small victory for the state. Some major claims in the lawsuit rested on whether the law was passed with discriminatory intent, that the law unfairly targeted Black Floridians as a class. And here, the public face of the entire campaign—a Black man, at that—just stated that he didn't think race was a factor in the law that was passed, and that the two leading legislators showed a "genuine intent" to get things "right."

Judge Hinkle was no casual observer. When he heard Meade's testimony he thought of an entirely different topic: employment discrimination cases brought against the State of Florida. "I have presided over scores, maybe at this point more than 100, employment cases against the State of Florida," said Hinkle. In many of those cases, he said, the person bringing the suit will testify that the reason they were fired or not promoted was because of their gender or race. And in those cases, the State of Florida claims that the testimony is not admissible, because one person is incapable of knowing what's inside the mind and the heart of someone else. Actions are one thing. But the internal world of thoughts is a place to which few courts will stray.

"If Mr. Meade's testimony about what was in Representative Grant's mind is admissible, then why isn't the same rule applicable in every employment discrimination case?" asked Judge Hinkle. If the state wanted him to rubber-stamp Meade's comments, Florida might never again win an employment discrimination case, said Hinkle: "Because the plaintiff will always be happy to testify that the real reason was discrimination."

Expert witnesses are a different ball game. The experts are supposed to have some sort of scientific or technical knowledge on a subject, usually coupled with thorough research. That means their opinion on an issue does mean something. The main expert witness the state relied upon was Michael Barber, a Brigham Young University political science professor.[2] Before taking the stand in the case, Barber was best known in the legal world as a hired gun for Republican lawmakers seeking to defend controversial voting measures. To be more specific, a hired gun with a mixed record.

In a federal case that tackled the question of whether Republican lawmakers unconstitutionally gerrymandered North Carolina, Barber defended the Republicans. In a judgment, the court said it found his opinions "unpersuasive," and overall, it gave "little weight to his testimony."[3]

"Dr. Barber admitted that he was not an expert on North Carolina's political geography, nor had he spent time in North Carolina other than two vacations in the Outer Banks and one visit to Duke's campus," the court wrote in that judgment. The Republicans lost.

Another case Barber testified for had to do with elections in Florida. The case asked if the order in which names appear on the ballot constituted an unconstitutional advantage for Republicans, since the governor's party always appears first, and names that appear first tend to get more votes. Florida Democrats, having been out of the governor's mansion for more than twenty years, were left with the sloppy seconds. The court in that case found Barber's expert testimony "emphatically not credible," calling his opinions "unreliable" and "nonsensical."[4] (The state lost that trial but ultimately won on appeal.)

Barber's work in the voting rights case would follow a similar pattern. The main piece of material Barber pointed to was a poll conducted in 2014, in which the ACLU and others tested the messaging for what would ultimately become Amendment 4. It was the only messaging and polling that was done in the entire run-up to the 2018 election that talked about anything along the lines of what the legislature did after Amendment 4 passed. When the poll asked respondents if they would support restoring voting rights to someone after they completed a prison term, 70 percent said they would approve. When asked if they would support restoring voting rights after someone completed all terms of their sentence, support rose to 77 percent.

Barber's response to this was to home in on the seven-point differential. If 7 percent fewer people supported it when it only applied to a prison sentence, then he would knock off seven points when it came to how many people ultimately voted for it, assuming that this is how the public understood the question. By doing that, just under 60 percent of Floridians would have voted for Amendment 4, he calculated. Since ballot items need 60 percent or more to pass in Florida, it meant that the measure would have failed. This was, in essence, Barber's analysis.

Judge Hinkle was vocally skeptical of this math. "Did you see anything that suggested how many voters in Florida have any idea how many criminal defendants get judgments against them that include fines, fees or costs?" asked Hinkle.

"No, I didn't see any—I didn't see any survey results that asked that question," said Barber. "Given the research on the typical voter, I think that voters are not especially informed of these topics or most political topics in general."

"Did you see anything that suggested that voters in Florida would think it okay to keep somebody from voting just because they did not have enough money to pay a fee or cost or fine?"

"Again, no, I didn't—I don't think that's in any of the research materials," said Barber.

For his analysis, Barber didn't have access to the underlying socioeconomic data for the various surveys' respondents, or information response rates. He didn't have a full list of questions asked, nor did he even know if the surveys and focus groups he referred to in his testimony were conducted over the phone or online. In fact, all of the surveys and polls he reviewed were provided by the State of Florida's attorneys, and they were all exhibits to Desmond Meade's deposition. He admitted this in court under oath. One of the few media articles he cited in his report about Amendment 4's messaging was a *Vox* article that was the first item that came up when he did an internet search. Again, he admitted this under oath. These revelations were extracted from him one by one in a methodical pinprick takedown of the expert witness by Orion Danjuma, an attorney with the ACLU.

Judge Hinkle pounced at the sight of blood. He repeatedly asked Barber a series of questions that explored whether race was at play in what legislators did: Why did every Democrat vote against this bill, and why did every Republican vote for it? If not for partisan reasons, what other reason could there be?

Barber responded that there are "faulty assumptions made by the public and legislators" about the racial makeup of people with felony convictions. Since African Americans are overrepresented among people with felony convictions, the mistaken assumption is that allowing former felons to vote would help Democrats and hurt Republicans, he argued.

"But in re-enfranchising former felons, if you look at the actual numbers, you are getting a lot of—a lot more white former felons re-enfranchised," said Barber. "So that number is just simply larger than the number of African-Americans being re-enfranchised." White voters' votes are statistically much more unpredictable than those of Black voters, who tend to vote for Democrats, he said. So that assumption is not quite true, but it's still what a lot of people believe. Lawmakers' mistaken racial assumptions could help explain why votes for the bill broke down along partisan lines, he testified. Because they believed more eligible Black voters would hurt Republicans.

In the closing arguments for the trial, Judge Hinkle brought up Barber's off-the-cuff comments about "faulty assumptions made by the public and legislators" about race and political party, forcing attorney Jazil into a corner. Instead of defending comments made by Barber—the state's star expert witness in the case—Jazil began to discredit him.

To repeat: The State of Florida's key expert witness in the trial was explicitly discredited by the state's own attorney.

"Dr. Barber is not an expert on racial discriminatory intent," said Jazil. "Dr. Barber did not look at the legislative history for 7066; he didn't listen to any of the floor debates; he didn't listen to any of the committee meetings. Dr. Barber doesn't have any information about what the legislators relied on as they were going about and doing their business."

"I think that Dr. Barber may have been saying things he didn't know. I'm not the one that signed him up to testify in the case," snapped Hinkle. "What is there in the record to show any other purpose other than partisan? And what is there in the record to show any basis for the partisan view other than that there's a disproportionate share of African-Americans?"

As the closing arguments went on, Hinkle butted in repeatedly with questions. He grew audibly frustrated that the state clearly didn't know what it was doing, or even if it had settled on an actual position.

With every new fact drawn out, Hinkle found a new issue to be probed. With every potential solution to SB 7066, a new problem. People can get information about what they owe from their public defenders, Jazil argued. Hinkle countered, What about cases from the 1960s, before people had the right to a public defender? To which Jazil responded that those people would have to be "rather aged." To which Hinkle responded, "You can be 94 and still vote." And the public defender system wasn't rolled out overnight, either.

And round and round it went, as the state's case began to go into a tailspin. The judge was pushed beyond his limit when Jazil asked whether, if the law was found to be unconstitutional, the state would have the chance to submit some kind of counterproposal or suggestions to Hinkle before he wrote new rules for Florida in his court order.

"You've filed hundreds of pages of briefs, you've had preliminary injunction hearing, summary judgment hearing, seven days of trial, and opportunity to make closing arguments, and that's not due process? You need more time?" asked Hinkle.

And with that, the judge laid it all out on the table. "Look, here's where I think we are," started Hinkle. "I'm gonna make a ruling. I expect it to be a whole lot easier to administer than anything you've dealt with so far. That may be a bit of a bold statement, and when I write it down I might find it's not as easy as I thought it might be. And I certainly don't think it's easy. But I hope to make it better for you."

The state had lost the trial. Hundreds of thousands of Floridians were just waiting for the details.

Hinkle's solution came down on the Sunday evening of a long weekend, the day before Memorial Day. In a 125-page smackdown, the judge called Florida's scheme an unconstitutional "pay-to-vote system." If someone could not afford their debt, they should still be able to vote, he ruled. He also declared that court fees should be considered a tax because they fund the regular operation of government and are not punitive in nature.[5]

The flip side was that if someone "is able to pay" what they owed, they could still be banned from voting. Nonetheless, Hinkle wrote, most impacted Floridians are likely not able to pay. For them, this would open the door to participating in the democratic process.[6]

Along with the decision, Hinkle shared a form that he ordered the state and supervisor of elections offices across the state to distribute and follow. The form would allow residents of Florida to submit a "request for an advisory opinion" about someone's voting rights status. The idea that came straight from the mouth of Maria Matthews, the director of the Florida Division of Elections. The intent was to take the guesswork out of the equation and put the burden on the state, which is the state, after all.[7]

Hinkle's version of the request read: "I may have been convicted of one or more felonies. I request an advisory opinion on whether I owe a fine or restitution that makes me ineligible to vote." From there the person would check a box asking for information about their debt, and they could also check a box if they believe they are "unable to pay the required amount." A financial declaration could also be included to help the Division of Elections process the request.[8]

Then came the catch: If the state did not respond to the request within twenty-one days, the presumption would be that the resident should be able to vote. In essence, Hinkle ruled that if the state was unable to provide basic information in a timely fashion, that void of information could not be weaponized. Also, the form would reduce the bureaucratic backlog that had already become an insurmountable obstacle, even for the 85,000 who registered to vote before the state law passed.

"The State is on pace to complete its initial screening of the citizens by 2026, or perhaps later," Hinkle wrote in his decision, referring to admissions made at trial. "In the meantime, year after year, federal and state elections will pass. The uncertainty will cause some citizens who are eligible to vote, even on the State's own view of the law, not to vote, lest they risk criminal prosecution."[9]

The judge said his approach that placed the entirety of the burden on the state only came because Florida squandered months on end that could have been spent coming up with its own solution. "With ample time to address the issue, that State did nothing," wrote the judge.[10]

By later in the week, only a single county supervisor of elections office that was a party in the lawsuit had placed the form on its website as ordered by the judge.[11] "We got it up there as soon as we could when the decision came down," said Susy Trutie, a spokesperson for Miami-Dade Supervisor of Elections office.

But one county north, in Broward County, there was an entirely different response. The office had no immediate plans to put the required document on its website. "It's not the law yet and the issue is still unsettled," Steve Vancore, then a representative for the Broward elections office, told me. "We of course are keeping a close eye on it and as soon as we get the final go-ahead will do what the court says."

One of the attorneys who worked on the trial, Leah Aden of the NAACP Legal Defense and Educational Fund, grew frustrated with that position. "It is the law," Aden told me. "There is no getting around it. This is the law."[12]

This is not something that was up to interpretation. Governor DeSantis said he planned to appeal the decision, but no appeal had yet been filed. And even if an appeal had been filed, no higher court had blocked the Hinkle ruling from going into effect. Broward County, along with Alachua, Leon, Indian River, Manatee, Orange, Sarasota and Hillsborough Counties, were breaking the law by refusing to place the form on their websites.[13]

Things were not over yet.

11

MASK OFF

President Donald Trump reshaped the federal courts between 2017 and 2021. It was one of the undeniable accomplishments of his first term. He turned the US Supreme Court sharply to the right over the span of his four years by appointing three conservative justices. In that same time span, Trump succeeded in appointing fifty-four justices to appellate courts, a rung just under the Supreme Court. Over his eight years in office, Democratic predecessor President Barack Obama was only able to appoint fifty-five. When Trump took office in 2017, nine of the thirteen appellate court circuits had a majority of Democratic-appointed justices; by the time he left office, he had "flipped" three circuits to being majority Republican-appointed.[1]

One of those appeals court circuits flipped by Trump and the Republican-led Senate was the Court of Appeals for the Eleventh Circuit, the court that handles appeals from Alabama, Georgia, and Florida. Two of the new judges on that newly conservative court had been plucked from the Florida Supreme Court: Barbara Lagoa and Robert Luck, who owed part of their good fortunes to DeSantis.[2]

As expected, DeSantis appealed Judge Hinkle's ruling. He requested not to redo a version of the three-justice panel that had ruled against him in the case just a few months prior. On the appeal after losing the trial, DeSantis and his attorneys requested to leapfrog the panel stage and receive a hearing by the entire bench of the circuit, a move that was extremely uncommon.[3] What was even more uncommon was the fact that the appeals court decided to go along with it. With all the justices on the bench, Republican-appointed judges now held a slight advantage over Democrat-appointed judges. Ideologically, the odds were in DeSantis's favor.

Attorneys representing the hundreds of thousands of potential Florida voters called foul. Since Lagoa and Luck had participated in the "advisory opinion" at the Florida Supreme Court about Amendment 4, attorneys at the Campaign Legal Center formally asked the judges to recuse themselves.

The cases were overwhelmingly similar, they argued.[4] Then, powerful lawmakers did the same. In a pair of letters sent to the two judges, Democratic members of the Senate Judiciary Committee accused the two new justices of violating the Code of Conduct for United States Judges. The lawmakers, including California Senator Dianne Feinstein, New Jersey Senator Cory Booker, and Vermont Senator Patrick Leahy, referred to commitments made under oath as part of the nomination process. Future Vice President Kamala Harris, then a California senator, also signed the letter. "You promised under oath that, if confirmed to the Eleventh Circuit, you would recuse yourself from cases in which you participated as a Florida Supreme Court Justice," the senators wrote.[5]

Then there was a problem with Andrew Brasher, another Trump nominee to the appeals court. As a solicitor general for the State of Alabama, Brasher participated in a similar case about a similar law in that state, making the same arguments that Florida was now relying on. Effectively, he would have to rule against, and possibly override, a set of arguments he made only a few years prior. Both attorneys for the plaintiffs and the senators called on Brasher to recuse himself.

Brasher immediately recused himself.[6] His recusal made the circuit an even split of Republican- and Democratic-appointed justices. But if Lagoa and Luck agreed to recuse themselves, the three recusals would mean a Democrat-nominated majority's opinion would carry the day.

Lagoa and Luck refused and issued a twenty-five-page order that laid out their side of the case.[7] The judges argued that the cases were in fact not similar at all; they just happened to both stem from the same state ballot amendment. The pair merely heard oral arguments at the Florida Supreme Court, they said. But that case was hardly a real case at all: It did not have any parties to it; they had simply been asked for an "advisory opinion" to help the governor interpret the state constitution, a kind of proceeding that has "no federal equivalent."[8]

"The request is an original proceeding. There is no trial or intermediate appeal. No facts are developed for the record—there is no record. The opinion of the state supreme court, as the name suggests, is advisory only," they wrote.[9] And, by the way, both judges had left the Florida Supreme Court by the time the advisory opinion itself was written.

At the federal appeals court, Lagoa and Luck were dealing with a real case with real people and were looking at questions of federal civil rights, not a simple interpretation of a state constitution. These differences mattered a lot, they argued. "We have carefully considered whether disqualification is legally required, and because we did not serve as lawyers or trial or appellate judges in this case, we've concluded that it is not," the duo wrote.[10]

The appeals court, with Luck and Lagoa on the case, issued a temporary block on Hinkle's landmark court order, at least until the appeals court case was settled. It gave no explanation why it did so. For the immediate term, the class-action plaintiffs decided to launch a Hail Mary effort to be able to vote in the upcoming elections: They would ask the US Supreme Court to intervene.[11]

The Supreme Court's temporary decision about whether or not to get involved in the case came down without any warning and without any explanation. The effective part of the order amounted to a total of one single sentence. It read, in its entirety: "The application to vacate stay presented to JUSTICE THOMAS and by him referred to the Court is denied." Since Justice Clarence Thomas was assigned to handle incoming cases from the Eleventh Circuit, the decision was his alone.[12]

The Supreme Court would not intervene, and an estimated 750,000 Floridians would not be able to participate in upcoming elections. The Florida primary election was a month away, in August, but for all anyone knew, the action could well bar felons from voting in the November presidential election.

Three of the most liberal members of the court, Sonia Sotomayor, Elena Kagan, and Ruth Bader Ginsburg, dissented from Thomas's decision to let the blockage of Hinkle's order stand. "This Court's order prevents thousands of otherwise eligible voters from participating in Florida's primary election simply because they are poor," Sotomayor started in her dissent.[13] She referred to it as "Florida's voter paywall."

Sotomayor's dissent oozed frustration with her colleagues. In a case just weeks earlier during the COVID-19 pandemic, the court rejected last-minute changes to an election that would have changed the rules for voting by mail because it created "confusion." As the thinking goes, the status quo should prevail when it gets too close to an election.

The thing was, both sides argued to the Supreme Court that their side was the true status quo. Almost a year earlier, Hinkle's preliminary ruling was made and was upheld at appeals court. Those outcomes lined up with his final decision after trial. Was that the status quo? Or was the status quo the perpetual state of confusion that voters were thrust into when SB 7066 was passed?

"Those who registered in reliance on the preliminary and permanent injunctions will remain on the voter rolls despite the Eleventh Circuit's stay," wrote Sotomayor. "Yet because of the Eleventh Circuit's decision, these voters will have no notice of their potential ineligibility or the resulting criminal prosecution they may face for failing to follow the abrupt change in law." She went on. The appeals court "failed to defer to the District Court's factual findings," she said. Further, the appeals court appeared to contradict itself on that very same case. Just a year earlier it ruled that the plaintiffs were "likely" to win the case when it solidified Hinkle's preliminary ruling. Then the plaintiffs won at trial. Nothing explained why the previous position was so haphazardly abandoned, wrote Sotomayor. In sum, Sotomayor said the Supreme Court was "condoning disenfranchisement." But there was little she could do about it. Thomas's ruling was final.

Arguments for the appeals court case were not scheduled until August 18, 2020—the same day as Florida's primary election.

Despite all the drama in the courts, for many, the primary election was their very first chance to exercise their newfound voting rights. In Miami's historically Black Brownsville neighborhood, about a dozen first-time voters gathered at a community center to march to the polls for early voting along with fellow civil rights supporters.[14]

The chatter at the gathering was not the contentious presidential race, but the sheer number of local seats that were up for election, as term-limit rules on the county commission started to kick in. The county could also soon elect its first woman mayor. People behind bars just a few years earlier had the chance to vote on circuit court judges who might have sentenced them.

"This is a historic moment for myself," said Ijamyn Gray, a forty-year-old Black man with a long salt-and-pepper beard. After spending a long stint in prison for various mistakes made in his twenties, he turned his life around and now helped promote local Black-owned businesses.[15]

The primary would be the first time in his life that he cast a vote, and the prospect of having a say in his own community was transformational, he said. "I understand now that voting is very important to us when it comes to local elections," said Gray. "Too many times they have us focused on the presidential race. But the presidential race is really not what matters to us. What matters to us is the things that go on around us, like the commissioners, the mayors, our state attorneys, our state representatives, our senators, our judges, and the list goes on and on."[16]

The group marched toward the polls with supporters arm in arm chanting, "Get out and go vote," and wearing facemasks that read "My Vote Matters." As they passed an apartment building, neighbors took to the balconies to whoop and cheer in support. Dexter Gunder, a key Miami organizer for the ballot campaign, smiled from ear to ear at the atmosphere. "Even though I'm not eligible to vote yet, this is a big deal for me because next time when it's my time to vote, I'll be able to vote," he said. A mere month after the presidential election he would finish his federal probation and become eligible. "Next time," he promised, "I'll be ready."[17]

One of the most talked-about local races was the heated prosecutor's race that would be decided in the primary since there were only two candidates. The race pitted a long-term Cuban American establishment figure against the reformist Melba Pearson, a former prosecutor and former deputy director of the ACLU of Florida who worked extensively on the campaign to pass Amendment 4. She joined the march to court potential voters but also to bask in the fruits of all her labor alongside Howard Simon and a small army of volunteers. Outside the polling location at the end of the march, she reflected on the moment.

"This is the beautiful conclusion of it because now we're able to see people vote for the first time, some of them in their lives. Some of them in twenty, thirty years. So for me it's a beautiful moment and at the end of the day voting is what's central to our democracy," she said.[18]

Deshaun Jones stood out from the crowd in her homemade pink-and-black T-shirt that read, "She's Been Reformed." Her handwritten Dade County Corrections inmate number was crossed out, and beneath it she wrote her voter registration number. The last time she voted was to help put Barack Obama in the Oval Office twelve years earlier. After being released from prison in 2014,[19] she cleaned up her life, went back to school, and got a good-paying job as a social worker. Jones stood tall and proud as she marched.[20]

"I'm no longer a felon. In my eyes, I'm not. I have gotten my rights back and I'm currently a citizen who can vote," she said.[21]

When she came back outside the public library after casting her ballot, her homemade shirt had a new sticker on it. It read, "I Voted." "My daughter is asking me to send pictures right now, she's texting me," she said, elated. "She's 20 years old, she's so excited, more than excited. She's sharing everything for me, she's talking about it to her friends, you know. I am what reform looks like to her, also. I was gone a year out of her life. So this makes a big deal to her too."[22]

Jones smiled as widely as she could and hugged the friend who came with her to vote. She took a few steps away, snapped a selfie, and sent it to her daughter.

Meanwhile in Atlanta, the appeals court heard arguments for the court case that could overturn Judge Hinkle's monumental decision. The political dynamics on the court were apparent to anyone who watched. The more liberal justices backed up Judge Hinkle's analysis. The more conservative tried to poke holes in it and took the interpretation previously voiced by the administration of Governor DeSantis, a defendant.

Justice Lagoa pointed to the ability to "modify" a sentence that was included in the law as potential evidence that things were not as bad as the advocates made them out to be. "Is there any evidence," she asked the state's lawyer, "to show that the state was in any way, shape or form impeding a felon's right to be able to seek a court modification of an original sentencing order?"[23]

The lawyer said *no*. The problem was that only three counties out of a total of sixty-seven had chosen to offer that option. Julie Ebenstein, an attorney with the ACLU, called that remedy wholly "insufficient." Not to mention the fact that community service was only credited at ten dollars per hour, a rate that could barely dent some classes of debt. "It's not a real option for most people. It's illusory for most people," Ebenstein said. During the trial itself, Miami-Dade Public Defender Carlos Martinez went into detail about the many aspects that made those programs—celebrated when they launched—so difficult in practice. Old case files were often held at several different locations; it was hard to determine who the money was technically owed to in order to get permission to waive the debt; there was no legal right to an attorney to help the defendant through the process. Further, the state's sloppy recordkeeping made it hard to track what had and had not already been paid. "From what we have been able to determine, their records are terrible," said Martinez at trial.

Lagoa pressed Ebenstein on what the court should do if the majority decided Florida was violating the constitution by the way it was defining "all terms on a sentence." "Tell me where would you strike, what would you strike, in order to make this constitutional?" Lagoa pressed. "Are you asking us to rewrite a constitutional provision?" Ebenstein responded that the court could follow Hinkle's lead and narrowly block the state for unconstitutional activity. But Lagoa insisted that if some aspect had to be blocked, then the whole shebang would take on a different meaning. The very words Floridians voted upon would be changed, after the fact. "You can't have one or the other," Lagoa said.[24]

Judge Charles Wilson, appointed to the appeals court by President Bill Clinton, asked the state's attorney if it was the governor's position that "we scrap the whole thing" if the majority found Florida was violating the constitution.

"The state does not believe that Amendment 4 could be rewritten with those conditions and caveats consistent with the law that governs severability," replied DeSantis's attorney, Charles Cooper. Translation: If one part goes, the whole thing must go. The movement would be back to square one.

Existential questions aside, some of the liberal justices seemed simply taken aback at the totality of the circumstances, the sheer absurdity of the underlying facts of the case.

"Do you know of any cases anywhere in the country that allow a state to impose a condition on the exercise of a benefit and then not tell people how to satisfy that condition?" Judge Adalberto Jordan, appointed by President Barack Obama, asked out loud. The simple answer was *no*.[25]

The state argued that it was all water under the bridge. The State of Florida admitted fault, up to a point. As Judge Jordan pointed to all the specifics of the case, the inability of the state to process voting applications it had received before the trial, the judge asked, "What does that tell you about the rationality of Florida's system?"[26]

"It tells me that Florida did not get its act together as quickly as one would hope, to be sure," said Cooper, the governor's lawyer. "But I'm here to tell you that Florida has now gotten its act together."[27]

The appeals court decision came down the afternoon of 9/11. For those seeking to regain the right to vote, the majority opinion was an unfettered disaster. William Pryor, a George W. Bush–nominated justice, wrote the opinion.

The court outlined what it called the "twin interests" for Florida that were at play: "disenfranchising those who disregard the law and restoring those who satisfy the demands of justice." Through this lens, money was just incidental to the question of justice. On virtually every point, the court ruled against Judge Hinkle's decision, and against the process he created to help people figure out whether they owed debt or not. Hinkle's advisory opinion process was "unprecedented," even if it was well intended, wrote Pryor. States can create this kind of process on their own, went the argument. But a court cannot mandate the creation of a process.[28]

"States are constitutionally entitled to set legitimate voter qualifications through laws of general application and to require voters to comply with those laws through their own efforts," Pryor wrote.

On the question of whether fees and court costs were indeed taxes, Pryor came down squarely in the camp that said they were not taxes. If someone is able to convert the court-imposed money into community service hours, it is clearly a form of punishment, not revenue, he stated. "To be sure, one purpose of fees and costs is to raise revenue, but that does not transform them from criminal punishment into a tax. Every financial penalty raises revenue for the government, sometimes considerable revenue. In addition to costs and fees, Florida uses criminal fines to fund both its courts and general government operations, but that additional purpose does not make them taxes," he wrote. Pryor wrote that since this is the case, fees and costs "are not taxes under the Twenty Fourth Amendment."[29]

The "poll tax" argument was a lost one. The majority opinion turned a core issue in the case on its head. For the 85,000 Floridians with felony convictions who had already registered to vote—people for whom the state could not determine if they owed money or not—the court wrote that the law was clear enough for them to go ahead and register. The state hadn't turned up information saying that they were barred from voting, and so "until it does, all 85,000 are entitled to vote," Pryor continued.[30] Left unstated in the decision was the reality that at some point in the future, any of those 85,000 might be deemed as ineligible to vote and perhaps they could be prosecuted with yet another felony for following his advice. Pryor didn't talk about the scores of truly eligible voters who would not register to vote because the state was unable to provide information.

In a brief earlier filed with the appeals court, the Florida Rights Restoration Coalition talked about the thousands of inquiries it got from the public looking to get access to its Fines and Fees Fund, in the hope that the fund might pay off the money that was owed. But as of a few months before the decision came out, nearly five hundred applicants either didn't have a disqualifying offense or owed no money whatsoever. They were simply seeking out help from the fund because they couldn't navigate the state's labyrinthian system on their own. The FRRC called this a "chilling effect" that even succeeded in "deterring eligible voters."[31] Pryor took great pains to write many thousands of words without addressing the real-world impacts that lie at the crux of the case.

"This is somewhat of a dishonest opinion," one of the attorneys who worked on the case told me a few hours after it dropped. The attorney did not want to be named. Airing that kind of criticism against judges they might work with again would be unwise. The attorney continued, "This case rises and falls in a large measure—at least on the due process claim—on the factual record, and the majority just pretends that those facts aren't there."[32] Appeals courts are supposed to defer to the specific fact findings of the lower courts when making their decisions, the attorney explained.

Pryor, who penned the deeply impactful decision, had long been on President Trump's public list of possible nominees to the Supreme Court.[33] Just two days before the opinion came out, Justice Barbara Lagoa was added to Trump's list.[34] Supreme Court Justice Ruth Bader Ginsburg died one week after the decision was released, opening the realistic possibility that Trump could appoint one of them to the highest court.

The connections with Trump hung over the outcome of the appeals court decision. Five of the six justices who joined the majority were Trump appointees. His success in filling judicial vacancies paid its dividends. But, ultimately, he appointed Amy Coney Barrett to the Supreme Court seat.

In Florida, three-quarters of a million people were now prohibited from voting in the presidential election, less than two months away.

In the eyes of basketball fans the world over, the debate over whether Lebron James or Michael Jordan truly holds the title of the Greatest of All Time is never-ending. But for Ángel Sánchez, that debate was forever ended in July 2020. "Jordan has to get it," said Sánchez, who worked with the Florida Rights Restoration Coalition.[35]

A few weeks before we spoke, a nonprofit run by Lebron James donated $100,000 to the Fines and Fees Fund, to help people pay their outstanding debts and regain the right to vote.[36] Not to be outdone, Michael Jordan and his Jordan Brands stepped into the fold to donate $500,000 to the cause.[37]

The moment leading up to Florida's voter registration deadline of October 5 amounted to a kind of benevolent bidding war. The social impact arm of the Miami Dolphins gave $100,000.[38] Orlando attorney John Morgan, one of the most consequential legal voices in the state, launched his own fundraising effort, adding that he would match the first $100,000 raised.[39] MTV, VH1, and Comedy Central made a joint donation of $250,000 to the fund.[40]

"This is the final push," Erika Soto Lamb, the vice president of social impact for parent company ViacomCBS, told me. "This is also a challenge to other companies. For us, this is an opportunity to put our money where our mouth is and both increase voter access, and fix the injustices that are long overdue for fixing."[41]

Sánchez said the big names making donations to the cause helped in two ways. "We need the money. That's the bottom line," he said. Then, whenever a marquee donation came in that generated media coverage, smaller donations followed. Sánchez could barely contain his frustration, despite the feel-good moments of corporations stepping in to help out.

"The vote is being held hostage with poor folks," said Sánchez. "And what we're saying is that look: People's vote matters so much that we're gonna get friends, we're gonna get family, we're gonna get celebrities—we're gonna get everyone we can to pay them off."[42]

Another track for getting the right to vote back in the final stretch was the court programs that allowed judges to modify the original sentence. Only three counties in Florida ever exercised that part of the law in the first place. And even among those that tried, the roadblocks were constant. The Miami program had a major problem with volume: There was none.

Less than a month out from the deadline to register to vote, there were more attorneys offering pro bono help than there were clients.[43] Democratic State Senator Jason Pizzo was the first to sound the alarm about what would happen with Amendment 4. He also helped get the language into the law that would allow for a program like this. He helped create the Miami-Dade program, and he was frustrated at how few people were using it.

"Less than one hundred people's cases have been modified in the largest county in Florida, the third-largest state in the country," Pizzo told me. "How is it that my tweet the other day has gotten more 'likes' than the number of people in a county of 2.7 million that have come forward to ask to have their case looked at? How is that possible?"[44] He now offered to help, personally. He launched a campaign and media blitz.

"I want everyone to reach out, honestly, I don't care what it is, just give me a try. Give me a chance to see if I can help you," he said. "Somebody who's got a ten-year-old case—if you stole that TV from Circuit City and they're not in business, I can get that restitution waived. Every case is different. People need to call and reach out and then we will put them in the right place."[45]

Pizzo knew his way around the system as a former prosecutor. He had long-standing relationships with players at every step of the process, from the public defender to the top prosecutor to the judges to the clerk of courts. "I know the prosecutor who's handling whether or not the state will mutually agree in a motion to waive certain things, and it's gonna be like, 'Yo, Daisy, waive this fucking condition right now,'" he said.[46]

A few people contacted him through his social media channels, asking in essence for legal advice. Here are the facts of their case, should they register to vote or not? But the numbers were anemic, even after the push.

"Is it apathy or is it beating down people and basically making them feel so disheartened and disenchanted with the system that's like 'I give up. I just give up and I don't want to engage?' I don't know," pondered Pizzo. "I think that our side will argue that it's because of extended prolonged litigation and confusion and suppressing the vote and all that stuff, and not caring for returning citizens. That it's resulted in low numbers and apathy. But that's where we are."[47]

The senator reflected back to a nonpublic discussion behind closed doors during the legislative process that might have doomed the whole thing. An early draft of the law would have allowed the Florida Department of Law Enforcement, a state police agency, to share information directly with the Florida Division of Elections. This could have gone a long way toward creating a clearinghouse of information. But some fellow Democrats were against this idea in principle, since they feared any central registry that could open voters up to public scrutiny in potentially troubling ways.

"The Democrats wanted to take it out because it was considered a scarlet letter. 'The felon registry.' Well, guess what? Now you make a returning citizen go have to call each and every single place he ever got arrested or convicted and go try to get a cooperative clerk to let him know how much he owes," said Pizzo. "We fucked ourselves," he said.[48] Whatever the cause, if people had questions, the answers were evasive.

The last-minute confusion of maneuvering Florida's new pay-to-vote system was personal for Ángel Sánchez of the FRRC. He had just been through an entire ordeal of his own. Sánchez just completed law school at the University of Miami, where he graduated with a top student award and served on the Law Review's editorial board while volunteering as a tutor at Dade Correctional Institute, a nearby state prison. His is a full rehabilitation success story if there ever was one. The Cuban American speaks with a rare combination of law school and the streets. He is smart enough to know the laws and his rights and yet familiar enough with the system to admit that this knowledge makes him nervous. "One of the solutions to many of my problems was when I saw law enforcement over there, I went the other way," he said. "I might have a right to keep walking, but I don't know. The way that I could ensure myself to not get caught up was just to avoid the law."[49]

It was that same instinct of self-preservation that stuck him in a bind. Even as he experienced homelessness, Sánchez made payments toward the $1,698 that he owed to the Miami-Dade County Clerk of the Court's office for previous felony cases. At first he made them with money orders because he had no bank account. Sánchez was released early from probation in 2014, and a court ordered his criminal sentence complete because of the extraordinary turn that he made in his life. As far as he was told, as far as he understood, he had truly and fully paid his debt to society.

The first day Amendment 4 went into effect, Sánchez registered to vote. The first vote that he ever cast in his life was in the presidential primary in March. He described it as one of the happiest days of his life. But as the court case wore on and the uncertainty behind the process solidified, he was nervous. What if the state still believed he owed money?

He started digging and found an unnerving reality: The Miami-Dade County Clerk of Court's office still listed him as owing money. Even worse and more confusingly, he went on to verify that he had actually paid over six hundred dollars more than what he originally owed. As far as Sánchez was concerned, someone owed *him* money, but the system was still trying to shake him down for more. "I really was bothered by that idea," he said. "They're bullying me, they're extorting me."[50]

At last, Sánchez figured out what had happened. The clerk's office had sent some of his outstanding fees to a collection agency, which he said never contacted him. Scared that the state might come after him for registering to vote and voting, Sánchez vowed not to vote again until he got to the bottom of the situation.

One of the only fig leaves that the state still left dangling to those caught in this bureaucratic labyrinth was the prospect of asking the state for an "advisory opinion" that would give a final word on whether someone was eligible to vote or not. After the appeals court decision, the state was under no obligation to respond quickly to a request for an advisory opinion.[51] It had no legal obligation to do anything, in fact.

Judge Hinkle's solution was now out the window, and now the state was handing out favors. The state published instructions on the Division of Elections website for how someone could apply for an advisory opinion on their own within less than a week of Florida's primary election day.[52] Tight as the deadline was, Sánchez applied, submitting the facts of his case and asking for a final determination of whether he could vote or not.

The day before the primary election he received a response.[53] The Florida Department of State wrote to him that "based on the facts and circumstances that you have asserted in your request, you would be eligible to vote."

"On August 17 I found out, and on August 18 I started scrambling to bring my niece and nephew with me to the polls. Not because it was exciting. This is not a carnival; kids don't like it. But they had never witnessed anybody in their family vote," said Sánchez. "I don't get that printout, I'll confess to you, I probably wouldn't have voted."[54]

The stubs Sánchez used to keep from his money order payments were long lost. His bank statements didn't go back that far. The state's online payment contractor website didn't go back that far either. In the end, Sánchez was saved only by the grace of a probation officer whom he pleaded with until the officer agreed to print out a sheet that listed all his payments, the last of which was made six years earlier. It was him against the mystery amount listed on the clerk of court's website, trying to shake out some logic from the mindless bureaucracy. He found it unacceptable.

"I just graduated from law school, I have a law degree, I have time, I have resources, I have internet, and despite all that it took me over two weeks," he said. "No regular citizen should have to go through this madness."[55]

In fact, very few did. By the time the deadline for registering to vote for the 2020 presidential election arrived, the State of Florida issued a paltry eighteen advisory opinions. Half of the applicants were told they could not vote. For that, they would have to pay money.[56]

As the court fight heated up in late 2019 and early 2020 parallel to the presidential campaign, Monique Upshaw sat watching it all from her dorm at Homestead Correctional Institution. The prison facility lies down the road from an alligator farm, right on the edge of civilization and the brutal Florida Everglades. She was serving a three-and-a-half-year sentence for aggravated battery, and she painted a seldom-seen picture of a thriving democracy from the inside of confinement.

"We had full-on debate. We had made signs for who we were voting for," she said of the presidential election. "We were participating, even though nobody knows we participated but us, but we participated."[57]

She and some of her dorm mates were due for release before the presidential election of 2020, and the way they saw it, they would soon cast their votes. With little else to do on the inside, politics took on a central role. Upshaw, a Black woman in her late twenties, was an early supporter of Democrat Joe Biden, but she was open to persuasion about President Donald Trump, depending on the topic of the day, the latest speech, the latest news and analysis.

"I was in between. I'd make a sign and put my sign back down. Make a sign and put my sign back down. My Joe Biden sign was up and down, up and down," she said. "I had a lot of arguments about Donald Trump and Joe Biden, and when you have an argument in prison it's not good because you have security guards coming through like, 'What's going on?' And it's like, 'It's just the president.' And then they come down to sit down with us and then they go at it with us as well."⁵⁸ "The presidency debate started an uproar in our dorm because we want the right person to represent us if we have a right to vote. So we're screaming like everyone else out there," she said.⁵⁹

When the news came down that the state was going to make all the women in her dorm pay fines, fees, and restitution before voting, Upshaw was gutted. All the debate, all the argument and dreams of becoming full responsible citizens again, gone. The feeling was, It's all about the money. The other women in the dorm, some who had been in prison for decades and who were counting down election cycles for when they might be able to vote in the future, were distraught. If it was all about the money, it was not going to happen.

"Really, they're digging us deeper into a hole that we're trying to get out of, like being in a hole of clay and you can't dig out of it," said Upshaw. "It's like, When will I be able to come up instead of coming up a little bit and then being knocked down again?"

She knew life was going to be hard when she got out. It was already going to be an issue to find housing and a job with halfway decent pay. As it turned out, she was released just a few weeks before the 2020 election, too late to register to vote even if she was eligible.

As I talked to her days before the election, she was working a job at a thrift store in Miami that doubles as a reentry center for formerly incarcerated women, helping them get back on their feet. Upon release, the Department of Corrections gave her a slip of paper listing the amount of money she owed before she could vote: $1,665. She wasn't making much money, but Upshaw drew on her patience and made peace with the situation.

"I might can't vote for three, four years, well into the next presidency. Which, I pray I get myself together so that I can vote in the next three, four years. Four or five, however long it takes for the next election to come out. So I pray that I work hard and I go with the flow and life and it gives me a treat so that I can pick up a bunch of little dollars out so I can put it in a savings account to vote," she said.⁶⁰

The entire ordeal of the law and the courts left her bitter. She and her dorm mates had dreams and aspirations, she said. The whole thing was disrespectful, hurtful, and dehumanizing for those like her who made mistakes in life, but who wanted to do better.

"We're human," said Upshaw. "We live here, too."⁶¹

If there was a day, a moment, a single event when the mask came off, it was the entirety of Wednesday, September 23, 2020. The day started off at 8:00 a.m. in Tallahassee, at a Florida Executive Clemency Board hearing. Like the rest of the world, Florida was in the throes of a global pandemic, and the board hadn't met since January. The backlog of residents hoping to get their civil rights restored from a panel of politicians had grown significantly since then, and two prominent names were scheduled to come before the Florida Cabinet.

Desmond Meade and Neil Volz were on the agenda. Both showed up clean-cut in suits, swapping the "Let My People Vote" T-shirts they wore as activists for courtroom attire. The duo was scheduled to go before the board to ask for full clemency for their past crimes. Full clemency would allow them to move on with their lives, beyond voting rights.

The first inclination that something was off was an unusual but understated action taken by Florida Attorney General Ashley Moody. After Volz was called to come before the board, Moody announced that she would be abstaining from both of their cases. "Just to avoid an appearance of a conflict of interest regarding my roles as attorney general," she explained.[62]

The four-member board included Republicans Moody, Governor Ron DeSantis, and Florida Chief Financial Officer Jimmy Patronis. Also included was the state Commissioner of Agriculture, Nikki Fried. If a majority voted for clemency, that would be the deal of the day.

Volz approached the podium with an air of humility and told an abbreviated story of his last decade of life. The scandal he was caught up in in Washington, the profound sense of shame it brought to him.

After that ordeal he moved to Florida, worked as a janitor for minimum wage, met his wife, who stood supportively behind him with her blue-colored hair, and he helped run a homeless shelter for veterans. "I got to see firsthand the power of redemption in that process. I became the chairman of our local homeless coalition, and I helped to lead a movement that freed 1.4 million people in our state with past felony convictions, who faced a lifetime ban on voting," he said. "These experiences have helped strengthen my belief in the power of forgiveness, redemption and restoration."[63]

Governor DeSantis took to the mic and made a bit of light of the situation with his quick comments. "Not to excuse what you did, but sometimes in Washington the crimes are what's legal, not what's illegal. There's a lot that goes on there," he laughed. "I am absolutely in favor of restoring your civil rights."[64] With Moody out, the three remaining board members voted unanimously to grant clemency to Volz.

Next up was Desmond Meade, the most recognizable face of voting rights restoration for the entire country, asking for a full pardon for his crimes. He came to the podium with his facemask on and removed it as his passion started to burst out the seams and he couldn't contain it any longer. Rather than talking about forgiveness and saying he was sorry, Meade declared that he would show them what he had done. He ran through a list of his work and accomplishments, working with the Miami-Dade State Attorney's office that once prosecuted him to start youth programs. Starting youth programs in his college, to battling homelessness in the state.

"As I stand here asking you all to give me a favorable decision, I'm asking you to give that person that is standing in front of you a favorable decision, not the one from 20 years ago, not the one that was caught up in drug addiction, but the one that's here that loves his community, embraces his community and would give his life for his community," said Meade.[65]

DeSantis looked down at his paper and grimaced. Meade's first-ever crime led to a court-martial when he was serving in the US Army in 1990, when he was pinged for grand larceny and conspiracy. DeSantis didn't like that and suggested Meade should take it up with the federal government and then come back to the state. He didn't like it one bit.

Patronis was not happy with other parts of Meade's record. There was a domestic violence charge on his record, in connection with his ex-wife, and a battery charge connected to his brother. The state CFO said he would have to personally hear that both had forgiven him.

"My brother passed away," said Meade, a shake forming in his voice. "If he was still living, he would be here. Right here with me. But he's not."[66]

DeSantis took to the mic again, this time to ask about something that must have been eating at him. "Just out of curiosity," started DeSantis, "Amendment 4 did not restore the rights to be on a jury or the right to run for public office. Why? Why weren't those included?"

"Because of the single subject rule, Governor. In Florida, you could only deal with one subject at a time. You can't even deal with two subjects inadvertently," said Meade. "If I were to have dealt with more than just one subject, it would have been struck down as unconstitutional. And voting to me is the most important indicator of citizenship. So that was the most important right to go for."

Meade's wife, Sheena, pleaded with the cabinet to give him his civil rights back so he could go hog hunting with his son in Seminole County. As someone with a felony conviction, he could not legally own a firearm. Meade had a law degree, but without his full civil rights back he could not practice law in Florida. DeSantis was not having it, adding that since he had been the subject of a federal court-martial, a federal ban would probably supersede any state ban on owning firearms anyway. With Patronis's support, the cabinet did not grant the pardon but instead took it "under advisement," with an undetermined timeline.

"Just to be clear, I, I still can not even just get like the restoration of my civil rights?" asked Meade.

"Well, that was not on the agenda," said DeSantis. "You're on the agenda for a full pardon. I'm willing to consider the civil rights, but I think what we would like to do is take it under advisement."[67]

A few hours later, Attorney General Ashley Moody broke her silence, putting her recusal for Meade's and Volz's cases in a new light. That was when she sent a letter to the FBI and the Florida Department of Law Enforcement, asking them to look into the Florida Rights Restoration Coalition and a $16 million promise from billionaire Michael Bloomberg to pay fines, fees, court costs, and restitution for thousands of Floridians, so they could participate in the 2020 election.

The announcement of an investigation prompted Governor DeSantis, President Trump, Representative Matt Gaetz, and others to chime in, suggesting criminal acts and sabotage. Two days after that announcement, Volz came on a statewide radio show with me and declared that not only was the investigation perverse and unwarranted, but the organization had not even received the allegedly nefarious money.[68] Even if they had, he explained, it would just be a large donation, no different from any of the tens of thousands of donations that had already been made into the fund from across the nation. Volz himself was a registered Republican.

"We started our Fines and Fees Fund in 2019, and we've been paying people's fines and fees in almost all the counties in the state of Florida since that time period. And we're gonna continue to do that way beyond the election," said Volz.[69]

A spokesperson for Bloomberg called the investigation a "transparent political ploy" that was just "the latest example of Republicans attempting to keep Floridians disenfranchised."[70] A visibly angry Meade posted a video on Twitter. It was a rare instance where he seemed unable to hold back on the politics that he tried for years to avoid. He railed against the political class in general. His organization was pumping millions of dollars into the struggling court system, he emphasized. Now they didn't want it?

"They really want to fight that? They really want to stop a large infusion of funding to the clerk of courts? To victims? They said they're for the victim but now we're trying to give them money so the victim can get compensated, they want to stop that? Then are they really for the victim, or is this political shenanigans? What do we have here? What we have is a select handful of politicians that's wanting to play politics with our lives and don't care if we're suffering, don't care what matters we're going through. All they care about is positioning themselves politically. And they don't care for the people. We're caring for the people. We're gonna continue caring for the people," said Meade. "They picked the right one this time, because I refuse to be bullied by any politician that wants to play partisan politics. I refuse to bow down to any politician that places the needs of their partisan leanings over the needs of the people, and we will continue to fight back and we will continue—we're gonna double down on 'em. Double down on our efforts."[71]

Amid the manufactured controversy, Bloomberg never sent the money. A subpoena from the FRRC turned over 7,614 pages of documents to state investigators. They found nothing wrong with any of the work Meade's group had been doing. It took them 706 work hours to figure that out.[72] The 2020 election was just a few short weeks away. The entire nation held its breath.

12
THE LONG GAME

The 2020 election came and went in Florida without a hitch, with President Donald Trump winning the state by over 3 percentage points. Ironically, the state's ability to quickly process the pandemic-era spike in vote-by-mail ballots happened because of separate provisions in the omnibus elections law that gutted much of Amendment 4's impact.[1] Governor DeSantis applauded the fast results on election night, as other states still scrambled to count mail-in ballots.

"Perhaps 2020 was the year that we finally vanquished the ghost of Bush versus Gore," he declared. "As we watch what unfolds in the rest of the country, I do think you're going to continue to hear from people looking at how: If the third most populous state in the country can count 11 million votes, produce a result across the board, why can't some of these other states that are much smaller?"

But below the surface, things were not right. A few days after Election Day I was a guest on a radio show, and a man from Broward County called in to express his frustration.[2] He was convicted of a felony in 1993 and had since then been unable to vote. All of his fines, fees, and restitution were fully paid, he said, but when he tried to double-check with the Florida Department of State to verify his eligibility, the answer was anything but satisfying.

"I went to the site, jumped through all the hoops, and got back an email that I will hear from them in 2023," he said. "Now I don't know which team—team Democrat, team Republican or team neutral—is trying to suppress votes, but that sure seems like a style of voter suppression."[3]

Sadly, I had to tell him that if everything he just told us was true, he should have been able to vote. He knew this much but expressed his unwillingness to court another potential felony on his record. Stuck on the backlog from the inept state bureaucracy, he chose to sit out the election. "I wish I was able to vote," he pleaded.

The full tally of how many people were in this exact situation is impossible to know. But by the state's own admission, tens of thousands of Floridians were on that backlog list. Judge Hinkle's prophecy that eligible voters would be scared out of participating in the democratic process had been fulfilled.

In data reviewed just before the election, an analysis by the *Miami Herald,* the *Tampa Bay Times,* and *ProPublica* found that 31,400 Floridians with felony convictions had registered to vote since Amendment 4 took effect. More than twice as many of the new voters registered as Democrats than as Republicans, and in areas with large Black populations the impact was even stronger. In Gadsden County in North Florida, a total of one in five new voters had felony convictions. For seven other counties with large Black populations, voters with felony convictions made up one in fifteen new voters.[4]

This analysis only took into account people who had been released from prison since 1997. The number, then, was likely an undercount. A separate tally by a Georgetown University law professor, Neel Sukhatme, found that 43,800 people with felony convictions registered to vote since the process was opened up (it's unclear why all these numbers differed from the 85,000 number that the state mentioned in court hearings).[5] Overall, both analyses found that under 8 percent of potentially new eligible voters actually did so, fewer than the 10 to 20 percent advocates originally hoped for. The kicker was that, according to Sukhatme's analysis, over 75 percent of those newly registered voters might still owe money in fines, fees, or restitution.[6]

One of those would-be voters, a thirty-three-year-old white man named Stephen Deane, registered to vote immediately after Amendment 4 went into effect. A proud son happy to move on from the substance abuse issues of his past, he said he showed his mother the voter registration card when it came in the mail. No state or local official ever notified him that he would not be able to vote due to $10,000 still owed on past convictions. It was only when an investigative reporter contacted him that he was made aware that he could not legally cast a ballot.

"I should have known better," Deane told the reporter. "This is Florida."[7]

When lawmakers in Florida got ready to meet again shortly after the presidential election, a series of reforms was floated by Republican lawmakers.

State Senator Dennis Baxley, himself among the first to suggest that "all terms" of a sentence might need to be properly defined, had a commonsense suggestion. His idea: The state should create a "clearinghouse" database where Floridians could simply plug in their name and get quick answers. "You could check there, and there would be a database that you could challenge or you could agree to, and it will show if you completed," Baxley told me. "Right now it's quite a hunt to find out what's outstanding, and how do you verify that you completed it?"[8]

Fellow Republican State Senator Keith Perry echoed the sentiments of the Charlie Crist era, suggesting that the state expand the number of rights that were automatically restored when someone completed their newly defined sentence. The right to run for public office, serve on a jury, and "under certain circumstances" the right to bear arms should also be granted, he said. Forcing people to go in front of the governor and cabinet wasn't only "unfair," but it costs taxpayers money in state bureaucratic manpower, he argued. "Why do we have a whole system designed to go through this interview process, to go through the things, the hearings, and then come before the cabinet? That just doesn't make a lot of sense for the overwhelming majority of these cases. . . . You're eighteen and you steal someone's laptop and thirty years later you're still paying your debt to society? It doesn't make any sense at all."[9]

"I own a roofing business, and we hire a lot of people coming out of the criminal justice system, a lot of people out on work release. If you talk to them, especially before Amendment 4, they really felt that they really weren't part of society, part of the community. Even though they were working, married, paying taxes, whatever else," Perry told me. "They just felt, and I talked to them on a personal level, about their disconnect and somehow feeling that they were set aside. So it makes sense. I think it's a fair thing to do and I think it's the right thing to do."[10]

Neither of these proposals became law. Neither received committee hearings or sparked a greater debate in the state Capitol. They simply died. For his part, Baxley did not even bother to file a bill about his idea. His grand idea was little more than idle talk. Perry did file a bill. His office wrote up a press release about it. He wanted his ideas to become law. The madness of Tallahassee politics had other ideas.[11]

To his credit, Governor DeSantis did take action, albeit only after the presidential election was in the rearview mirror. Under his leadership, the Florida Cabinet approved a sweeping rehaul of clemency rules that undid measures that were put in place a decade earlier by former Governor Rick Scott and the former cabinet. Under the new rules, the right to serve on a jury and run for public office would automatically be restored the very moment all the fines, fees, and restitution are paid and the felony sentence completed. The move also did away with the Rick Scott–era five- to seven-year waiting period required before someone could even apply to have those rights restored.[12]

"I believe that those who have had their voting rights restored under Amendment 4, it makes sense to restore their other rights," DeSantis said at a Clemency Board meeting. Taking the preceding history as context, it was a significant move.[13]

Agriculture Commissioner Nikki Fried, the sole Democrat in the cabinet, welcomed the changes, even if they were "long overdue." She expressed frustration that the changes "mirror" the state law that passed after Amendment 4, even though the cabinet could go much further. Amendment 4 set a floor; the cabinet could easily go above and beyond, if only it had the political will. The state constitution allowed it. Keeping the same rigid criteria would still keep tens of thousands of people languishing in a bureaucratic backlog, trying to verify whether they still owe money for old crimes or whether they are in the clear.[14]

"We don't need to follow what the legislature does. The power is in our hands to do right," Fried told me. "It was very frustrating to see that even with the passage of some changes to clemency, that the one big hiccup is that we have so many people on this list that have court costs and fees that are still owed, and they have no recourse. Half the time they can't even find how much they owe. They can't even find where to go to pay it, or proof that they've already paid it."[15]

In campaign ads, Jason Mariner was straightforward about his many past run-ins with the law. "I've been addicted to drugs, I've spent time in a cell. Multiple times. I've had a knee on my neck. I know what it's like," he said in a straight-to-camera video.[16] Mariner was a Republican candidate running for Congress in a heavily Democratic district in South Florida following the death of Representative Alcee Hastings. "Not your typical candidate" was regularly touted during his campaign.[17]

After Mariner won the Republican primary for the seat, questions swirled about his eligibility to hold public office, since he never had that civil right restored after felony convictions. Ultimately, it appeared that since he was running for federal office and not a state or local government position, that restriction would not apply. For me, though, related questions were unsettled.

In December 2011, Mariner broke into a home in Delray Beach and stole $20,000 worth of paintings by the Florida Highwaymen, some of the most revered artists in Florida history.[18] The loose collective of Black artists painted vivid landscapes across the state and sold them for dollars on the roadside in the mid-twentieth century. Today, the paintings sell for thousands of dollars at auction houses.

Mariner took the stolen paintings to a secondhand shop and sold many for a total of $400. After police investigated, Mariner was arrested and found guilty of felony grand theft, among other charges. Several of the stolen paintings were returned, but others were never recovered. Mariner received a sentence of up to fourteen months imprisonment for the bundle of charges he faced at the time.[19]

Court records showed that Mariner paid the outstanding fees and court costs related to that case in order to reinstate his driver's license upon release. But the records also showed that a judge in 2012 ordered Mariner to pay $14,500 to the victim of that theft. I tracked down the seventy-nine-year-old victim, who did not want to be identified. She told me that she never received a dime in restitution payments for the stolen paintings.

"They're worth a heck of a lot more now than they were in 2011," she said. "Son of a gun."[20]

The potential problem was that Mariner voted in the 2020 election, as the Palm Beach Supervisor of Elections office confirmed.[21] If he did in fact still owe restitution money, Mariner had likely committed a felony.

For his part, Mariner said he believed he paid the restitution as part of a work release program he participated in after release from prison. Yet after several weeks of asking, neither the Florida Department of State nor the Florida Department of Corrections was able to deny or confirm that restitution payments were made. The full truth, for our purposes, was unknowable.[22]

The utter inability of the state to verify whether or not a federal congressional candidate illegally voted serves as a cruel reminder of the 2019 state law, said Kara Gross, the legislative director for ACLU of Florida. "It's not a Democratic or Republican issue. It affects everybody. It affects all Floridians," Gross said. "This is a person who served their time, returned to society and is now a successful business owner and now civic leader. And there's no reason that he shouldn't have had his voting rights restored automatically as Amendment 4 was designed to do."²³

In other cases, the state bureaucracy works in a startlingly efficient manner, forcing questions about selective attention based on political considerations.

Between February and July 2020, the Supervisor of Elections office in Alachua County organized a series of voter registration drives at the county jail. This took place right in the middle of court battles and ensuing confusion—just prior to the federal trial. As things were up in the air about who might be eligible to vote come Election Day, this was probably not the smartest thing to do. But nonetheless, elections officials did it. They went to jails and registered voters under the premise that the inmates would have finished their sentences by the time Election Day came.

The people who got in trouble over the decision to run a jailhouse voter registration drive were the inmates. By mid-2022, at least ten would end up facing felony charges for registering to vote, and in some cases voting in the 2020 election, when they were not eligible. They still owed debt for previous felony convictions.²⁴ It was the very scenario Supreme Court Justice Sonia Sotomayor warned about: The people who registered to vote while there was a temporary court ruling allowing them to do so faced criminal consequences once the appeals court pulled the rug out from under them. Elections officials themselves set the inmates up for the trap, yet they faced no consequences of their own.

John Boyd Rivers, a forty-four-year-old, was one of the inmates charged. He told a reporter that inmates were assured by election officials that there would be no issue. "They actually helped us fill out the voter rights registration forms. They came in and recruited us to vote, and then you know, told us that we could vote and now they're charging us for voting," Rivers said.²⁵

The prosecution of the inmates was the result of an eight-month-long investigation by the Florida Department of Law Enforcement.²⁶ Five of the six counties that were swept up in an investigation into jailhouse voter registration practices reliably vote for Democrats in statewide and national elections.²⁷

In the coming years, Floridians might expect more of this kind of shrewd omniscience. Governor DeSantis successfully convinced the state legislature in 2022 to create a new state police office focused entirely on prosecuting election-related crimes. This new office, called the Office of Election Crime and Security, was the first police force of its kind in the nation.[28] The idea grew out of pressure for the governor to do something—anything—to address President Trump's unfounded claims of widespread fraud in the 2020 election, unfounded claims that became a kind of dogma in the mainstream Republican Party. As DeSantis said himself the night of the election, Florida did not have problems with its election. Fraud remains a remarkably rare occurrence in elections. But now a dedicated force of investigators would be tasked with going out and finding problems, with an additional staff of state police officers who could be brought in. The top prosecutor in Palm Beach County warned that the new elections police force is "swatting a mosquito with a sledgehammer" and that the team will likely "feel pressure to go out and create its own cases without predicate complaints of wrongdoing."[29]

Days before primary elections in 2022, the new police force announced it was in the process of making twenty arrests for alleged cases of "voter fraud." All the defendants registered to vote and voted in the 2020 election. They were all previously convicted of either sexual offenses or homicide, charges that were specifically excluded by Amendment 4's automatic restoration process. "Yet they went ahead and voted anyways. That is against the law, and now they're going to pay the price for it," DeSantis announced at a press conference at the Broward County Courthouse in Fort Lauderdale.[30]

As the criminal cases pressed on, many began to fall apart. The arrests were captured on body camera video, and the defendants were visibly confused about why they were being targeted.[31] Arresting officers themselves seemed understanding if not outright apologetic about the arrest warrants. All of the defendants had been given voter registration cards by the state.[32] This made prosecution tough, since it was difficult to prove intent to commit a crime. If the state tells you it is okay to vote, how can you be prosecuted for knowingly casting an illegal vote? And what further proof of the state giving you the thumbs-up can there be, if not the state cross-checking all its databases and in the end sending a voter registration card?

Attorney Roger Weedon represented two defendants caught up in the sweep. Several of his clients had their cases outright dismissed because the state's case was so weak. Many cases were thrown out on evidentiary and procedural grounds, others because the statewide prosecutor that filed the cases was not permitted by law to bring the cases. Some defendants took plea deals that carried no prison time, no fines, or community service. Just a further stain on the record. Weedon argued all the cases should be dropped. "The government shouldn't be able to prosecute cases in which they are almost co-conspirators by sending the registration cards and allowing them to vote," Weedon said.[33]

Neil Volz of the Florida Rights Restoration Coalition used the arrests to prove a broader point. People with sex offenses or who were convicted of some degree of homicide were not included in Amendment 4. But the cases alarmed him because of the long-standing lack of clarity from the state government. Either people should be told they can vote or they cannot. Criminalizing the ambiguity hurt everyone. What was really needed was an authoritative database, he argued.

"This is a real sign for all of us to be careful when we begin to criminalize voting," said Volz. "We really need to focus on the voters. And in this case fixing the system so that we don't find ourselves in this kind of situation in the future."[34]

No such database ever emerged.

Months after the twenty arrests were announced, the FRRC announced that it was going to sue the state over alleged "bureaucratic ineptitude" and a "years' long campaign of acts and omissions" that made voting a dangerous proposition for people with felony records. The suit noted that Alabama next door—which also requires people to pay fines and fees before they cast votes—has a master database. In Alabama, anyone asking whether or not they are eligible to vote receives an answer within forty-four days. Florida's grand compromise that came out of the federal trial was that the state would also give "advisory opinions" for people who needed guidance. But FRRC alleged the opinions were neither consistent nor timely. Many simply received no response. State election officials were not required to follow any kind of timeline or to meet any particular standards.[35]

In order to resolve the legal battle, the state and the FRRC agreed to enter into mediation talks. FRRC dropped its lawsuit as they hammered out an agreement. Members of the Florida Department of State, the FRRC, and different county election offices met in mid-2024 to figure out the details. Elections officials stressed that they had to hire extra staff strictly to help with the "felon review process." Volz stressed that the demands of FRRC were "simple": "That anybody can get a 'yes' or a 'no' from the government, that they can bank on that, that we can take that uncertainty out of the process," he said. Basically, the same thing they had been asking about for years. The difference was that now it was being discussed in an open and public forum, with advocates on somewhat even footing with the state.[36]

Coming out of that meeting, the state declared that it would approve a new rule simplifying and codifying the process for getting a final answer, once and for all.[37] The resulting answer would be timely and legally bulletproof. The Division of Elections drew up a new form on which someone could indicate if they were "unsure" whether they were eligible to vote, and it set a ninety-day timeline for responding to someone's question about eligibility.[38]

The solution to the mediation session bore striking resemblance to the very thing ordered by Judge Hinkle when the state lost the federal trial: The state had to accept a standard form and return it to would-be voters with a clear answer, within a specific time frame. Nearly every single pitfall the judge warned would happen if the state did not create this simplified process, happened.

Desmond Meade and the FRRC were pleased with the outcome of the mediation. At long last, clarity was within reach, albeit six years after Amendment 4 was passed by voters, and four frustrating years after the federal trial. "I think this is a big step on the part of the state to help people come to a solid answer on whether or not they're eligible and have them feel comfortable," said Meade.[39]

Time will tell if the solution works as well in practice as it does on paper.

The road to this historical victory of Amendment 4 was long, winding, and anything but straightforward. Decades of debates and lobbying led to policy changes that were only reversed when the political tides turned in new directions. Voters across Florida banded together to fundamentally change the state of voting rights. No matter what happened after that, it marked a monumental shift.

For Howard Simon, who began raising awareness and gearing up for the fight after the fiasco of the 2000 election in Florida, things had the feel of coming full circle. He remembered back to being a college student, volunteering to run a mimeograph machine in the basement of a church in Selma, Alabama, in 1965, a time and place in which he crossed paths with Martin Luther King Jr. and John Lewis as they marched in the famous bloody march that made the passage of the Voting Rights Act of 1965 politically possible.

"I came into this issue dealing with the right to vote," said Simon, "and the last thing that I did before I retired was to help drag Amendment 4 over the finish line." He lamented everything that followed, while still finding his life's work worthy of celebrating.[40]

"It ended the horrible situation in which people had to go hat in hand and on bended knee to appeal and beg for their right to vote back from state officials who had no standards whatsoever—and were proud that they had no standards. That system ended," said Simon. "So Amendment 4 did make some major changes. But the legislature and the courts left Florida with some intolerably unjust situation, in which while people have to pay to vote, the state has no obligation to tell them whether they have to pay anything. That's an intolerable situation."[41]

Nonetheless, history was made. The passage of Amendment 4 marked one of the largest expansions of voting rights in a single swoop. It might be hard to see, and with everything that happened since then, the victory might be hard to celebrate for what it was. But with politicians being barred from making case-by-case decisions about the voting rights of individuals, it was indeed a major victory.

The victory was never going to be felt in a fell instant, it was never going to be a sea change that would reshape the next election cycle, the sudden emergence of a new voting bloc that could determine outcomes on its own. Not at first, at least. "Even if there were not any litigation issues or legislative issues, I think that the full impact of Amendment 4 would still take a while to be felt," said Desmond Meade. "That immediate impact probably pales in comparison to what we would actually experience some years down the line."[42] Even if all things went perfectly, the way he hoped, there would still be newly eligible voters who needed to be educated about their new rights. They would have to be registered. Then, they would have to actually turn out to cast ballots.

After women gained the right to vote in 1920, Arkansas, Georgia, Mississippi, and South Carolina barred them from voting in the 1920 election. Other states enacted roadblocks that prevented many women from participating in elections. Some states, like Connecticut and Massachusetts, required a literacy test.[43] In Richmond, Virginia, offices were overwhelmed by the number of women who wanted to register to vote in the 1920 elections, and officials decided to assist the white women, while giving unequal assistance to the line of Black women. The Black newspaper the *Chicago Defender* reported murders, assaults, and threats against those who attempted to educate and register women to vote. In the first elections after the passage of the Nineteenth Amendment, women did not vote in overwhelming numbers; in Virginia, fewer than 5 percent of women voted in 1920. As late as 1936, women's turnout still lagged a whopping 20 percentage points behind men's.[44]

Contemporary magazines and newspapers openly asked if the whole experiment in allowing women to vote was a failure. Scholars pondered why the influx of new voters failed to shake up the two-party system. As late as 1960, an article in the *Los Angeles Times* crudely concluded that women could make a difference, if only they were interested: "Today women of voting age outnumber men. Yet, offsetting this to some extent has been the fact that women have generally stayed in the kitchen in unhealthy numbers on Election Day."[45]

Today, women have higher voter turnout than men in presidential elections. That's been true since 1984, when they first surpassed men.[46] What changed was that it took years for women to fully integrate into the political culture of the nation. Citizen groups like the League of Women Voters and innumerable local organizations played the long game, educating, registering, and turning women out to vote in elections to reflect the things they cared about. Elections for local, state, and national office now hinge on who can swing the "women's vote." As a political class, women will no longer be ignored. Who now would argue it was all for nothing?

This is the long game Meade keeps in mind when he thinks about the estimated 1.4 million people to whom he gave some semblance of a chance, whether they are able to pay money they owe right now or not. Whether the state decided to play ball in good faith or not. With every passing week, people in Florida are released from prison, and so that original 1.4 million grows and grows. Just as it took women two generations to realize their full potential at the ballot box, so it might before convicted felons who have satisfied the obligations imposed by the state. Meade keeps the long view close to his heart.

"This is not just for the 1.4 million who could take advantage of this opportunity now," said Meade. "It's for the countless number of people years from now, even a decade from now, who will be able to benefit."[47]

NOTES

PREFACE

1. Stacey Abrams, "Desmond Meade: The 100 Most Influential People of 2019," *Time*, https://time.com/collection/100-most-influential-people-2019/5567673/desmond-meade/.
2. Abrams, "Desmond Meade."
3. Editorial Board, "The Racist Anti-Vote Effort by Florida Republicans Hits a New Low," *Washington Post*, September 28, 2020, https://www.washingtonpost.com/opinions/the-racist-anti-vote-effort-by-florida-republicans-hits-a-new-low/2020/09/27/5d5a7450-fe9d-11ea-8d05-9beaaa91c71f_story.html.
4. Editorial Board, "The Racist Anti-Vote Effort by Florida Republicans Hits a New Low."
5. Danielle Lang, interview by the author, September 24, 2020.
6. Chris Hart, "Chris Hart: Florida's Court Clerks Are Facing a Budget Crisis—That Means Changes for Everyone," *Florida Politics*, September 21, 2020, https://floridapolitics.com/archives/368782-chris-hart-floridas-court-clerks-are-facing-a-budget-crisis-that-means-changes-for-everyone.
7. Matt Dixon and Gary Fineout, "Florida AG Calls for Criminal Inquiry into Bloomberg's $16M Felon Voter Donation," *Politico*, September 23, 2020, https://www.politico.com/states/florida/story/2020/09/23/florida-ag-calls-for-criminal-inquiry-into-bloombergs-16m-felon-voter-donation-1317995.
8. Michael Scherer, "Mike Bloomberg Raises $16 Million to Allow Former Felons to Vote in Florida," *Washington Post*, September 22, 2020, https://www.washingtonpost.com/politics/mike-bloomberg-raises-16-million-to-allow-former-felons-to-vote-in-florida/2020/09/21/6dda787e-fc5a-11ea-8d05-9beaaa91c71f_story.html.
9. Matt Gaetz (@RepMattGaetz), "I just spoke to @AGAshleyMoody, she is all over the @MikeBloomberg-connected activities in Florida," Twitter (now X), September 22, 2020, https://twitter.com/RepMattGaetz/status/1308586784184512512.
10. A. G. Gancarski, "Gov. DeSantis Says Mike Bloomberg Felon Fine Payoff Effort Racially Discriminates," *Florida Politics*, September 26, 2020, https://floridapolitics.com/archives/370044-desantis-bloomberg-racial-discriminate.
11. Peter Caterina, "President Trump Says He Will Respect the Election Results If

the Supreme Court Rules Joe Biden Won," Fox News Radio, September 24, 2020, https://radio.foxnews.com/2020/09/24/president-donald-trump-on-the-brian-kilmeade-show-9-24-20/.

12 Desmond Meade (@desmondmeade), "My response to attacks on democracy and the paying off of fines and fees." Twitter (now X), September 27, 2020, https://twitter.com/desmondmeade/status/1310369975320768513.

13 Investigative report, case EI–32–0084, Florida Department of Law Enforcement, May 3, 2021.

14 Investigative report, case EI–32–0084.

15 Desmond Meade, interview by the author, October 18, 2021.

1 THE LIST

1 Mireya Navarro, "Fraud Ruling Invalidates Miami Mayoral Election," *New York Times,* March 5, 1998, sec. "U.S.," https://www.nytimes.com/1998/03/05/us/fraud-ruling-invalidates-miami-mayoral-election.html.

2 Brett Sokol, "No More Mayor Loco," *Miami New Times,* July 22, 2004, https://www.miaminewtimes.com/news/no-more-mayor-loco-6343710.

3 Dave Barry, *Dave Barry Hits Below the Beltway* (New York: Ballantine Books, 2011).

4 Miami Herald Staff Special Report, "Felons Vote Too—But It's a Crime," *Miami Herald,* February 15, 1998.

5 Miami Herald Staff Special Report, "Felons Vote Too."

6 Miami Herald Staff Special Report, "Felons Vote Too."

7 Miami Herald Staff Special Report, "Felons Vote Too."

8 Lisa Getter, "Florida Net Too Wide in Purge of Voter Rolls," *Los Angeles Times,* May 21, 2001, https://www.latimes.com/archives/la-xpm-2001-may-21-mn-620-story.html.

9 U.S. Commission on Civil Rights, *Voting Irregularities in Florida During the 2000 Presidential Election* (Washington, DC, 2001), https://www.usccr.gov/files/pubs/vote2000/report/main.htm.

10 Harry Sawyer, "Oral History," interview by Julian Pleasants, Samuel Proctor Oral History Program at the University of Florida, May 22, 2001.

11 Getter, "Florida Net Too Wide in Purge of Voter Rolls."

12 U.S. Commission on Civil Rights, *Voting Irregularities in Florida During the 2000 Presidential Election.*

13 U.S. Commission on Civil Rights, *Voting Irregularities in Florida During the 2000 Presidential Election.*

14 U.S. Commission on Civil Rights, *Voting Irregularities in Florida During the 2000 Presidential Election.*

15 U.S. Commission on Civil Rights, *Voting Irregularities in Florida During the 2000 Presidential Election.*

16 U.S. Commission on Civil Rights, *Voting Irregularities in Florida During the 2000 Presidential Election.*

17 U.S. Commission on Civil Rights, *Voting Irregularities in Florida During the 2000 Presidential Election*.
18 U.S. Commission on Civil Rights, *Voting Irregularities in Florida During the 2000 Presidential Election*.
19 Getter, "Florida Net Too Wide in Purge of Voter Rolls."
20 Scott Hiaasen, "Felon Purge Sacrificed Innocent Voters," *Palm Beach Post*, May 27, 2001, 1A.
21 Hiaasen, "Felon Purge Sacrificed Innocent Voters."
22 Hiaasen, "Felon Purge Sacrificed Innocent Voters."
23 Hiaasen, "Felon Purge Sacrificed Innocent Voters."
24 Hiaasen, "Felon Purge Sacrificed Innocent Voters."
25 Hiaasen, "Felon Purge Sacrificed Innocent Voters."
26 Getter, "Florida Net Too Wide in Purge of Voter Rolls."
27 *Saturday Night Live*, season 26, episode 5, originally aired November 11, 2000, NBC, https://www.youtube.com/watch?v=SuVaBPNgsuc.

2 THE BACKLASH

1 "Today in History—June 2, [n.d.]," Library of Congress, Washington, DC, https://www.loc.gov/item/today-in-history/june-02/#indian-citizenship-act.
2 Andrew Goodman Foundation, "Historical Archives," https://andrewgoodman.org/historical-archives/.
3 Howard Simon, interview by the author, April 21, 2020.
4 "ACLU Chief Howard Simon Recalls MLK and Bloody Sunday," *Miami New Times*, January 15, 2011, https://www.miaminewtimes.com/news/aclu-chief-howard-simon-recalls-mlk-and-bloody-sunday-6535294.
5 Amy Driscoll, "ACLU Watchdog Has Plenty of Bite," *Miami Herald*, April 5, 1999, 1B.
6 Paul Magnusson, "FBI Knew Policeman Was Leak to Klan on Freedom Riders," *Washington Post*, August 20, 1978, https://www.washingtonpost.com/archive/politics/1978/08/20/fbi-knew-policeman-was-leak-to-klan-on-freedom-riders/b7c9511b-8805-4ff6-a4dd-3da31a05f1af/.
7 Magnusson, "FBI Knew Policeman Was Leak to Klan on Freedom Riders."
8 Simon, interview, April 21, 2020.
9 Judy Odierna, "Felons Get Support on Voting Rights," *Miami Herald*, January 18, 2001, 2B.
10 Draeger Martinez, "Ex-Convicts' Forum Seeks Voting Rights," *Miami Herald*, January 25, 2001, 2NC.
11 Martinez, "Ex-Convicts' Forum Seeks Voting Rights."
12 Daniel Grech, "Felons Aim to Restore Voting Rights," *Miami Herald*, January 28, 2001, 3B.
13 Grech, "Felons Aim to Restore Voting Rights."
14 Grech, "Felons Aim to Restore Voting Rights."

15 Grech, "Felons Aim to Restore Voting Rights."
16 Grech, "Felons Aim to Restore Voting Rights."
17 Grech, "Felons Aim to Restore Voting Rights."
18 James Gregory, "Florida Migration History," 2017, Washington.edu, https://depts.washington.edu/moving1/Florida.shtml.
19 David R. Colburn and Richard K. Scher, *Florida's Gubernatorial Politics in the Twentieth Century* (Tallahassee: University Presses of Florida, 1980).
20 Gordon E. Harvey, "The Nut with a Huey Long Outlook versus the Goblins of Fear and Distortion: Reubin Askew and the Campaign to Establish the Florida Corporate Profits Tax," *Florida Historical Quarterly* 86, no. 3 (2008): 309–45, http://www.jstor.org/stable/25594627.
21 David R. Colburn, *From Yellow Dog Democrats to Red State Republicans* (Gainesville: University Press of Florida, 2013).
22 Gordon E. Harvey, *The Politics of Trust: Reubin Askew and Florida in the 1970s* (Tuscaloosa: University of Alabama Press, 2015).
23 Colburn, *From Yellow Dog Democrats to Red State Republicans*.
24 Colburn, *From Yellow Dog Democrats to Red State Republicans*.
25 Colburn, *From Yellow Dog Democrats to Red State Republicans*.
26 Allison J. Riggs, "Felony Disenfranchisement in Florida: Past, Present, and Future," *Journal of Civil Rights and Economic Development* 28, no. 1 (2015): 6.
27 "Josiah Thomas Walls | the New York Public Library," www.nypl.org, https://www.nypl.org/events/exhibitions/galleries/josiah-thomas-walls#:~:text=Walls%20was%20the%20first%20African.
28 Richard Pettigrew, interview by the author, June 24, 2020.
29 Janet Reno, oral history, interviews by Hillarie Bass, American Bar Association American Bar Association Women Trailblazers in the Law Project, interviews conducted 2005–8, https://stacks.stanford.edu/file/druid:vy278js2249/vy278js2249_RenoJ_Transcript.pdf.
30 James C. Adkins, "In Re Advisory Opinion of Governor Civil Rights," Supreme Court of Florida, https://law.justia.com/cases/florida/supreme-court/1975/45808-0.html.
31 "Advisory Opinions to the Governor," n.d., Supreme Court of Florida, https://www.floridasupremecourt.org/News-Media/Advisory-Opinions-to-the-Governor.
32 Richard Ervine, "In Re Advisory Opinion of Governor Civil Rights," Supreme Court of Florida, https://law.justia.com/cases/florida/supreme-court/1975/45808-0.html.
33 Ervine, "In Re Advisory Opinion of Governor Civil Rights."
34 Associated Press, "Felons to Regain Rights upon Sentence Completion," *Tallahassee Democrat*, September 11, 1975, 19.
35 Rules of Executive Clemency, Florida Commission on Offender Review, https://www.fcor.state.fl.us/docs/clemency/clemency_rules.pdf.
36 Manning Dauer, *Florida's Politics & Government* (Gainesville: University Presses of Florida, 1984).

37 Allison J. Riggs, "Felony Disenfranchisement in Florida: Past, Present, and Future," *Journal of Civil Rights and Economic Development* 28, no. 1 (2015): 6.
38 Associated Press, "Felons to Regain Rights upon Sentence Completion," *Tallahassee Democrat*, September 11, 1975, 19.
39 Bruce Smathers, Florida Board of Executive Clemency, December 8, 1976.
40 Amy Sherman, "Dan Gelber Says Charlie Crist Got Automatic Restoration of Felon Rights for 1st Time in Florida History," @Politifact, https://www.politifact.com/factchecks/2013/dec/12/dan-gelber/dan-gelber-says-charlie-crist-got-approved-automat/.
41 Phil Willon, "Politicians Would Face Review to Get Civil Rights Back," *Tampa Tribune*, December 19, 1991, 7.
42 Willon, "Politicians Would Face Review to Get Civil Rights Back."
43 Willon, "Politicians Would Face Review to Get Civil Rights Back."
44 Rules of Executive Clemency, Florida Commission on Offender Review, https://www.fcor.state.fl.us/docs/clemency/clemency_rules.pdf.
45 Andrea Robinson, "Lawsuit Seeks Voting Rights for Felons," *Miami Herald*, March 15, 2001, 1B; "ACLU of Florida Launches Equal Voting Rights Project to Address Irregularities, Reform Election Practices in Florida," American Civil Liberties Union, https://www.aclu.org/press-releases/aclu-florida-launches-equal-voting-rights-project-address-irregularities-reform.
46 "ACLU of Florida Launches Equal Voting Rights Project to Address Irregularities."
47 Gary Kane and Scott Hiaasen, "Clemency Process Unfair to Blacks?" *Palm Beach Post*, December 23, 2001, 1A.
48 Andrea Robinson, "Felons May See Vote Rights Restored," *Miami Herald*, July 25, 2003, 1A.
49 Robinson, "Felons May See Vote Rights Restored."
50 Editorial Memorandum, "An 'Unhealthy Democracy' Florida Court Case Highlights Felon Disenfranchisement Crisis in U.S.; National Effort to Restore Voting Rights to Ex-Felons Grows," 2002, Brennan Center for Justice at NYU School of Law, https://www.brennancenter.org/sites/default/files/legal-work/download_file_10042.pdf.
51 U.S. Commission on Civil Rights, *Voting Irregularities in Florida During the 2000 Presidential Election* (Washington, DC, 2001), https://www.usccr.gov/files/pubs/vote2000/report/main.htm.
52 U.S. Commission on Civil Rights, *Voting Irregularities in Florida During the 2000 Presidential Election*.
53 U.S. Commission on Civil Rights, *Voting Irregularities in Florida During the 2000 Presidential Election*.
54 U.S. Commission on Civil Rights, *Voting Irregularities in Florida During the 2000 Presidential Election*.
55 U.S. Commission on Civil Rights, *Voting Irregularities in Florida During the 2000 Presidential Election*.

56 U.S. Commission on Civil Rights, *Voting Irregularities in Florida During the 2000 Presidential Election.*

57 Abigail Thernstrom and Russell G. Redenbaugh, *Dissenting Statement on Voting Irregularities in Florida During the 2000 Presidential Election* (self-published, July 19, 2001), [not considered official record but acknowledged in official record], https://media4.manhattan-institute.org/pdf/final_dissent.pdf, https://www.usccr.gov/files/pubs/vote2000/report/dissent.htm.

58 Thernstrom and Redenbaugh, *Dissenting Statement.*

3 CLINGING TO THE PAST

1 Katherine Harris, *Center of the Storm: Practicing Principled Leadership in Times of Crisis* (Nashville: WND Books, 2002).

2 Harris, *Center of the Storm.*

3 Harris, *Center of the Storm.*

4 Harris, *Center of the Storm.*

5 Julie Hauserman, "Cabinet Eases Rules for Restoring Felons' Rights," *St. Petersburg Times,* June 15, 2001, 4B.

6 Hauserman, "Cabinet Eases Rules for Restoring Felons' Rights."

7 Hauserman, "Cabinet Eases Rules for Restoring Felons' Rights."

8 Hauserman, "Cabinet Eases Rules for Restoring Felons' Rights."

9 Gary Kane and Scott Hiaasen, "Clemency Process Unfair to Blacks?," *Palm Beach Post,* December 23, 2001, 1A.

10 Kane and Hiaasen, "Clemency Process Unfair to Blacks?"

11 Kane and Hiaasen, "Clemency Process Unfair to Blacks?"

12 Kane and Hiaasen, "Clemency Process Unfair to Blacks?"

13 Kane and Hiaasen, "Clemency Process Unfair to Blacks?"

14 Committee of Government Reform, U.S. House of Representatives, "Election 2000: An Investigation of Voting Irregularities," 2005.

15 "About the EAC | U.S. Election Assistance Commission," www.eac.gov, https://www.eac.gov/about.

16 Daniel J. Palazzolo, "Election Reform After the 2000 Election," in *Election Reform: Politics and Policy,* edited by Daniel J. Palazzolo and James W. Ceaser, 3–15 (Lanham, MD: Lexington Books, 2005), https://scholarship.richmond.edu/cgi/viewcontent.cgi?article=1084&context=polisci-faculty-publications.

17 Steve Bousquet, "Bush Task Force to Seek Remedy," *Miami Herald,* December 15, 2000, 6A.

18 Bousquet, "Bush Task Force to Seek Remedy," 6A.

19 Bousquet, "Bush Task Force to Seek Remedy," 6A.

20 Steve Bousquet, "State Election Task Force Is at Odds on Its Mission," *Miami Herald,* January 8, 2001, 1B.

21 Steve Bousquet, "Panel Gets Input on Election Flaws," *Miami Herald,* January 24, 2001, B1.

22 Governor's Select Task Force on Election Procedures, Standards and Technology, "Revitalizing Democracy in Florida," March 1, 2001, http://edocs.dlis.state.fl.us/fldocs/dos/de/2001RevitalizingDemocracy.pdf.
23 Governor's Select Task Force on Election Procedures, Standards and Technology, "Revitalizing Democracy in Florida."
24 Mark Silva, "Panel OKs Felon Voting Rights," *Miami Herald*, March 22, 2001, 1B.
25 Rep. Chris Smith, Florida HB 51, "Citizens' Empowerment Act," original bill text, Florida House of Representatives, 2001, https://www.myfloridahouse.gov/Sections/Documents/loaddoc.aspx?FileName=_h0051__.pdf&DocumentType=Bill&BillNumber=0051&Session=2001.
26 Silva, "Panel OKs Felon Voting Rights."
27 Silva, "Panel OKs Felon Voting Rights."
28 Linda Kleindienst and Gregory Lewis, "Voting Remains Off-Limits to Felons High Court Won't Review Florida Ban," *South Florida Sun-Sentinel*, November 15, 2005, 1A.
29 Maya Bell, "Activists Seek Vote for Ex-Felons After Lobbying Failed, a Lawmaker Wants a Referendum to Lift Ban Some Say Is Unfair," *Orlando Sentinel*, December 29, 2003, B1.
30 Marcu Franklin, "Felons Line up for Right to Vote," *St. Petersburg Times*, July 27, 2003, 1B.
31 Florida Division of Elections, "Committee Tracking System: Committee to Restore Voter Dignity, Inc.," https://dos.elections.myflorida.com/committees/ComDetail.asp?account=37784.
32 Florida Division of Elections, "Restoration of Voting Rights 03–36," https://dos.elections.myflorida.com/initiatives/initdetail.asp?account=37784&seqnum=1; Muslima Lewis, interview by the author, September 12, 2020.
33 Howard Simon, interview by the author, December 10, 2020.
34 Simon, interview, December 10, 2020.
35 Simon, interview, December 10, 2020.
36 John Kennedy, "20,000 Felons May Get to Vote Nov. 2: Gov. Bush Touts His Restoration of Their Rights, Downplaying Any Political Fallout," *Orlando Sentinel*, June 18, 2004, A1.
37 Chris Davis and Matthew Doig, "E-mail on Felon List Contradicts Governor—Bush Denied Being Warned About the List, But an Official Had Urged the State to 'Pull the Plug,'" *Sarasota Herald-Tribune*, October 16, 2004, A1.
38 Linda Robinson, "Rights Leader Scolds Bush on Use of Felon Voter Purge List," *Miami Herald*, June 22, 2004, 3B.
39 Robinson, "Rights Leader Scolds Bush on Use of Felon Voter Purge List."
40 State of Florida, Office of the Governor, Executive Order Number 05-28, February 7, 2005.
41 State of Florida, Governor's Ex-Offender Task Force, "Final Report to the Governor," November 30, 2006.

4 THE REFORMER

1. "PolitiFact Florida Checks up on 'Chain Gang Charlie,'" September 21, 2016. https://www.wusf.org/politics/2016-09-21/politifact-florida-checks-up-on-chain-gang-charlie.
2. Charlie Crist, interview by the author, June 4, 2020.
3. Vicki Chachere, "Chain Gang Bent on Punishing Wrongdoers, Florida Will Return to the Past," *Tampa Tribune*, June 12, 1995, 1A.
4. Crist, interview, June 4, 2020.
5. Curtis Krueger, "Charlie Crist's Signature Accomplishment Is One He Never Mentions," *Tampa Bay Times*, September 28, 2014, https://www.miamiherald.com/news/politics-government/state-politics/article2290614.html.
6. Brent Kallestad, "Fla. Attorney General to Run for Governor," Associated Press, May 10, 2005.
7. William March, "Crist Would Let All Felons Vote—Davis Campaign Questions Switch," *Tampa Tribune*, October 14, 2006.
8. Crist, interview, June 4, 2020.
9. Crist, interview, June 4, 2020.
10. Howard Simon, interview by the author, August 6, 2020.
11. Crist, interview, June 4, 2020.
12. Abby Goodnough, "In Break from the Past, Florida Will Let Felons Vote," *New York Times*, April 6, 2007, https://www.nytimes.com/2007/04/06/us/06florida.html.
13. Bill McCollum, "McCollum: Be Responsible About Felons' Rights," *Orlando Sentinel*, April 1, 2007, https://www.orlandosentinel.com/news/os-xpm-2007-04-01-myword01-story.html.
14. McCollum, "McCollum: Be Responsible About Felons' Rights."
15. "Charles Bronson," Florida Agricultural Hall of Fame, October 8, 2012, http://floridaaghalloffame.org/2012/10/charles-bronson/.
16. Simon, interview, August 6, 2020.
17. Joe Follick, "Crist Wins Shift on Felons' Rights—Cabinet Votes to Allow Nearly Automatic Restoration of Voting Rights for Many Felons," *Sarasota Herald-Tribune*, April 6, 2007, A1.
18. "4/5/07 Executive Clemency Board Meeting—the Florida Channel," The Florida Channel, https://thefloridachannel.org/videos/4-5-07-executive-clemency-board-meeting/.
19. Steve Bousquet, "Restoring Felons' Rights Slowed by Bureaucracy," *Tampa Bay Times*, September 28, 2007, https://www.tampabay.com/archive/2007/09/27/restoring-felons-rights-slowed-by-bureaucracy/.
20. "4/5/07 Executive Clemency Board Meeting."
21. Joe Follick, "Crist Wins Shift on Felons' Rights—Cabinet Votes to Allow Nearly Automatic Restoration of Voting Rights for Many Felons," *Sarasota Herald-Tribune*, April 6, 2007. A1.

22. Follick, "Crist Wins Shift on Felons' Rights."
23. Follick, "Crist Wins Shift on Felons' Rights."
24. Follick, "Crist Wins Shift on Felons' Rights."
25. Follick, "Crist Wins Shift on Felons' Rights."
26. "Florida Shifts Stance on Ex-Convicts' Civil Rights," NPR, April 5, 2007, https://www.npr.org/templates/story/story.php?storyId=9396745.
27. "Florida Shifts Stance on Ex-Convicts' Civil Rights."
28. Florida Parole Commission, "Annual Report, 2007–2008," State of Florida, https://www.fcor.state.fl.us/docs/reports/FCORannualreport200708.pdf.
29. Florida Parole Commission, "Annual Report, 2007–2008."
30. Florida Parole Commission, "Annual Report, 2007–2008."
31. "ACLU Expresses Concern to Governor Crist About HB 5075, Future of Restoration of Civil Rights," American Civil Liberties Union of Florida, April 16, 2008, https://www.aclufl.org/en/press-releases/aclu-expresses-concern-governor-crist-about-hb-5075-future-restoration-civil-rights.
32. "ACLU Expresses Concern to Governor Crist about HB 5075, Future of Restoration of Civil Rights."
33. Safety & Security Council and Mitch Needelman, "HB 5075," 2008, original bill text, Florida House of Representatives https://www.myfloridahouse.gov/Sections/Documents/loaddoc.aspx?FileName=_h5075__.docx&DocumentType=Bill&BillNumber=5075&Session=2008.
34. Safety & Security Council and Mitch Needelman, "HB 5075," 2008, Staff Analysis, Florida House of Representatives, https://www.myfloridahouse.gov/Sections/Documents/loaddoc.aspx?FileName=h5075a.PBC.doc&DocumentType=Analysis&BillNumber=5075&Session=2008.
35. "3/26/08 House Safety and Security Council," at 1:17:00, The Florida Channel, https://thefloridachannel.org/videos/32608-house-safety-security-council/.
36. "ACLU Expresses Concern to Governor Crist about HB 5075, Future of Restoration of Civil Rights."
37. Florida Parole Commission, "Annual Report, 2008–2009," State of Florida, https://www.fcor.state.fl.us/docs/reports/FCORannualreport200809.pdf.
38. Manuel Roig-Franzia, *The Rise of Marco Rubio* (New York: Simon and Schuster, 2015), 120.
39. Marco Rubio, *An American Son* (New York: Sentinel, 2012), 130.
40. Christopher Curry, "GOP Taps Shores for Idea Book—Baxley and Future House Speaker Seek Input to Shape Republican Agenda," *Ocala Star Banner,* June 13, 2006.
41. Marco Rubio, *100 Innovative Ideas for Florida's Future* (Washington, DC: Regnery, 2006), 6.
42. Jim Geraghty, "When Rubio Was the Man of Florida's House," *National Review,* April 13, 2015, https://www.nationalreview.com/2015/04/when-rubio-was-man-floridas-house-jim-geraghty/.
43. Drew Wilson, "Supermajority Tax Amendment Approved by Supermajority of

Voters," *Florida Politics*, November 7, 2018, https://floridapolitics.com/archives/280406-supermajority-tax-amendment; Aaron Sharockman, "Rubio Claims 57 of His 100 Ideas Were Made Law by the Florida Legislature," PolitiFact, November 4, 2009, https://www.politifact.com/factchecks/2010/feb/26/marco-rubio/rubio-claims-57-his-100-ideas-were-made-law-florid/.

44 "Innovative Ideas for Florida's Future," 100Ideas.org, August 9, 2006, https://web.archive.org/web/20061009045126/http://www.100ideas.org/ideas.php?start=250&PageSize=50&Category=&MCategory=&textsearch=.

45 "Innovative Ideas for Florida's Future."

46 William March, "'Teflon Charlie' Remains Popular," *Tampa Tribune*, April 16, 2009, 4.

47 George Bennett, "DeSantis Gets Highest Approval for Florida Governor in 10 Years," *Palm Beach Post*, https://www.palmbeachpost.com/news/20190313/poll-desantis-gets-highest-approval-for-florida-governor-in-10-years.

48 Damian Cave and Christine Jordan Sexton, "New Florida Rules Return More Than 115,000 Ex-Offenders to Voting Rolls," *New York Times*, June 18, 2008, https://www.nytimes.com/2008/06/18/us/18florida.html.

49 Cave and Sexton, "New Florida Rules Return More Than 115,000 Ex-Offenders to Voting Rolls."

50 State of Florida, Office of the Governor, Executive Order Number 08–179, August 27, 2008.

51 Aaron Deslatte and Vicki McClure, "Crist Makes It Easier for Ex-Cons to Vote," *Orlando Sentinel*, August 28, 2008, A1.

52 Charlie Crist and Ellis Henican, *The Party's Over* (New York: Penguin, 2014).

53 Molly Ball, "Is This What Post-Partisanship Looks Like?," *The Atlantic*, March 12, 2014, https://www.theatlantic.com/politics/archive/2014/03/is-this-what-post-partisanship-looks-like/284350/.

54 Lydia DePillis, "How America's Foreclosure Capital Came Back from the Dead," *CNNMoney*, August 14, 2018, https://money.cnn.com/2018/08/14/news/economy/fort-myers-florida-foreclosures-recession/index.html.

55 "Presidential Town Hall Meeting," C-SPAN, February 10, 2009, https://www.c-span.org/video/?283942-1/presidential-town-hall-meeting.

56 "Presidential Town Hall Meeting."

57 Damian Cave and Gary Fineout, "Restless in Tallahassee, or With Eye on 2012, Governor Rolls Dice," *New York Times*, May 12, 2009, https://www.nytimes.com/2009/05/13/us/13cristq.html.

58 *Morning Joe*, MSNBC, October 27, 2009, https://www.youtube.com/watch?v=hyEj-p5p77s.

59 Marco Rubio, "Transcript: Florida Senate Showdown on 'Fox News Sunday,'" *Fox News*, March 28, 2010, https://www.foxnews.com/transcript/transcript-florida-senate-showdown-on-fox-news-sunday.

60 Marco Rubio, "Rubio Comments on Flawed Felons' Rights Restoration Pro-

gram," MarcoRubio.com, September 29, 2009, https://web.archive.org/web/20091018041546/http://www.marcorubio.com/092509felonrights/.
61 Rubio, "Rubio Comments on Flawed Felons' Rights Restoration Program."
62 Charlie Crist, "Crist Announces Independent Bid," *Palm Beach Post*, April 29, 2010, https://www.youtube.com/watch?v=tt6QSZXSrBg.
63 Florida Department of State, Division of Elections, "November 2, 2010 General Election, Official Results," State of Florida, 2010, https://results.elections.myflorida.com/Index.asp?ElectionDate=11/2/2010&DATAMODE=.

5 NO RULES

1 Adam Sorensen, "Florida's Rick Scott Sends High-Speed Rail Packing," *Time*, February 16, 2011, https://swampland.time.com/2011/02/16/floridas-rick-scott-sends-high-speed-rail-packing/.
2 Hartford Courant Editorial Board, "Thank [sic] for Everything, Gov. Scott. Love, Connecticut," *Miami Herald*, June 28, 2018, https://www.miamiherald.com/opinion/op-ed/article213562689.html.
3 "2/24/11 Executive Clemency Board Meeting," The Florida Channel, https://thefloridachannel.org/videos/22411-executive-clemency-board-meeting/.
4 "2/24/11 Executive Clemency Board Meeting."
5 "2/24/11 Executive Clemency Board Meeting."
6 "2/24/11 Executive Clemency Board Meeting."
7 Alexander Burns, "3 GOP Candidates Spend $243M," *Politico*, October 24, 2010, https://www.politico.com/story/2010/10/3-gop-candidates-spend-243m-044072.
8 Aaron Sharockman, "Rick Scott, Former Healthcare CEO, Faces Questions About Past," *PolitiFact*, May 20, 2010, https://www.politifact.com/factchecks/2010/may/20/alex-sink/rick-scott-healthcare-ceo-faces-questions-a/.
9 "HCA—The Healthcare Company and Subsidiaries to Pay $840 Million in Criminal Fines and Civil Damages and Penalties: Largest Government Fraud Settlement in U.S. History," press release, U.S. Department of Justice, December 14, 2000, https://web.archive.org/web/20030702173234/www.justice.gov/opa/pr/2000/December/696civcrm.htm.
10 "Florida Executive Clemency Board," transcript, State of Florida, March 9, 2011.
11 Florida Parole Commission, "Annual Report, 2010–2011," State of Florida, https://www.fcor.state.fl.us/docs/reports/FCORannualreport2001011.pdf.
12 "Florida Executive Clemency Board," transcript.
13 "Florida Executive Clemency Board," transcript.
14 "Florida Executive Clemency Board," transcript.
15 "Florida Executive Clemency Board," transcript.
16 "Florida Executive Clemency Board," transcript.
17 "Florida Executive Clemency Board," transcript.
18 "Florida Executive Clemency Board," transcript.

19 "Florida Executive Clemency Board," transcript.
20 "Florida Executive Clemency Board," transcript.
21 Melissa Locker, "John Oliver Urges Floridians to Vote on 'Last Week Tonight,'" *Time*, September 10, 2018, https://time.com/5391261/john-oliver-last-week-tonight-florida/.
22 "9/21/16 Executive Clemency Board Meeting," The Florida Channel, September 21, 2016, at 4:05:15 to 4:11:05, accessed 2021, since removed; previously available at http://thefloridachannel.org/videos/92116-executive-clemency-board-meetingpart-2/.
23 "6/24/15 Executive Clemency Board Meeting," The Florida Channel, June 24, 2015, at 1:08:59 to 2:12:31, http://thefloridachannel.org/videos/62415-executive-clemency-board-meeting/.
24 "12/7/16 Executive Clemency Board Meeting—the Florida Channel," The Florida Channel, December 7, 2016, at 2:02:53 to 2:06:45, http://thefloridachannel.org/videos/12716-executive-clemency-board-meeting/.
25 "6/2/11 Executive Clemency Board Meeting," The Florida Channel, June 2, 2011, at 2:09:06 to 2:16:49, https://thefloridachannel.org/videos/621111-executive-clemency-board-meeting/.
26 Mark Walker, "Order on Cross-Motions for Summary Judgment | Hand v. Scott [Later, Desantis] N.D. Fla. | Civil Rights Litigation Clearinghouse," Clearinghouse.net, February 1, 2018, https://clearinghouse.net/doc/98818/.
27 "3/3/16 Executive Clemency Board Meeting Part 1—the Florida Channel," The Florida Channel, March 3, 2016, at 4:30 to 5:00, https://thefloridachannel.org/videos/3316-executive-clemency-board-meeting-part-1/.
28 Emily Bazelon, "Will Florida's Ex-Felons Finally Regain the Right to Vote?," *New York Times*, September 26, 2018, https://www.nytimes.com/2018/09/26/magazine/ex-felons-voting-rights-florida.html.
29 Desmond Meade, interview by the author, April 24, 2020.
30 Meade, interview, April 24, 2020.
31 Howard Simon, interview by the author, December 10, 2020.
32 Simon, interview, December 10, 2020.
33 Meade, interview, April 24, 2020.
34 "Florida Rights Restoration Coalition, Inc. Florida Not-For Profit Corporation," Florida Department of State, Sunbiz.com, https://search.sunbiz.org/Inquiry/CorporationSearch/SearchResultDetail?inquirytype=EntityName&directionType=Initial&searchNameOrder=FLORIDARIGHTSRESTORATIONCOALIT%20N110000117450&aggregateId=domnp-n110000117745-f403480a-6815-49f3-a992-6a6255b4b8bf&searchTerm=florida%20rights%20restoration&listNameOrder=FLORIDARIGHTSRESTORATIONCOALIT%20N110000117450.
35 Simon, interview, December 10, 2020.
36 Simon, interview, December 10, 2020.
37 "Hon. Myrna Perez," United States Court of Appeals for the Second Circuit, https://www.ca2.uscourts.gov/judges/bios/mp.html.

38 Michael Morse, "The Future of Felon Disenfranchisement Reform: Evidence from the Campaign to Restore Voting Rights in Florida," *California Law Review* 109, no. 3 (June 2021), available at SSRN: https://ssrn.com/abstract=3875714.
39 Morse, "The Future of Felon Disenfranchisement Reform."
40 Lulu Ramadan, Mike Stucka, and Wayne Washington, "Florida Felon Voting Rights: Here's Who Got Theirs Back Under Scott," *Palm Beach Post,* https://www.palmbeachpost.com/news/20181025/florida-felon-voting-rights-who-got-theirs-back-under-scott.
41 Ramadan, Stucka, and Washington, "Florida Felon Voting Rights."
42 Ramadan, Stucka, and Washington, "Florida Felon Voting Rights."
43 Ramadan, Stucka, and Washington, "Florida Felon Voting Rights."
44 Mitch Perry, "Lawsuit Against Rick Scott and Clemency Board Seeks to Restore Former Felons' Voting Rights," *Florida Politics,* March 13, 2017, https://floridapolitics.com/archives/233813-lawsuit-rick-scott-clemency-board-seeks-restore-former-felons-voting-rights.
45 Annual report 2016–17, Florida Commission on Offender Review, https://www.fcor.state.fl.us/docs/reports/Annual%20Report%202017%20for%20web.pdf.
46 Ramadan, Stucka, and Washington, "Florida Felon Voting Rights."
47 Ramadan, Stucka, and Washington, "Florida Felon Voting Rights."
48 Mark Walker, "Order on Cross-Motions for Summary Judgment | Hand v. Scott [Later, DeSantis] N.D. Fla. | Civil Rights Litigation Clearinghouse," Clearinghouse.net, February 1, 2018https://clearinghouse.net/doc/98818/.
49 Walker, "Order on Cross-Motions for Summary Judgment."
50 "12/12/13 Executive Clemency Board Meeting," The Florida Channel, December 12, 2013, at 3:47:38 to 3:50:19, https://thefloridachannel.org/videos/121213-executive-clemency-board-meeting/.
51 Walker, "Order on Cross-Motions for Summary Judgment."
52 Walker, "Order on Cross-Motions for Summary Judgment."

6 LET MY PEOPLE VOTE

1 Daniel Rivero, "1.5 Million Voters Are Missing in Florida—and It Could Be the Difference Between Trump and Clinton," Splinter News/Fusion, October 18, 2016, https://splinternews.com/1-5-million-voters-are-missing-in-florida-and-it-could-1793862951.
2 Rivero, "1.5 Million Voters Are Missing in Florida."
3 Domenico Montanaro, "The 13 Bellwether Counties That Could Decide the Election," NPR, November 7, 2016, https://www.npr.org/2016/11/07/500379215/the-13-bellwether-counties-that-could-decide-the-election.
4 Rivero, "1.5 Million Voters Are Missing in Florida."
5 Rivero, "1.5 Million Voters Are Missing in Florida."
6 Rivero, "1.5 Million Voters Are Missing in Florida."
7 Rivero, "1.5 Million Voters Are Missing in Florida."

8 Rivero, "1.5 Million Voters Are Missing in Florida."
9 Rivero, "1.5 Million Voters Are Missing in Florida."
10 Rivero, "1.5 Million Voters Are Missing in Florida."
11 Desmond Meade, *Let My People Vote: My Battle to Restore the Civil Rights of Returning Citizens* (Boston: Beacon, 2020), 75.
12 Meade, *Let My People Vote*, 52.
13 Desmond Meade, interview by the author, October 18, 2021.
14 Amy Sherman, "Voting-Rights Activist Says One-Quarter of Disenfranchised Felons in U.S. Live in Florida," *Tampa Bay Times*, January 23, 2014.
15 Charles Ellison, "In Congress, a Sudden Push for Felon Voting Rights—Guest Commentary" *Woonsocket (RI) Call*, July 27, 2014.
16 Ellison, "In Congress, a Sudden Push for Felon Voting Rights."
17 Ellison, "In Congress, a Sudden Push for Felon Voting Rights."
18 John Davis, "U.N. Human Rights Committee Calls on Florida, U.S. to Restore Voting Rights to Former Felons," WGCU, March 28, 2014, https://news.wgcu.org/government/2014-03-28/u-n-human-rights-committee-calls-on-florida-u-s-to-restore-voting-rights-to-former-felons.
19 "Follow-Up Report to the United Nations Human Rights Committee in Connection with the Fourth Periodic Review of the United States' Compliance with the International Covenant on Civil and Political Rights," 110th Session, March 10–28, 2014, https://tbinternet.ohchr.org/_layouts/15/TreatyBodyExternal/Download.aspx?symbolno=INT/CCPR/CSS/USA/16508&Lang=en.
20 "NAACP Commends Concluding Observations from UN Human Rights Committee," Targeted News Service (USA), March 28, 2014.
21 Robert Steinback, "Advocates Working to Restore Voting Rights to Reformed Ex-Felons," *Fort Lauderdale Sun Sentinel*, November 14, 2014, 19A.
22 Steinback, "Advocates Working to Restore Voting Rights to Reformed Ex-Felons."
23 Neil Volz, interview by the author, April 24, 2024.
24 Volz, interview, April 24, 2024.
25 Volz, interview, April 24, 2024.
26 Bethany Rodgers, "Activists: Restore Felons' Right to Vote: Former Offender Calls Restrictions 'an Invisible Prison,'" *Orlando Sentinel*, August 2, 2016, 1B.
27 Editorial Board, "Fight to Restore Ex-Felons' Voting Rights Must Not Be Abandoned," *Palm Beach Post*, October 5, 2015, 12A.
28 Volz, interview, April 24, 2024.
29 Volz, interview, April 24, 2024.
30 Volz, interview, April 24, 2024.
31 Desmond Meade, interview by the author, April 24, 2020.
32 Neil Volz, interview by the author, April 24, 2024.
33 Mary Ellen Klas, "Last Day to Register to Vote? Not for the 1.5 Million Citizens Who Are Barred from Voting," *Tampa Bay Times: Blogs*, August 1, 2016; Dan Sweeney, "Push on for Felon Voting Rights Florida High Court to Rule on Ballot Access for Amendment," *South Florida Sun-Sentinel*, January 1, 2017, 1.

34. "Floridians for a Fair Democracy Inc.," Florida Division of Elections, Committee Tracking System, https://dos.elections.myflorida.com/committees/ComDetail.asp?account=64388.
35. "Voting Restoration Amendment 14–01," Florida Division of Elections, Initiatives / Amendments / Revisions Database, https://dos.elections.myflorida.com/initiatives/initdetail.asp?account=64388&seqnum=1.
36. Sweeney, "Push on for Felon Voting Rights."
37. Amy Wang, "Trump Asked for a 'Muslim Ban,' Giuliani Says—and Ordered a Commission to Do It 'Legally,'" *Washington Post*, https://www.washingtonpost.com/news/the-fix/wp/2017/01/29/trump-asked-for-a-muslim-ban-giuliani-says-and-ordered-a-commission-to-do-it-legally/.
38. Michael D. Shear, Nicholas Kulish, and Alan Feuer, "Judge Blocks Trump Order on Refugees amid Chaos and Outcry Worldwide," *New York Times*, January 28, 2017, sec. "U.S.," https://www.nytimes.com/2017/01/28/us/refugees-detained-at-us-airports-prompting-legal-challenges-to-trumps-immigration-order.html.
39. Rebecca Hersher, "Federal Judge Stays Trump Travel Order, but Many Visas Already Revoked," NPR, February 3, 2017, https://www.npr.org/sections/thetwo-way/2017/02/03/513306413/state-department-says-fewer-than-60-000-visas-revoked-under-travel-order.
40. Howard Simon, interview by the author, December 10, 2020.
41. "Voting Restoration Amendment 14–01."
42. Simon, interview, December 10, 2020.
43. Simon, interview, December 10, 2020.
44. Michael Morse, "The Future of Felon Disenfranchisement Reform: Evidence from the Campaign to Restore Voting Rights in Florida," *California Law Review* 109, no. 3 (June 2021), table 1, available at SSRN: https://ssrn.com/abstract=3875714.
45. Morse, "The Future of Felon Disenfranchisement Reform."
46. Morse, "The Future of Felon Disenfranchisement Reform."
47. George W. Koehn, "Fla. Shouldn't Heed Liberals to Restore Ex-Felons' Rights," *Orlando Sentinel*, September 16, 2016, 13A.
48. Steve Bousquet, "Diverse Donors Fund Final Push in Campaign to Win Voting Rights for Florida Felons," *Miami Herald*, November 7, 2018, https://www.miamiherald.com/news/politics-government/state-politics/article220614240.html.
49. Morse, "The Future of Felon Disenfranchisement Reform."
50. Meade, interview, April 24, 2020.
51. Bousquet, "Diverse Donors Fund Final Push in Campaign to Win Voting Rights for Florida Felons."
52. "Official Results," Florida Department of State, Division of Elections, November 3, 2018, General Election, https://results.elections.myflorida.com/Index.asp?ElectionDate=11/6/2018&DATAMODE=.
53. C. J. Ciaramella, "Florida Approves Ballot Amendment to Restore Voting Rights of 1.4 Million People with Felony Records," *Reason*, November 7, 2018, https://reason.com/2018/11/06/florida-approves-ballot-amendment-to-res/.

54 Conor Friedersdorf, "Florida Votes for Democracy," *The Atlantic: Web Edition Articles,* November 7, 2018.
55 Tamara Lush, "Florida Passes Amendment to Restore Felons' Voting Rights," Associated Press, US News Online, November 7, 2018.

7 A VERY BIG PROBLEM

1 Marjory Stoneman Douglas, *The Everglades: River of Grass* (Sarasota, FL: Pineapple, 2021), 1.
2 Lizette Alvarez, "House Approves Plan to Restore Everglades," *New York Times,* November 4, 2000, https://www.nytimes.com/2000/11/04/us/house-approves-plan-to-restore-everglades.html.
3 News Service of Florida, "Judge Sides with Environmentalists, Says Lawmakers Failed to Comply with Amendment 1," *Tampa Bay Times,* https://www.tampabay.com/florida-politics/buzz/2018/06/15/judge-sides-environmentalists-says-lawmakers-failed-to-comply-with-amendment-1/.
4 "A Recent History of Redistricting in Florida," Common Cause Florida, https://www.commoncause.org/florida/a-recent-history-of-redistricting-in-florida/.
5 Joe Reedy, "Florida Judge Rules State's Smokable Medical Marijuana Ban Unconstitutional," *Insurance Journal,* May 29, 2018, https://www.insurancejournal.com/news/southeast/2018/05/29/490452.htm.
6 Howard Simon, interview by the author, November 7, 2018.
7 Simon, interview, November 7, 2018.
8 Simon, interview, November 7, 2018.
9 Simon, interview, November 7, 2018.
10 Daniel Rivero, "No One Seems to Know How Amendment 4 Will Be Implemented to Restore Felons' Right to Vote," WLRN, November 29, 2018, https://www.wlrn.org/news/2018-11-29/no-one-seems-to-know-how-amendment-4-will-be-implemented-to-restore-felons-right-to-vote.
11 Rivero, "No One Seems to Know How Amendment 4 Will Be Implemented."
12 Rivero, "No One Seems to Know How Amendment 4 Will Be Implemented."
13 Rivero, "No One Seems to Know How Amendment 4 Will Be Implemented."
14 Rivero, "No One Seems to Know How Amendment 4 Will Be Implemented."
15 Dennis Baxley, interview by the author, November 28, 2018.
16 Baxley, interview, November 28, 2018.
17 George Bennett, "DeSantis Wants Quick Action on Toxic Algae, Caution on Felon Voting Rights," *Palm Beach Post,* n.d., https://www.palmbeachpost.com/news/20181214/desantis-to-act-quickly-on-toxic-algae-cautiously-on-felon-voting-rights.
18 Jason Pizzo, interview by the author, January 3, 2019.
19 Daniel Rivero, "Unpaid Court Fees Could Throw a Wrench into Restoration of Voting Rights for Felons in Florida," WLRN, January 3, 2019, https://www.wlrn.org

/news/2019-01-03/unpaid-court-fees-could-throw-a-wrench-into-restoration-of-voting-rights-for-felons-in-florida.

20 Rivero, "Unpaid Court Fees Could Throw a Wrench."
21 Rivero, "Unpaid Court Fees Could Throw a Wrench."
22 Daniel Rivero, "'A Sense of Renewal': Convicted Felons Register to Vote as Amendment 4 Goes into Effect," WLRN, January 8, 2019, https://www.wlrn.org/local-news/2019-01-08/a-sense-of-renewal-convicted-felons-register-to-vote-as-amendment-4-goes-into-effect.
23 Rivero, "'A Sense of Renewal.'"
24 Rivero, "'A Sense of Renewal.'"
25 Joshua Repogle and Adriana Gomez Licon, "Florida Felons Rejoice After Regaining Their Right to Vote," Associated Press, January 8, 2019, https://apnews.com/article/a0086670a6df42c9a3d2857d1606e027.
26 Andrew Pantazi, "Felony Convictions Won't Stop Jacksonville's Newest Voters," *Florida Times-Union,* January 8, 2019, https://www.jacksonville.com/news/20190108/felony-convictions-wont-stop-jacksonvilles-newest-voters.
27 Steven Lemongello and Adelaide Chen Orlando, "Study: 2,000 Ex-Felons Registered to Vote in 3 Months," *St. Augustine Record,* May 25, 2019, https://www.staugustine.com/story/news/local/2019/05/25/2000-florida-ex-felons-registered-to-vote-in-first-3-months-of-amendment-4-study-finds/5061321007/.
28 Daniel Rivero, "Felons Might Have to Pay Hundreds of Millions Before Being Able to Vote in Florida," WLRN, January 20, 2019, https://www.wlrn.org/news/2019-01-20/felons-might-have-to-pay-hundreds-of-millions-before-being-able-to-vote-in-florida.
29 Rivero, "Felons Might Have to Pay Hundreds of Millions."
30 Rivero, "Felons Might Have to Pay Hundreds of Millions."
31 Rivero, "Felons Might Have to Pay Hundreds of Millions."
32 Rivero, "Felons Might Have to Pay Hundreds of Millions."
33 Rivero, "Felons Might Have to Pay Hundreds of Millions."
34 Rivero, "Felons Might Have to Pay Hundreds of Millions."
35 Rivero, "Felons Might Have to Pay Hundreds of Millions."

8 POLL TAX?

1 Kelly Phillips Erb, "For Election Day, a History of the Poll Tax in America," *Forbes,* November 5, 2018, https://www.forbes.com/sites/kellyphillipserb/2018/11/05/just-before-the-elections-a-history-of-the-poll-tax-in-america/?sh=13bb361a4e44; Rivero, "Felons Might Have to Pay Hundreds of Millions."
2 Farrell Evans, "How Jim Crow–Era Laws Suppressed the African American Vote for Generations," History, A&E Television Networks, May 13, 2021, https://www.history.com/news/jim-crow-laws-black-vote.
3 United Press International, "24th Amendment, Banning Poll Taxes, Has Been

Ratified; Vote in South Dakota Senate Completes the Process of Adding to Constitution," *New York Times,* January 24, 1964, https://www.nytimes.com/1964/01/24/archives/24th-amendment-banning-poll-tax-has-been-ratified-vote-in-south.html.

4   Erb, "For Election Day, a History of the Poll Tax in America."
5   "Harper v. Virginia Bd. Of Elections, 383 U.S. 663 (1966)," *Justia Law,* https://supreme.justia.com/cases/federal/us/383/663/.
6   Lawrence Mower, "House Committee Passes Amendment 4 Bill Along Party Lines," *Tampa Bay Times,* https://www.tampabay.com/florida-politics/2019/03/19/house-committee-passes-amendment-4-bill-along-party-lines/.
7   "Amendment 4 Is Under Attack!," Florida Rights Restoration Coalition, November 11, 2019, https://web.archive.org/web/20191111163011/https://floridarrc.com/a4-under-attack/.
8   "CS/HB 7089 (2019)—Voting Rights Restoration," Florida House of Representatives, https://www.myfloridahouse.gov/Sections/Bills/billsdetail.aspx?BillId=66272.
9   Sam Levine, "Florida House Approves Measure Requiring People to Repay Criminal Fines and Fees Before They Can Vote," *HuffPost,* April 25, 2019, https://www.huffpost.com/entry/florida-felon-disenfranchisement-poll-tax_n_5cc1106ae4b01b6b3efc6ebe.
10 James Grant, interview by the author, March 27, 2019.
11 Grant, interview, March 27, 2019.
12 Florida House Judiciary Committee Meeting, Florida House of Representatives, April 9, 2019, at 2:29:00 to 2:29:10, https://www.myfloridahouse.gov/VideoPlayer.aspx?eventID=582.
13 Grant, interview, March 27, 2019.
14 Grant, interview, March 27, 2019.
15 Grant, interview, March 27, 2019.
16 "Jon L. Mills, Faculty," University of Florida, https://www.law.ufl.edu/faculty/jon-l-mills.
17 "Advisory Opinion to the Attorney General Re: Voting Restoration Amendment & Advisory Opinion to the Attorney General Re: Voting Restoration Amendment (FIS)," transcript, Florida Supreme Court, March 6, 2017, https://wfsu.org/gavel2gavel/transcript/pdfs/16-1785_16-1981.pdf; https://wfsu.org/gavel2gavel/viewcase.php?eid=2421.
18 "Advisory Opinion to the Attorney General Re: Voting Restoration Amendment."
19 Daniel Rivero, "Co-Author and Attorney for Florida's Amendment 4 Helped Create Statewide Fines and Fees Policy," WLRN, March 27, 2019, https://www.wlrn.org/news/2019-03-27/co-author-and-attorney-for-floridas-amendment-4-helped-create-statewide-fines-and-fees-policy.
20 Grant, interview, March 27, 2019.
21 Rivero, "Co-Author and Attorney for Florida's Amendment 4 Helped Create Statewide Fines and Fees Policy."

22 Rivero, "Co-Author and Attorney for Florida's Amendment 4 Helped Create Statewide Fines and Fees Policy."
23 "Schedule of Events—Meeting Proceedings," transcript, Florida Constitutional Revision Commission, February 12, 1998, University of Florida Digital Collections, http://library.law.fsu.edu/Digital-Collections/CRC/CRC-1998/minutes/crcminutes021298.html.
24 "Schedule of Events—Meeting Proceedings, Florida Constitutional Revision Commission. February 12, 1998."
25 "Official Results," Florida Department of State, Division of Elections, November 3, 1998, General Election, https://results.elections.myflorida.com/Index.asp?ElectionDate=11/3/1998&DATAMODE=.
26 United States Department of Justice Civil Rights Division, "Investigation of the Ferguson Police Department," United States Department of Justice, March 4, 2015, https://www.justice.gov/sites/default/files/opa/press-releases/attachments/2015/03/04/ferguson_police_department_report.pdf.
27 Judge Steven Leifman, interview by the author, January 27, 2021.
28 Daniel Rivero, "Felons Might Have to Pay Hundreds of Millions."
29 Rivero, "Felons Might Have to Pay Hundreds of Millions."
30 Rebecca Diller, "The Hidden Costs of Florida's Criminal Justice Fees," Brennan Center for Justice, 2010, https://www.brennancenter.org/sites/default/files/legacy/Justice/FloridaF&F.pdf.
31 SB 7086, Meeting packet, Senate Criminal Justice Subcommittee, Florida Senate, March 25, 2019, https://www.flsenate.gov/Committees/Show/CJ/MeetingPacket/4531/8021_MeetingPacket_4531.pdf.
32 Jeff Brandes, interview by the author, February 14, 2019.
33 Mitch Perry, "Jeff Brandes Driver's License Suspension Reform Bill Passes Unanimously in Committee," *Florida Politics,* January 14, 2016, https://floridapolitics.com/archives/198652-iver-license-suspension-reform-bill-by-brandes-just-passed-transportation-committee-unanimous/.
34 Brandes, interview, February 14, 2019.
35 "Senate Criminal Justice Subcommittee Meeting," Florida Senate, March 25, 2019, at 1:03:35 to 1:17:20, https://www.flsenate.gov/media/videoplayer?EventID=2443575804_2019031354&Redirect=true.
36 "SB 7086 (2019), Vote History," Florida Senate, https://www.flsenate.gov/Session/Bill/2019/7086/?Tab=VoteHistory.
37 Grant, interview, March 27, 2019.
38 "SB 7066 (2019) Bill Text," Florida Senate, https://www.flsenate.gov/Session/Bill/2019/7066/BillText/er/PDF.
39 Jason Pizzo and Jeff Brandes, joint interview by the author, June 26, 2021.
40 Florida Senate Floor Debate, SB 7066, Florida Senate, May 2, 2019, at 6:36 to 6:38, http://www.flsenate.gov/media/VideoPlayer?EventID=2443575804_2019051020&Redirect=true.

41 Gray Rohrer, "Florida Lawmakers Pass Amendment 4 Restrictions on Ex-Felon Voting Rights as Democrats Fume on Wild Day," *Orlando Sentinel,* May 4, 2019, https://www.orlandosentinel.com/politics/os-ne-florida-legislature-session-friday-20190503-story.html.

42 Howard Simon, interview by the author, May 15, 2019.

9 "AN ADMINISTRATIVE NIGHTMARE"

1 Betty Riddle, interview by the author, September 29, 2020.
2 Betty Riddle, "Inmate Release Information Detail," Florida Department of Corrections.
3 Riddle, interview, September 29, 2020.
4 Riddle, interview, September 29, 2020.
5 "Formerly Incarcerated Floridians Register to Vote," Keith Ivey interview by NPR News, January 13, 2019, https://www.npr.org/2019/01/13/684894858/46-year-old-felon-from-florida-ready-to-vote-for-the-first-time.
6 Complaint, 1:19-cv-00121, United States District Court for the Northern District of Florida.
7 Daniel Tilley, interview by the author, May 25, 2019.
8 Governor Ron DeSantis to Secretary of State Laurel Lee, Executive Office of Governor Ron DeSantis, June 28, 2019, https://www.flgov.com/wp-content/uploads/2019/06/6.282.pdf.
9 Governor Ron DeSantis to Secretary of State Laurel Lee.
10 Governor Ron DeSantis to Secretary of State Laurel Lee.
11 Daniel Rivero, "Federal Lawsuit Pushes Back on Florida's Amendment 4 Roll-Out," WLRN, June 29, 2019, https://www.wlrn.org/news/2019-06-28/federal-lawsuit-pushes-back-on-floridas-amendment-4-roll-out.
12 Complaint, 1:19-cv-00121, United States District Court for the Northern District of Florida.
13 Case number 4:19-cv-00300, United States District Court for the Northern District of Florida.
14 "Transcript of Second Day of Preliminary Injunction Hearing Before the Honorable Robert L. Hinkle, United States District Judge, Case Number 4:19-cv-00300," United States District Court for the Northern District of Florida, October 8, 2019.
15 "Hinkle, Robert Lewis," Federal Judicial Center, https://www.fjc.gov/history/judges/hinkle-robert-lewis.
16 "Transcript of Second Day of Preliminary Injunction Hearing Before the Honorable Robert L. Hinkle, United States District Judge, Case Number 4:19-cv-00300."
17 "Transcript of Second Day of Preliminary Injunction Hearing Before the Honorable Robert L. Hinkle."
18 "Transcript of Second Day of Preliminary Injunction Hearing Before the Honorable Robert L. Hinkle."

19 "Transcript of Second Day of Preliminary Injunction Hearing Before the Honorable Robert L. Hinkle."
20 "Transcript of Second Day of Preliminary Injunction Hearing Before the Honorable Robert L. Hinkle."
21 Daniel Rivero, "New Miami-Dade County Process Grants Right to Vote to Felons, Despite Ongoing Lawsuits," WLRN, November 8, 2019, https://www.wlrn.org/news/2019-11-08/new-miami-dade-county-process-grants-right-to-vote-to-felons-despite-ongoing-lawsuits.
22 Rivero, "New Miami-Dade County Process Grants Right to Vote to Felons."
23 Rivero, "New Miami-Dade County Process Grants Right to Vote to Felons."
24 Rivero, "New Miami-Dade County Process Grants Right to Vote to Felons."
25 Rivero, "New Miami-Dade County Process Grants Right to Vote to Felons."
26 Rivero, "New Miami-Dade County Process Grants Right to Vote to Felons."
27 Rivero, "New Miami-Dade County Process Grants Right to Vote to Felons."
28 Daniel Rivero, "People Across Florida Are Getting Their Voting Rights Back: Few Republicans Could Benefit," WLRN, January 5, 2020, https://www.wlrn.org/local-news/2020-01-05/people-across-florida-are-getting-their-voting-rights-back-few-republicans-could-benefit.
29 Rivero, "People Across Florida Are Getting Their Voting Rights Back."
30 Rivero, "People Across Florida Are Getting Their Voting Rights Back."
31 Rivero, "People Across Florida Are Getting Their Voting Rights Back."
32 Rivero, "People Across Florida Are Getting Their Voting Rights Back."
33 "Formerly Incarcerated Floridians Register to Vote," Keith Ivey interview by NPR News, January 13, 2019, https://www.npr.org/2019/01/13/684894858/46-year-old-felon-from-florida-ready-to-vote-for-the-first-time.
34 "Formerly Incarcerated Floridians Register to Vote."
35 "Formerly Incarcerated Floridians Register to Vote."
36 "Formerly Incarcerated Floridians Register to Vote."
37 Lawrence Mower, "Being Poor Shouldn't Stop Florida Felons from Voting, Judge Rules in Amendment 4 Case," *Miami Herald*, October 19, 2019, https://www.miamiherald.com/news/politics-government/state-politics/article236421363.html.
38 Betty Riddle, interview by the author, February 11, 2020.
39 Micah Kubic, "ACLU: Gov. Ron DeSantis Keeps Flip-Flopping on a Crucial Voting Rights Issue," *Florida Phoenix*, November 25, 2019, https://floridaphoenix.com/2019/11/25/aclu-gov-ron-desantis-keeps-flip-flopping-on-a-crucial-voting-rights-issue/.
40 Brief of Appellants, Case number 4:19-cv-00300, United States Court of Appeals for the Eleventh Circuit, December 13, 2019, 46.
41 Dara Kam, News Service of Florida, "Does DeSantis Want to Void Amendment 4? His Lawyers Suggest Yes, He Does," *Tampa Bay Times*, December 4, 2019, https://www.tampabay.com/florida-politics/buzz/2019/12/04/does-desantis-want-to-void-amendment-4-his-lawyers-suggest-yes-he-does/.

42 Kam, "Does DeSantis Want to Void Amendment 4?"
43 Karina Elwood, "Florida's Amendment 4 'Fines and Fees' Limitation Found Unconstitutional in US Appeals Court Opinion," WUFT, February 20, 2020, https://www.wuft.org/fresh-take-florida/2020-02-19/floridas-amendment-4-fines-and-fees-limitation-found-unconstitutional-in-us-appeals-court-opinion.
44 Elwood, "Florida's Amendment 4 'Fines and Fees' Limitation Found Unconstitutional in US Appeals Court Opinion."
45 Daniel Rivero, "Florida Supreme Court Seems Comfortable Tying Money to Felon Voting," WLRN, November 6, 2019, https://www.wlrn.org/news/2019-11-06/florida-supreme-court-seems-comfortable-tying-money-to-felon-voting.
46 Staff report, "Ron DeSantis Appoints Carlos Muñiz to Florida Supreme Court," *Florida Politics,* January 22, 2019, https://floridapolitics.com/archives/286089-ron-desantis-carlos-muniz-supreme-court/.
47 Rivero, "Florida Supreme Court Seems Comfortable Tying Money to Felon Voting."
48 Rivero, "Florida Supreme Court Seems Comfortable Tying Money to Felon Voting."
49 Rivero, "Florida Supreme Court Seems Comfortable Tying Money to Felon Voting."
50 Rivero, "Florida Supreme Court Seems Comfortable Tying Money to Felon Voting."
51 Jacqueline Thomsen, "With Lagoa Confirmed to 11th Circuit, Trump Flips a Third Appeals Court to GOP Majority," *National Law Journal,* November 20, 2019, https://www.law.com/nationallawjournal/2019/11/20/with-lagoa-confirmed-to-11th-circuit-trump-flips-a-third-appeals-court-to-gop-majority/?slreturn=20210830002640.
52 Thomsen, "With Lagoa Confirmed to 11th Circuit, Trump Flips a Third Appeals Court to GOP Majority."
53 "Advisory Opinion to the Governor vs RE: Implementation of Amendment 4, The Voting Restoration Amendment, No. SC19–1341," Supreme Court of Florida, January 16, 2020.
54 @GovRonDeSantis, X (formerly Twitter), January 16, 2020, https://twitter.com/GovRonDeSantis/status/1217867897906913282.
55 A. G. Gancarski, "Ron DeSantis Says He Didn't Write 'Voting Is a Privilege' Tweet," *Florida Politics,* January 21, 2020, https://floridapolitics.com/archives/316332-governor-voting-privilege/.
56 Gancarski, "Ron DeSantis Says He Didn't Write 'Voting Is a Privilege' Tweet."
57 Daniel Rivero, "Everything You Need to Know About Florida's Amendment 4 Lawsuit," WLRN, October 5, 2019, https://www.wlrn.org/news/2019-10-04/everything-you-need-to-know-about-floridas-amendment-4-lawsuit.
58 Rivero, "Everything You Need to Know About Florida's Amendment 4 Lawsuit."
59 Rivero, "Everything You Need to Know About Florida's Amendment 4 Lawsuit."
60 Rivero, "Everything You Need to Know About Florida's Amendment 4 Lawsuit."

61 Rivero, "Everything You Need to Know About Florida's Amendment 4 Lawsuit."
62 Rivero, "Everything You Need to Know About Florida's Amendment 4 Lawsuit."
63 Rivero, "Everything You Need to Know About Florida's Amendment 4 Lawsuit."
64 Rivero, "Everything You Need to Know About Florida's Amendment 4 Lawsuit."
65 Daniel Rivero, "Voting Rights for Hundreds of Thousands of Felons at Stake in Florida Trial," WLRN, April 27, 2020, https://www.wlrn.org/2020-04-27/voting-rights-for-hundreds-of-thousands-of-felons-at-stake-in-florida-trial.
66 Rivero, "Voting Rights for Hundreds of Thousands of Felons at Stake in Florida Trial."
67 "Brief of Alabama, Arizona, Arkansas, Georgia, Kentucky, Louisiana, Nebraska, South Carolina, Texas and Utah as Amici Curiae in Support of Defendants-Appellants," Case number 4:19-cv-00300, United States Court of Appeals for the Eleventh Circuit, March 3, 2020.
68 "Thompson v. Alabama," Campaign Legal Center, https://campaignlegal.org/cases-actions/thompson-v-alabama.
69 "Thompson v. Alabama."
70 Constitution of the State of Georgia, Art. II, Sec. I, Para. III. State of Georgia.
71 Andrea Young, interview by the author, May 27, 2020.
72 Young, interview, May 27, 2020.
73 "Probation and Parole in the United States, 2017–2018," U.S. Department of Justice, Bureau of Justice Statistics, August 2020, https://bjs.ojp.gov/content/pub/pdf/ppus1718.pdf.
74 Young, interview, May 27, 2020.
75 Tanya Mosley and Francesca Paris, "Kentucky Governor Andy Beshear Restores Voting Rights to Felons," WBUR, December 13, 2019, https://www.wbur.org/hereandnow/2019/12/13/kentucky-felon-voting-rights.
76 Mosley and Paris, "Kentucky Governor Andy Beshear Restores Voting Rights to Felons."
77 "Check Your Status—Civil Rights Restoration," Commonwealth of Kentucky, https://secure.kentucky.gov/Corrections/VoterEligibility/search.

10 THE TRIAL

1 Court case number 4:19-cv-00300, April 27, 2020, through May 6, 2020, United States District Court, Northern District of Florida, Tallahassee Division.
2 "Michael Barber," Brigham Young University, https://politicalscience.byu.edu/directory/michael-barber.
3 Case number 18-CVS-014001, Judgment, State of North Carolina, Wake County, Court of Justice Superior Court Division, issued September 3, 2019.
4 "Jacobson v. Lee, 411 F. Supp. 3d 1249," CaseText.com, November 15, 2019, https://casetext.com/case/jacobson-v-lee-2.
5 Jason Breslow, "Federal Judge Rules Florida Law Restricting Voting Rights for Felons Unconstitutional," NPR, May 24, 2020, https://www.npr.org/2020/05/24

/861776313/federal-judge-rules-florida-law-restricting-voting-rights-for-felons-unconstitut.
6. Breslow, "Federal Judge Rules Florida Law Restricting Voting Rights for Felons Unconstitutional."
7. Case number 4:19-cv-00300, Document 420–1, "Request for an Advisory Opinion," United States District Court, Northern District of Florida, Tallahassee Division, May 25, 2020.
8. Case number 4:19-cv-00300, Document 420–1, "Request for an Advisory Opinion."
9. Case number 4:19-cv-00300, "Opinion on the Merits," United States District Court, Northern District of Florida, Tallahassee Division, May 25, 2020.
10. Case number 4:19-cv-00300, "Opinion on the Merits."
11. "Potential New Battleground for Florida Voting Rights Fight Starts to Show," WLRN, May 28, 2020, https://www.wlrn.org/local-news/2020-05-28/potential-new-battleground-for-florida-voting-rights-fight-starts-to-show.
12. "Potential New Battleground for Florida Voting Rights Fight Starts to Show."
13. "Potential New Battleground for Florida Voting Rights Fight Starts to Show."

11 MASK OFF

1. Lawrence Hurley, "On Guns, Abortion and Voting Rights, Trump Leaves Lasting Mark on U.S. Judiciary," Reuters, January 15, 2021, https://www.reuters.com/article/idUSKBN29K16N/.
2. Tim Ryan, "Trump Flips Another Circuit to Majority GOP Appointees," *Courthouse News,* November 21, 2019, https://www.courthousenews.com/trump-flips-another-circuit-to-majority-gop-appointees/.
3. Dara Kam, News Service of Florida, "Judges Targeted for Disqualification in Felons Case," WLRN, July 16, 2020, https://www.wlrn.org/news/2020-07-16/judges-targeted-for-disqualification-in-felons-case.
4. Kam, "Judges Targeted for Disqualification in Felons Case."
5. Michael Moline, "U.S. Senate Dems Ask Lagoa, Luck Why They Didn't Recuse from Amendment 4 Appeal, as Promised," *Florida Phoenix,* July 22, 2020, https://floridaphoenix.com/2020/07/22/u-s-senate-dems-ask-lagoa-luck-why-they-didnt-recuse-from-amendment-4-appeal-as-promised/.
6. Zoe Tillman, "Two Trump-Appointed Judges Rejected Calls to Step Aside from a Florida Voting Rights Fight," BuzzFeed News, July 27, 2020, https://www.buzzfeednews.com/article/zoetillman/trump-judges-wont-recuse-florida-election-felon-voting.
7. "20-12003," Eleventh Circuit United States Court of Appeals, July 27, 2020, https://www.ca11.uscourts.gov/content/20-12003-0.
8. "20-12003," Eleventh Circuit United States Court of Appeals, July 27, 2020.
9. "20-12003," Eleventh Circuit United States Court of Appeals, July 27, 2020.
10. "20-12003," Eleventh Circuit United States Court of Appeals, July 27, 2020.

11 John Nichols, "Why the Hell Is the Supreme Court Allowing a New Poll Tax to Disenfranchise Florida Voters?" *The Nation,* July 17, 2020, https://www.thenation.com/article/politics/supreme-court-florida-felony-voting-rights/.
12 "On Application to Vacate Stay, No. 19A1071," Supreme Court of the United States, July 16, 2020, https://www.supremecourt.gov/opinions/19pdf/19a1071_4h25.pdf.
13 "On Application to Vacate Stay, No. 19A1071."
14 Daniel Rivero, "First Time Voters March to Polls in Miami Thanks to Amendment 4," WLRN, August 12, 2020, https://www.wlrn.org/2020-08-12/first-time-voters-march-to-polls-in-miami-thanks-to-amendment-4.
15 Rivero, "First Time Voters March to Polls in Miami Thanks to Amendment 4."
16 Rivero, "First Time Voters March to Polls in Miami Thanks to Amendment 4."
17 Rivero, "First Time Voters March to Polls in Miami Thanks to Amendment 4."
18 Melba Pearson, interview by the author, August 12, 2020.
19 Daniel Rivero, "First Time Voters March to Polls in Miami Thanks to Amendment 4," WLRN, August 12, 2020, https://www.wlrn.org/2020-08-12/first-time-voters-march-to-polls-in-miami-thanks-to-amendment-4.
20 Rivero, "First Time Voters March to Polls in Miami Thanks to Amendment 4."
21 Rivero, "First Time Voters March to Polls in Miami Thanks to Amendment 4."
22 Rivero, "First Time Voters March to Polls in Miami Thanks to Amendment 4."
23 Dara Kam, News Service of Florida, "Will Convicted Felons Get to Vote in November? Appeals Judges Hear Arguments in Florida Showdown," *South Florida Sun-Sentinel,* August 18, 2020, https://www.sun-sentinel.com/news/politics/fl-ne-appeals-court-oral-arguments-felon-voting-20200818-u7rivkpjbbbkdiykmglw43e7vy-story.html.
24 Kam, "Will Convicted Felons Get to Vote in November?"
25 Kam, "Will Convicted Felons Get to Vote in November?"
26 Kam, "Will Convicted Felons Get to Vote in November?"
27 Kam, "Will Convicted Felons Get to Vote in November?"
28 Case number 4:19-cv-00300, En Banc Opinion, United States Court of Appeals for the Eleventh District, September 11, 2020.
29 Case number 4:19-cv-00300, En Banc Opinion.
30 Case number 4:19-cv-00300, En Banc Opinion.
31 Case number 4:19-cv-00300, Amicus Brief, Florida Rights Restoration Coalition, United States Court of Appeals for the Eleventh District, August 3, 2020.
32 Anonymous attorney, interview by the author, September 11, 2020.
33 Adam Liptak, "Trump's Supreme Court Nominees List Gets New Scrutiny," *New York Times,* September 18, 2020, sec. "U.S.," https://www.nytimes.com/2020/09/18/us/trump-supreme-court-nominees-list.html.
34 "Additions to President Donald J. Trump's Supreme Court List—The White House," The White House, September 9, 2020, https://trumpwhitehouse.archives.gov/briefings-statements/additions-president-donald-j-trumps-supreme-court-list/.
35 Ángel Sánchez, interview by the author, September 17, 2020.
36 Veronica Stracqualursi, "LeBron James' Voting Rights Group to Help Florida's

Ex-Felons Who Owe Fines and Fees Register to Vote | CNN Politics," CNN, July 25, 2020, https://www.cnn.com/2020/07/25/politics/lebron-james-florida-voting-rights-felons/index.html.

37. Donovan Dooley, "With Assist from LeBron, Michael Jordan's Finally Getting Political," *Deadspin,* https://deadspin.com/with-assist-from-lebron-michael-jordan-s-finally-getti-1844570314.

38. "Miami Dolphins Social Impact Committee Gives $100,000 to Florida Rights Restoration Coalition's Fines and Fees Program," MiamiDolphins.com, https://www.miamidolphins.com/news/miami-dolphins-social-impact-committee-florida-rights-restoration.

39. News Service of Florida, "Morgan Touts Effort to Help Felons Pay Legal Debts," WJXT, August 24, 2020, https://www.news4jax.com/news/florida/2020/08/24/morgan-touts-effort-to-help-felons-pay-legal-debts/.

40. Daniel Rivero, "MTV, Comedy Central and VH1 Join Last-Minute Push to Register Florida's Returning Citizens," WLRN, September 18, 2020, https://www.wlrn.org/2020-09-18/mtv-comedy-central-and-vh1-join-last-minute-push-to-register-floridas-returning-citizens.

41. Rivero, "MTV, Comedy Central and VH1 Join Last-Minute Push to Register Florida's Returning Citizens."

42. Rivero, "MTV, Comedy Central and VH1 Join Last-Minute Push to Register Florida's Returning Citizens."

43. Rivero, "MTV, Comedy Central and VH1 Join Last-Minute Push to Register Florida's Returning Citizens."

44. Jason Pizzo, interview by the author, September 14, 2020.

45. Pizzo, interview, September 14, 2020.

46. Pizzo, interview, September 14, 2020.

47. Pizzo, interview, September 14, 2020.

48. Pizzo, interview, September 14, 2020.

49. Ángel Sánchez, interview by the author, September 17, 2020.

50. Sánchez, interview, September 17, 2020.

51. "Constitutional Amendment 4/Felon Voting Rights—Division of Elections—Florida Department of State," Florida Department of State, https://dos.fl.gov/elections/for-voters/voter-registration/constitutional-amendment-4felon-voting-rights/.

52. Gary Fineout and Matt Dixon, "Florida Quietly Gives Voting Advice to Ex-Felons—Grant Leaving House for State Job He Helped Shape—Progressive Group Gets $1M to Flip Florida House—Reporting Glitch with Coronavirus Numbers," *Politico,* August 13, 2020, https://www.politico.com/newsletters/florida-playbook/2020/08/13/florida-quietly-gives-voting-advice-to-ex-felons-grant-leaving-house-for-state-job-he-helped-shape-progressive-group-gets-1m-to-flip-florida-house-reporting-glitch-with-coronavirus-numbers-490059.

53. "Response to Request for Advisory Opinion F-20-9," Florida Department of State,

August 17, 2020, https://dos.myflorida.com/media/703434/f-20-9-redacted-final-response-to-ao.pdf.

54 Sánchez, interview, September 17, 2020.
55 Sánchez, interview, September 17, 2020.
56 "Advisory Opinions by Year," Florida Department of State, Division of Elections, https://dos.fl.gov/elections/laws-rules/advisory-opinions/advisory-opinions-by-year/.
57 Monique Upshaw, interview by the author, October 16, 2020.
58 Upshaw, interview, October 16, 2020.
59 Upshaw, interview, October 16, 2020.
60 Upshaw, interview, October 16, 2020.
61 Upshaw, interview, October 16, 2020.
62 "9/23/20 Executive Clemency Board Meeting," The Florida Channel, at 13:10 through 41:30, https://thefloridachannel.org/videos/9-23-20-executive-clemency-board-meeting/.
63 "9/23/20 Executive Clemency Board Meeting."
64 "9/23/20 Executive Clemency Board Meeting."
65 "9/23/20 Executive Clemency Board Meeting."
66 "9/23/20 Executive Clemency Board Meeting."
67 "9/23/20 Executive Clemency Board Meeting."
68 Denise Royal, "Governor's 'Law & Order' Proposal Gains Statewide Supporters and Detractors," WLRN, September 25, 2020, at 42:20 through 45:50, https://www.wlrn.org/podcast/the-florida-roundup/2020-09-25/governors-law-order-proposal-gains-statewide-supporters-and-detractors.
69 Royal, "Governor's 'Law & Order' Proposal Gains Statewide Supporters and Detractors."
70 Matt Dixon and Gary Fineout, "Florida AG Calls for Criminal Inquiry into Bloomberg's $16M Felon Voter Donation," Politico, September 23, 2020, https://www.politico.com/states/florida/story/2020/09/23/florida-ag-calls-for-criminal-inquiry-into-bloombergs-16m-felon-voter-donation-1317995.
71 Desmond Meade (@desmondmeade), "My response to attacks on democracy and the paying off of fines and fees," X (formerly Twitter), September 27, 2020, https://twitter.com/desmondmeade/status/1310369975320768513.
72 Investigative report, case EI-32–0084, Florida Department of Law Enforcement, May 3, 2021.

12 THE LONG GAME

1 Daniel Rivero and Caitie Switalski, "Florida's 2018 Election Woes May Foreshadow November's Vote," Reveal, October 2, 2020, https://revealnews.org/article/was-florida-in-2018-a-dry-run-for-troubles-in-november/.
2 Alexander Gonzalez and Tom Hudson, "After November Election Results, Is South

Florida Actually Purple?," WLRN, November 6, 2020, https://www.wlrn.org/2020-11-06/after-november-election-results-is-south-florida-actually-purple.

3. Gonzalez and Hudson, "After November Election Results, Is South Florida Actually Purple?"
4. Lawrence Mower and Langston Taylor, "In Florida, the Gutting of a Landmark Law Leaves Few Felons Likely to Vote," ProPublica, https://www.propublica.org/article/in-florida-the-gutting-of-a-landmark-law-leaves-few-felons-likely-to-vote.
5. Mower and Taylor, "In Florida, the Gutting of a Landmark Law Leaves Few Felons Likely to Vote."
6. Mower and Taylor, "In Florida, the Gutting of a Landmark Law Leaves Few Felons Likely to Vote."
7. Mower and Taylor, "In Florida, the Gutting of a Landmark Law Leaves Few Felons Likely to Vote."
8. Dennis Baxley, interview by the author, November 20, 2020.
9. Keith Perry, interview by the author, March 2, 2021.
10. Perry, interview with author, March 2, 2021.
11. SB 1932, Florida Senate, 2021 Session, https://flsenate.gov/Session/Bill/2021/1932.
12. Giulia Heyward, "Florida Restores More Rights for Felons," *Politico*, March 11, 2021, https://www.politico.com/news/2021/03/11/florida-restores-more-rights-for-felons-475413.
13. Heyward, "Florida Restores More Rights for Felons."
14. Nikki Fried, interview by the author, April 14, 2021.
15. Fried, interview, April 14, 2021.
16. "Vote Jason Mariner for Congress. Time to Fight for Each Other! #NotYourTypicalCandidate," Mariner for Congress, August 16, 2021, https://www.youtube.com/watch?v=oDcwmdtjHZU.
17. "Vote Jason Mariner for Congress. Time to Fight for Each Other! #NotYourTypicalCandidate."
18. Daniel Rivero, "Did This Republican Congressional Candidate Cast an Illegal Vote? Florida Can't Tell," WLRN, November 30, 2021, https://www.wlrn.org/news/2021-11-30/did-this-republican-congressional-candidate-cast-an-illegal-vote-florida-cant-tell.
19. Rivero, "Did This Republican Congressional Candidate Cast an Illegal Vote?"
20. Rivero, "Did This Republican Congressional Candidate Cast an Illegal Vote?"
21. Rivero, "Did This Republican Congressional Candidate Cast an Illegal Vote?"
22. Rivero, "Did This Republican Congressional Candidate Cast an Illegal Vote?"
23. Rivero, "Did This Republican Congressional Candidate Cast an Illegal Vote?"
24. Carolina Ilvento and Alexander Lugo (Fresh Take Florida), "Tenth Person Charged with Voter Fraud Investigation over Jailhouse registrations," WUFT, April 2, 2022, https://www.wuft.org/fresh-take-florida/2022-04-02/tenth-person-charged-with-voter-fraud-investigation-over-jailhouse-registrations.
25. Carolina Ilvento and Alexander Lugo (Fresh Take Florida), "Alachua County Supervisor of Elections Office Employees Cleared of Wrongdoing in Voter Fraud

Probe," WUFT, March 31, 2022, https://www.wuft.org/news/2022/03/31/alachua-county-supervisor-of-elections-office-employees-cleared-of-wrongdoing-in-voter-fraud-probe/.

26 Ilvento and Lugo, "Alachua County Supervisor of Elections Office Employees Cleared of Wrongdoing in Voter Fraud Probe."

27 Ilvento and Lugo, "Alachua County Supervisor of Elections Office Employees Cleared of Wrongdoing in Voter Fraud Probe."

28 Marita Vlachou, "Florida to Launch the First Election Police Force in the U.S," *Huffpost*, March 10, 2022, https://www.huffpost.com/entry/florida-opens-first-office-of-election-crimes-and-security-in-the-us_n_622a0eb1e4b0d1329e817c6b.

29 Lawrence Mower, "DeSantis' New Election Crimes Office: 52 Positions and 'Unprecedented' Authority," *Tampa Bay Times*, December 20, 2021, https://www.tampabay.com/news/florida-politics/2021/12/20/desantis-new-election-crimes-office-52-positions-and-unprecedented-authority.

30 Miles Cohen and Isabella Murray, "DeSantis Announces 20 Floridians Charged with Voter Fraud, Lauds New Election Policing Office," ABC News, August 18, 2022, https://abcnews.go.com/Politics/desantis-announces-20-floridians-charged-voter-fraud-lauds/story?id=88563886.

31 Lawrence Mower, "Police Cameras Show Confusion, Anger over DeSantis' Voter Fraud Arrests," *Tampa Bay Times*, October 18, 2022, https://www.tampabay.com/news/florida-politics/2022/10/18/body-camera-video-police-voter-fraud-desantis-arrests/.

32 Mower, "Police Cameras Show Confusion, Anger over DeSantis' Voter Fraud Arrests."

33 Ashley Lopez, "Florida's Effort to Charge 20 People with Voter Fraud Has Hit Some Roadblocks," NPR, December 21, 2022, https://www.npr.org/2022/12/21/1144265521/florida-voter-fraud-cases-prosecution-update.

34 Lopez, "Florida's Effort to Charge 20 People with Voter Fraud Has Hit Some Roadblocks."

35 Romy Ellenbogen, "Voting Rights Group Sues Florida over Haphazard Implementation of Amendment 4," *Miami Herald*, July 20, 2023, https://www.miamiherald.com/news/politics-government/state-politics/article277473203.html.

36 Dara Kam, "Changes Sought in Felon Voting Process," News Service of Florida, June 14, 2024, https://www.newsservicefloridacom/latest/headlines/changes-sought-in-felon-voting-process/article_10331ae6-2a91-11ef-86af-0f5d36411d60.html.

37 Ashley Lopez, "Florida Felons Could Get a Bit More Clarity on Their Voting Rights with a New Proposal," NPR, August 28, 2024, https://www.npr.org/transcripts/nx-s1-5084199.

38 Felon Eligibility Opinion Request, Rule 1S-2.010, Florida Division of Elections, https://files.floridados.gov/media/708400/ds-de-xxx-felon-eligibility-opinion-request-form.pdf.

39 Lopez, "Florida Felons Could Get a Bit More Clarity on Their Voting Rights with a New Proposal."

40 Howard Simon, interview by the author, April 21, 2020.
41 Howard Simon, interview by the author, February 5, 2024.
42 Desmond Meade, interview by the author, April 24, 2020.
43 J. Kevin Corder and Christina Wolbrecht, "Did Women Vote Once They Had the Opportunity?," American Bar Association, October 21, 2021, https://www.americanbar.org/groups/public_education/publications/insights-on-law-and-society/volume-20/issue-1/did-women-vote-once-they-had-the-opportunity-/.
44 Corder and Wolbrecht, "Did Women Vote Once They Had the Opportunity?"
45 Corder and Wolbrecht, "Did Women Vote Once They Had the Opportunity?"
46 Ruth Gielnik, "Men and Women in the U.S. Continue to Differ in Voter Turnout Rate, Party Identification," Pew Research Center, August 18, 2020, https://www.pewresearch.org/fact-tank/2020/08/18/men-and-women-in-the-u-s-continue-to-differ-in-voter-turnout-rate-party-identification/.
47 Desmond Meade, interview by the author, April 24, 2020.

INDEX

24th Amendment. *See* Poll taxes
2000 election. *See* Bush, George W.; Bush, Jeb; Gore, Al; Harris, Katherine; Simon, Howard; US Commission on Civil Rights

Alabama: among last states with poll tax, 84; former Solicitor General resigns, 131; Simon experience as student, 8–10, 72, 117; supporting Florida system, 115–116, 117; voter database, 156
American Civil Liberties Union (ACLU): Georgia chapter, 116–117; Michigan chapter, 9; National ACLU role in Amendment 4 campaign, 61, 66–68
American Civil Liberties Union (ACLU) of Florida: advocacy after passage of Amendment 4, 72–73, 92–94, 104, 153; advocacy after 2000 election, 10–11, 18; attempt at 2003 ballot initiative, 28; creation of Florida Rights Restoration Coalition, 29; independence of Florida Rights Restoration Coalition, 52–53; lawsuits, 18, 30, 104–107, 112, 119–129, 134; support for Amendment 4 campaign, 53–54, 65, 67, 134; work during Crist administration, 34–37; work during Scott administration, 48–49
Askew, Reubin: creation of Executive Clemency Board and automatic restoration process, 15–16; history, 12; rights restoration law declared unconstitutional, 12–15
Automatic rights restoration: automatic processes, 12–16, 38–40, 44, 48, 55, 60, 68, 151–154; debate about Amendment 4, 73, 86, 122; in other states, 118; proposed bills, 151; prosecutions, 155

Bloomberg, Michael, 10–12, 147–148
Baxley, Dennis, 74–75, 150
Bondi, Pam: role in rolling back automatic restoration, 47–48, 61
Brandes, Jeff: role in passing SB 7066, 91–93, 109, 122–123
Bronson, Charles: deciding vote on Crist reforms, 35–38
Bush, George W.: 2000 election, 5–7
Bush, Jeb: aftermath of 2000 election, 18, 23–33; botched data scandal, 30–31; relationship with Rubio, 40; rights restoration record, 54
Butterworth, Bob, 16–18, 24

Campaign for Amendment 4: bulk of the campaign, 58–68; early meetings, 10–11, 18; victory, 69–70
Carollo, Joe, 1
Chiles, Lawton, 17, 88, 112
Confusion on voting eligibility: advisory opinions from Florida Department of State, 120, 128, 137, 142–143, 156; sloppy clerk records, 104–105, 114, 120–127, 136, 140, 153–154
Crist, Charlie: bringing back automatic rights restoration, 35–40; evolution of hardline stances on crime, 33–36; popularity, 42; relationship with Obama, 41–44; relationship with Rubio, 40–41, 44; rights restoration record, 54

Dawson, Mandy, 28
DBT Online, 3–4, 19
Debate over meaning of "all terms" of a criminal sentence, 53–54, 67, 74–77, 85–94
Debt: creation of Florida criminal justice debt system, 88–89; debt after release from prison, 76–77, 90, 103, 141, 144, 153; debt collectors, 80, 120, 142; low expectations on collecting debts, 81–83; reliance on debt for government revenue, x–xi, 88–92, 106–107, 115–117. *See also* Confusion on voting eligibility; Waivers in lieu of paying debts
DeSantis, Ron: at Board of Executive Clemency, 145–147, 151–152; court battles, 105, 110–112, 119–130, 135–136; FBI letter, xi–xii, 147; investigations after 2020 election, 154–156; judge picks, 79, 112–113, 130; statements on restoration of rights, 68, 75, 78–79, 104–105, 113, 146, 152

Federal Bureau of Investigation (FBI): FBI data, 50; letter from Moody in 2020, ix–xxi, 147; Mississippi Klan attacks, 10
Florida Cabinet: partisan dynamics of Cabinet, 35, 46–47, 152; unique structure of Florida Cabinet, 15–16. *See also* Florida Executive Board of Clemency
Florida Constitution: early constitutions, 13, 49; 1968 version, 72
Florida Department of Corrections: 2000 election, 6; lawsuit, 18, 30; overcrowding, 33; recommendations for changes, 31–33, 39, 91; role in implementing Amendment 4, 74, 153
Florida Department of Law Enforcement: FBI letter investigation, xi–xiii, 147–148; lead up and 2000 election, 3, 6
Florida Division of Elections: admissions of inadequate records, 114–115, 120–121; erroneous felon lists, 3–5, 19, 30–31; mediation agreement on new procedures, 156–157; proposed reforms, 128, 141. *See* Confusion on voting eligibility
Florida Executive Board of Clemency: backlog of cases, 17, 31, 36–37, 42; clemency rule changes, 16–17, 24, 29, 35–38, 47–48, 151–152; creation, 15–16; errors, 18, 44; investigations after fraudulent election, 4, 15–16; proposals, 27, 151; total discretion in cases, 50–57
Florida Keys: erroneous state list, 3–4, 73–74. *See also* Sawyer, Harry; Supervisors of Elections offices: Monroe
Florida Office of Executive Clemency: community outreach, 42. *See* Florida Executive Board of Clemency
Florida Parole Commission: additional funds, 38; role, 24–5; staff reductions, 38–40, 42, 44–45
Florida Rights Restoration Coalition: 2003 ballot initiative effort, 28–29; becoming independent from ACLU, 52–53; campaign for Amendment 4, 61–70; continued advocacy, 85, 92–93, 138; fundraising to pay off debts, xi, 138–139, 147–148; lawsuit, 156–157; origins, 28–29
Florida Supreme Court: advisory opinions, 13–15, 111–113; allowing Amendment 4 on the ballot, 60, 63–66, 86–91; Gov. DeSantis nominees, 79, 130–131; ruling on 1974 law, 13–15
Fort Lauderdale, 38, 155
Fried, Nikki, 145, 152

Gore, Al: 2000 election, 5–7
Grant, Jamie: defense against accusations of racism, 85–86, 109, 123; role in passing SB 7066, 85–86, 88, 91–94, 109, 122

Harris, Kamala, 131
Harris, Katherine, 23
Hinkle, Robert: early rulings in federal lawsuit, 106–107, 110–111; granted class

action status, 115–117; reversal of decision and impact, 137, 142, 150, 157; trial and opinion of federal case, 119–125, 130–132, 135

Ingoglia, Blaise, 74

Jackson, Jesse, 30
Jacksonville, 78, 104, 114
Jazil, Mohammad, 106, 111

King, Martin Luther, Jr.: time in Selma, 8–9, 157
Ku Klux Klan, 9–10

Lagoa, Barbara: Florida advisory opinion hearing, 112–113; nominated to Florida Supreme Court, 78–79, 112; nominated by President Trump to federal appeals court, 113, 130; recusal controversy, 130–132
Legend, John, 107
Lewis, John: time in Selma, 9, 157
Liuzzo, Viola, 9–10
Luck, Robert: Florida advisory opinion hearing, 112–113; nominated to Florida Supreme Court, 112; nominated by President Trump to federal appeals court, 113, 130; recusal controversy, 130–132

Martinez, Carlos (public defender), 109, 135–136
McCollum, Bill, 33–37, 45
Meade, Desmond: advocacy after Amendment 4, 78, 94, 109; Amendment 4 campaign, 53–54, 60–64, 66–70, 87; before Executive Board of Clemency, 145–147; lawsuits, 122–123, 156–157; leadership of Florida Rights Restoration Coalition, 52–53; legacy, 158–159; letter to FBI, ix–xiii, 147–148; life before activism, 51–52, 60–61

Meek, Kendrick, 11, 28, 45
Miami: 2000 election and aftermath, 7, 10–11, 18–21, 30; ACLU of Florida headquarters, 28–29, 72; Amendment 4 campaign and aftermath, 69, 78–79, 82, 107–109, 114, 133–135, 139–144; contested 1997 election, 1–2, 4–7; influential people from, 11, 13–14, 28, 51, 60, 76, 90; supervisor of elections, 5, 7, 77–79, 128
Miami Dade College, 60–61
Michigan, 9–10
Mills, Jon: drafting of 1998 ballot amendment on funding courts, 88–91; role in passage of Amendment 4, 53, 87, 112
Mississippi, 8, 84, 158
Modification of criminal sentence: attempts to work around debt, 93, 106–109, 139–141
Montgomery, Alabama, 8–9
Moody, Ashley: at Board of Executive Clemency 145; letter to FBI, 9–10, 147–148

Obama, Barack, 38, 43–44, 46, 61, 78, 90, 108, 130, 134
Opinion poll: during Amendment 4 campaign, 53–54, 124–125

Paul, Rand, 61
Pettigrew, Richard, 13–16
Pizzo, Jason: during SB 7066 debate, 93, 122; pro-bono work to help restore voting rights, 140–141; raising alarm about debt, 76–77, 79
Poll taxes: debate about poll taxes, 83–94, 105–107, 137; history of poll taxes, 84–85
Potential of Amendment 4 being declared unconstitutional, 110–111, 136
Putnam, Adam, 47–50

Reno, Janet, 14
Restoration case backlog, 17, 36, 48, 55, 128, 145, 149, 150

INDEX 193

Role of Clerk of Courts offices, 76, 79–82, 89, 107, 114, 140, 142–143, 148
Rubio, Marco: 2010 Senate Campaign, 44–45; early career, 26, 40–41; relationship with Crist, 40, 44; relationship with Jeb Bush, 40
Ruvin, Harvey: fraudulent 1997 election, 2; role after Amendment 4 passed, 76, 79–80

Sawyer, Harry, 3, 4
Selma, Alabama, 8
Scott, Rick: career, 47–48; ideology and 2010 campaign, 45–47; impact on Amendment 4, 52–53, 86; rights restoration record, 50–51, 54–55
Simon, Howard: activism during Crist and Scott administrations, 34, 36–37, 39, 47, 49; advocacy following 2000 election, 10–11, 18; campaign for ballot amendments, 28–29, 52–54, 62, 65–67; lawsuits, 18, 30, 94, 134; post–Amendment 4 advocacy, 72–73, 157–158; student life and early work, 8–10
Sink, Alex, 35–37, 45
Smathers, George, 16
Smith, Chris, 26–27
St. Petersburg, 5
Suarez, Xavier, 1–2
Supervisors of Elections offices: Alachua, 154; Broward, 4, 128; Hillsborough, 5; Leon, 49, 115; Madison, 3–4; Miami-Dade, 5, 7, 77–79, 128; Monroe, 3–4, 74; Okaloosa, 26; Orange, 74; Palm Beach, 153; Statewide, 21, 23, 115, 128–129

Tampa, 5–7; lead up and 2000 election, 5–7, 46–47, 58–60, 85, 104
Trump, Donald: 2020 presidential campaign, 108, 143, 147, 149; comments about fundraising to pay debt, xi–xii; impact on Amendment 4 campaign, 63–64, 66–68; impact on federal courts, 113, 130, 138

United States Court of Appeals for the Eleventh Circuit: appeal after Amendment 4 case decision, 113, 130–138; impact of appeals court ruling, 142, 154; political makeup, 113, 30; temporary ruling in favor of plaintiffs, 111
US Commission on Civil Rights, 19–23
US Supreme Court: 2000 election decision, 7; on Amendment 4 court case, 132–133, 154; potential nominees involved in court case, 138; ruling on poll taxes, 84–85

Volz, Neil: activism and Amendment 4 campaign, 62–65, 68; before Executive Board of Clemency, 145–146; continued activism, 147, 156–157

Waivers in lieu of paying debts, 93, 107–110, 135–136, 140–141
Wilson, Frederica: early voting rights support, 11; helping Crist reforms, 38–39

DANIEL RIVERO is an award-winning investigative reporter who works with WLRN Public Radio in Miami. The Cuban American's investigations have appeared in the *Miami Herald*, NPR, the *Guardian*, *ABC News*, *Splinter*, and other outlets. This is his first book.

GOVERNMENT AND POLITICS IN THE SOUTH
EDITED BY SHARON D. WRIGHT AUSTIN
AND ANGELA K. LEWIS-MADDOX

Writing for the Public Good: Essays from David R. Colburn and Senator Bob Graham, edited by Steven Noll (2022)

"Chambers v. Florida" and the Criminal Justice Revolution, by Richard Brust (2025)

Crafting Constitutions in Florida, 1810–1968, edited by Robert Cassanello (2025)

Just Freedom: Inside Florida's Decades-Long Voting Rights Battle, by Daniel Rivero (2025)

MICHAEL V. GANNON FUND

In honor of Michael Gannon's lasting legacy and his dedication to the scholarship of our state's history, the University Press of Florida has established the Michael V. Gannon Fund to provide continued support for first publications in Florida history. Royalties and gifts donated to this fund underwrite the costs of these monographs, helping to keep the price as affordable as possible. Special thanks to Dr. Gary R. Mormino for his very generous contribution to further publications about the Sunshine State's long and fascinating history.